business solutions

Pivot **Table** Data
Crunching **for**
Microsoft® Office
Excel® 2007

Bill Jelen

Michael Alexander

que®

800 E. 96th Street
Indianapolis, Indiana 46240

Contents at a Glance

Introduction 1
1 Pivot Table Fundamentals 11
2 Creating a Basic Pivot Table 21
3 Customizing a Pivot Table 45
4 Controlling the Way You View Your Pivot Data 83
5 Performing Calculations Within Your Pivot Tables 117
6 Using Pivot Charts and Other Visualizations 141
7 Analyzing Disparate Data Sources with Pivot Tables 167
8 Sharing Pivot Tables with Others 189
9 Working with and Analyzing OLAP Data 201
10 Enhancing Your Pivot Table Reports with Macros 215
11 Using VBA to Create Pivot Tables 231
12 Common Pivot Table Issues and Questions 291
A Finding Pivot Table Commands on the Ribbon 315

D1543370

Pivot Table Data Crunching for Microsoft® Office Excel® 2007

International Standard Book Number: 0-7897-3601-2

Library of Congress Cataloging-in-Publication data is on file.

Printed in the United States of America

First Printing: December 2006

09   08   07   06   4   3   2   1

Trademarks

All terms mentioned in this book that are known to be trademarks or service marks have been appropriately capitalized. Que Publishing cannot attest to the accuracy of this information. Use of a term in this book should not be regarded as affecting the validity of any trademark or service mark.

Microsoft is a registered trademark of Microsoft Corporation. Excel is a registered trademark of Microsoft Corporation.

Warning and Disclaimer

Every effort has been made to make this book as complete and as accurate as possible, but no warranty or fitness is implied. The information provided is on an "as is" basis. The authors and the publisher shall have neither liability nor responsibility to any person or entity with respect to any loss or damages arising from the information contained in this book.

Bulk Sales

Que Publishing offers excellent discounts on this book when ordered in quantity for bulk purchases or special sales. For more information, please contact

> **U.S. Corporate and Government Sales**
> **1-800-382-3419**
> **corpsales@pearsontechgroup.com**

For sales outside of the U.S., please contact

> **International Sales**
> **international@pearsoned.com**

This Book Is Safari Enabled

Safari The Safari® Enabled icon on the cover of your favorite technology book means the book is available through Safari Bookshelf. When you buy this book, you get free access to the online edition for 45 days.

Safari Bookshelf is an electronic reference library that lets you easily search thousands of technical books, find code samples, download chapters, and access technical information whenever and wherever you need it.

To gain 45-day Safari Enabled access to this book:

- Go to http://www.quepublishing.com/safarienabled
- Complete the brief registration form
- Enter the coupon code IHEF-YEKC-DHZD-9JCD-8X42

If you have difficulty registering on Safari Bookshelf or accessing the online edition, please e-mail customer-service@safaribooksonline.com.

Associate Publisher
Greg Wiegand

Acquisitions Editor
Loretta Yates

Development Editor
Kevin Howard

Managing Editor
Gina Kanouse

Project Editor
Andy Beaster

Copy Editor
Chuck Hutchinson

Indexer
Erika Millen

Proofreader
Heather Arle

Technical Editor
Juan Pablo González

Team Coordinator
Cindy Teeters

Interior Designer
Anne Jones

Cover Designer
Anne Jones

Compositor
Juli Cook

Table of Contents

Introduction 1

What You Will Learn from This Book 1

What Is New in Excel 2007's Pivot Tables 2

Skills Required to Use This Book 2

Case Study: Life Before Pivot Tables 2

The Invention of the Pivot Table 5

Case Study: Life After Pivot Tables 7

Sample Files Used in This Book 9

Conventions Used in This Book 9

    Referring to Ribbon Commands 9

    Special Elements 10

1 Pivot Table Fundamentals 11

What Is a Pivot Table? 11

Why Should You Use a Pivot Table? 12

When Should You Use a Pivot Table? 13

The Anatomy of a Pivot Table 14

    Values Area 14

    Row Area 15

    Column Area 15

    Report Filter Area 16

Pivot Tables Behind the Scenes 16

Limitations of Pivot Table Reports 17

    A Word About Compatibility 18

Next Steps 19

2 Creating a Basic Pivot Table 21

Preparing Your Data for Pivot Table Reporting 21

    Ensure Your Data Is in a Tabular Layout 22

    Avoid Storing Data in Section Headings 22

    Avoid Repeating Groups as Columns 23

    Eliminate Gaps and Blank Cells in Your Data Source 23

    Apply Appropriate Type Formatting to Your Fields 24

    Summary of Good Data Source Design 24

Case Study: Cleaning Up Data for Pivot Table Analysis 25

Creating a Basic Pivot Table 26

    Adding Fields to the Report 29

    Adding Layers to Your Pivot Table 32

    Rearranging Your Pivot Table 32

    Creating a Report Filter 33

Case Study: Analyzing Activity by Market 35

Keeping Up with Changes in Your Data Source 39
   Changes Have Been Made to Your Existing Data Source 40
   Your Data Source's Range Has Been Expanded with the Addition of
      Rows or Columns 40

Sharing the Pivot Cache 41
   Side Effects of Sharing a Pivot Cache 41

Saving Time with New Pivot Table Tools 42
   Deferring Layout Updates 42
   Starting Over with One Click 42
   Relocating Your Pivot Table 43

Next Steps 44

3 Customizing a Pivot Table **45**

Making Common Cosmetic Changes 46
   Applying a Table Style to Restore Gridlines 47
   Changing the Number Format to Add Thousands Separators 47
   Replacing Blanks with Zeros 49
   Changing a Field Name 51

Making Layout Changes 52
   Using the New Compact Layout 52
   Using the Outline Form Layout 54
   Using the Traditional Tabular Layout 54

Case Study: Converting a Pivot Table to Values 56
   Controlling Blank Lines, Grand Totals, Subtotals, and Other Settings 59

Customizing the Pivot Table Appearance with Styles and Themes 61
   Customizing a Style 62
   Choosing a Default Style for Future Pivot Tables 64
   Modifying Styles with Document Themes 64

Changing Summary Calculations 65
   Understanding Why One Blank Cell Causes a Count 65
   Using Functions Other Than Count or Sum 66

Adding and Removing Subtotals 68
   Suppress Subtotals When You Have Many Row Fields 68
   Adding Multiple Subtotals for One Field 69

Using Running Total Options 70
   Display Change from Year to Year with Difference From 71
   Compare One Year to a Prior Year with % Difference From 72
   Track YTD Numbers with Running Total In 72
   Determine How Much Each Line of Business Contributes to the Total 72
   Create Seasonality Reports 73
   Measure Percentage for Two Fields with % of Total 73
   Compare One Line to Another Line Using % Of 75
   Track Relative Importance with the Index Option 75

Case Study: Producing Revenue by Line of Business Report 77

Next Steps 81

4 Controlling the Way You View Your Pivot Data 83

Grouping Pivot Fields 83
  Grouping Date Fields 84
  Including Years When Grouping by Months 86
  Grouping Date Fields by Week 86
  Grouping Two Date Fields in One Report 88

Case Study: Creating an Order Lead-Time Report 88
  Grouping Numeric Fields 89

Case Study: Grouping Text Fields 90
  Ungrouping 92

Looking at the PivotTable Field List 93
  Docking and Undocking the PivotTable Field List 93
  Rearranging the PivotTable Field List 93
  Using the Areas Section Drop-Downs 94
  Using the Fields Drop-Down 94

Sorting in a Pivot Table 96
  Sorting Using the Sort Icons on the Options Ribbon 96
  Sorting Using the Field List Hidden Drop-Down 98
  Understanding the Effect of Layout Changes on AutoSort 100
  Using a Manual Sort Sequence 100
  Using a Custom List for Sorting 101

Filtering the Pivot Table 102
  Adding Fields to the Report Filter Area 103
  Choosing One Item from a Report Filter 104
  Choosing Multiple Items from a Report Filter 104
  Quickly Selecting or Clearing All Items from a Filter 106
  Using the Field List Filters 106
  Using Label Filters 108
  Using Date Filters 109
  Using Value Filters 111

Case Study: Creating a Top 10 Report 113

Next Steps 116

5 Performing Calculations Within Your Pivot Tables 117

Introducing Calculated Fields and Calculated Items 117
  Method 1: Manually Add the Calculated Field to Your Data Source 118
  Method 2: Use a Formula Outside Your Pivot Table to Create the
    Calculated Field 118
  Method 3: Insert a Calculated Field Directly into Your Pivot Table 119

Creating Your First Calculated Field 121

Case Study: Summarizing Next Year's Forecast 124

Creating Your First Calculated Item 129

Understanding Rules and Shortcomings of Pivot Table Calculations 133

    Remembering the Order of Operator Precedence 134

    Using Cell References and Named Ranges 135

    Using Worksheet Functions 135

    Using Constants 135

    Referencing Totals 135

    Rules Specific to Calculated Fields 135

    Rules Specific to Calculated Items 136

Managing and Maintaining Your Pivot Table Calculations 137

    Editing and Deleting Your Pivot Table Calculations 137

    Changing the Solve Order of Your Calculated Items 138

    Documenting Your Formulas 139

Next Steps 140

6   Using Pivot Charts and Other Visualizations 141

What Is a Pivot Chart . . . Really? 141

Creating Your First Pivot Chart 142

Keeping Pivot Chart Rules in Mind 145

    Changes in the Underlying Pivot Table Affect Your Pivot Chart 145

    The Placement of Data Fields in Your Pivot Table May Not Be Best Suited for
      Your Pivot Chart 145

    A Few Formatting Limitations Still Exist in Excel 2007 146

Case Study: Creating a Report Showing Invoice Frequency and Revenue
    Distribution by Product 148

Examining Alternatives to Using Pivot Charts 153

    Method 1: Turn Your Pivot Table into Hard Values 153

    Method 2: Delete the Underlying Pivot Table 154

    Method 3: Distribute a Picture of the Pivot Chart 154

    Method 4: Use Cells Linked Back to the Pivot Table as the Source Data for Your Chart 154

Using Conditional Formatting with Pivot Tables 157

Next Steps 166

7   Analyzing Disparate Data Sources with Pivot Tables 167

Using Multiple Consolidation Ranges 168

Analyzing the Anatomy of a Multiple Consolidation Range Pivot Table 174

    The Row Field 174

    The Column Field 174

    The Value Field 175

    The Page Fields 175

    Redefining Your Pivot Table 176

Case Study: Consolidating and Analyzing Datasets 176

Building a Pivot Table Using External Data Sources 179

    Building a Pivot Table with Microsoft Access Data 180

Building a Pivot Table with SQL Server Data 183

Next Steps 187

8 Sharing Pivot Tables with Others 189

Sharing a Pivot Table with Other Versions of Office 189

Features Unavailable in Excel 2003 Pivot Tables 190

Excel 2007 Compatibility Mode 190

No Downgrade Path Available from Version 12 Pivot Tables 190

Strategies for Sharing Pivot Tables 190

Saving Pivot Tables to the Web 191

Publishing Pivot Tables to Excel Services 193

Requirements to Render Spreadsheets with Excel Services 194

Preparing Your Spreadsheet for Excel Services 194

Publishing Your Spreadsheet to Excel Services 194

What the End User Sees in Excel Services 196

What You Cannot Do with Excel Services 197

Viewing the Pivot Table in the Browser 199

Next Steps 199

9 Working with and Analyzing OLAP Data 201

What Is OLAP? 201

Connecting to an OLAP Cube 202

Understanding the Structure of an OLAP Cube 205

Understanding Limitations of OLAP Pivot Tables 207

Creating Offline Cubes 207

Breaking Out of the Pivot Table Mold with Cube Functions 211

Next Steps 213

10 Enhancing Your Pivot Table Reports with Macros 215

Why Use Macros with Your Pivot Table Reports? 215

Recording Your First Macro 216

Creating a User Interface with Form Controls 218

Altering a Recorded Macro to Add Functionality 220

Case Study: Synchronizing Two Pivot Tables with One Combo Box 225

Next Steps 229

11 Using VBA to Create Pivot Tables 231

Introducing VBA 231

Enabling VBA in Your Copy of Excel 231

Enabling the Developer Ribbon 232

Visual Basic Editor 232

Visual Basic Tools 233

The Macro Recorder 234

Understanding Object-Oriented Code 234

Learning Tricks of the Trade 234
    Writing Code to Handle Any Size Data Range 235
    Using Super-Variables: Object Variables 236

Understanding Versions 236
    New in Excel 2007 237

Building a Pivot Table in Excel VBA 239
    Getting a Sum Instead of a Count 241
    Learning Why You Cannot Move or Change Part of a Pivot Report 243
    Determining Size of a Finished Pivot Table 244

Creating a Report Showing Revenue by Product 246
    Eliminating Blank Cells in the Values Area 248
    Ensuring Table Layout Is Utilized 248
    Controlling the Sort Order with AutoSort 248
    Changing Default Number Format 248
    Suppressing Subtotals for Multiple Row Fields 249
    Suppressing Grand Total for Rows 250

Handling Additional Annoyances When Creating Your Final Report .250
    Creating a New Workbook to Hold the Report 250
    Creating a Summary on a Blank Report Worksheet 251
    Filling the Outline View 252
    Handling Final Formatting 252
    Adding Subtotals 253
    Putting It All Together 254

Addressing Issues with Two or More Data Fields 257
    Calculated Data Fields 258
    Calculated Items 260

Summarizing Date Fields with Grouping 263
    Group by Week 265

Using Advanced Pivot Table Techniques 267
    Using AutoShow to Produce Executive Overviews 267
    Using ShowDetail to Filter a Recordset 270
    Creating Reports for Each Region or Model 272
    Manually Filtering Two or More Items in a PivotField 275

Controlling the Sort Order Manually 276

Using Sum, Average, Count, Min, Max, and More 276

Creating Report Percentages 277
    Percentage of Total 277
    Percentage Growth from Previous Month 278
    Percentage of a Specific Item 278
    Running Total 278

Using New Pivot Table Features in Excel 2007 279
    Using the New Filters 279

Applying a Table Style 284
Changing the Layout 285
Applying a Data Visualization 286
Understanding Special Considerations for Excel 97 288

Next Steps 289

12 Common Pivot Table Issues and Questions 291

Troubleshooting Common Pivot Table Issues 291
I keep getting the error "The PivotTable field name is not valid." 291
When I refreshed my pivot table, my data disappeared. 291
My pivot table always uses Count instead of Sum. 292
My pivot table constantly adjusts the columns in my workbook to autofit
the headings. 292
The Defer Layout Update option locked me out of other functionality such as
sorting, filtering, and grouping. 293
Older versions of Excel do not open my pivot table properly. .293
When I try to group a field, I get an error message. 294
My pivot table shows the same data item twice. 294
Deleted data items still show up in the filter area. 295
I refreshed my pivot table, and now my calculated fields are displayed as error values. 296

Common Pivot Table Questions 297
How do I make my pivot table refresh automatically? 297
How do I refresh all pivot tables in a workbook at the same time? 297
How can I sort data items in a unique order that is not ascending or descending? 298
How do I turn my pivot table into hard data? 298
Is there an easy way to fill the empty cells left by row fields? .299
Is there an easy way to fill the empty cells left by row fields in many columns? 300
Why does my pivot chart exclude months for certain data items? 303
How do I add a rank number field to my pivot table? 305
How do I hide calculation errors in my pivot table? 307
How can I reduce the size of my pivot table reports? 308
How can I easily create a separate pivot table for each market? 309
How do I avoid the need to constantly redefine my pivot table's data range? 310

A Finding Pivot Table Commands on the Ribbon 315

Inserting a Pivot Table 315

Finding Commands from the Legacy PivotTable Toolbar 316

Index 321

About the Authors

Bill Jelen is Mr. Excel! He is principal behind the leading Excel website, MrExcel.com. He honed his pivot table wizardry during a 12-year tenure as a financial analyst for a fast growing public computer firm. Armed with only a spreadsheet, he learned how to turn thousands of rows of transactional data into meaningful summaries in record time. He is an accomplished author of books on Excel and is a regular guest on "Call For Help" on TechTV Canada. As an Excel consultant, he has written Excel VBA solutions for hundreds of clients around the English-speaking world. His website hosts over 12 million page views annually.

Michael Alexander is a Microsoft Certified Application Developer (MCAD) with over 14 years experience developing business solutions with Microsoft Office, VBA, and .Net. He currently lives in Frisco, Texas, where he works as a senior program manager for a top technology firm. In his spare time, he runs a free tutorial site, www.datapigtechnologies.com, where he shares basic Access and Excel tips with intermediate users.

Dedication

BILL JELEN:

To Zeke Jelen

MIKE ALEXANDER:

To my lovely wife, Mary, who will open this book just long enough to read this dedication

Acknowledgments

Bill Jelen:

Thank you to Pito Salas, who invented Lotus Improv, the first desktop product to offer functionality similar to pivot tables. Thanks to Dan Bricklin, Bob Frankston, and Mitch Kapor for being pioneers in the spreadsheet world. Thanks to Dave Gainer and the entire Excel team at Microsoft for bringing pivot tables along to what they are today. Juan Pablo González provided great technical review. Thanks to Mary Ellen, Josh, and Zeke Jelen for tolerating me while I was writing six books simultaneously. My sister, Barb Jelen, provides excellent back office support at MrExcel.com; there is a good chance that she packed and shipped this book to you. Lora White keeps things moving and produces our Podcasts. Thanks to Jerry Kohl at Leegin and everyone who ever asked me for a report back at Telxon, and our clients at MrExcel Consulting; you all contributed to my expertise with pivot tables. Thanks to William Brown at Waterside; Loretta Yates, Andy Beaster, Chuck Hutchinson, and Kevin Howard at Que Publishing. Thanks to Mike Alexander for being a great coauthor.

Mike Alexander:

Thank you to Bill Jelen for the opportunity to help write this book. It's hard to find anyone who has more passion and drive for what he does than Bill Jelen. Thank you to Juan Pablo González for keeping Bill and me honest and sparking some great ideas. Many thanks to Loretta Yates and the many professionals at Que Publishing for all the support during the writing process. A special thank you to Mary for putting up with all my crazy projects this year.

We Want to Hear from You!

As the reader of this book, *you* are our most important critic and commentator. We value your opinion and want to know what we're doing right, what we could do better, what areas you'd like to see us publish in, and any other words of wisdom you're willing to pass our way.

As an associate publisher for Que Publishing, I welcome your comments. You can email or write me directly to let me know what you did or didn't like about this book—as well as what we can do to make our books better.

Please note that I cannot help you with technical problems related to the topic of this book. We do have a User Services group, however, where I will forward specific technical questions related to the book.

When you write, please be sure to include this book's title and author as well as your name, email address, and phone number. I will carefully review your comments and share them with the author and editors who worked on the book.

Email: feedback@quepublishing.com

Mail: Greg Wiegand
           Associate Publisher
           Que Publishing
           800 East 96th Street
           Indianapolis, IN 46240 USA

Reader Services

Visit our website and register this book at www.quepublishing.com/register for convenient access to any updates, downloads, or errata that might be available for this book.

Pivot tables are the single most powerful feature in all of Excel. They came along during the 1990s when Microsoft and Lotus were locked in a bitter battle for dominance of the spreadsheet market. The race to continually add enhanced features to their respective products during the mid-90s led to many incredible features, but none as powerful as the pivot table.

With a pivot table, you can take 1 million rows of transactional data and transform it into a summary report in seconds. If you can drag a mouse, you can create a pivot table. In addition to quickly summarizing and calculating data, pivot tables allow you to change your analysis on the fly by simply moving fields from one area of a report to another.

There is simply no other tool in Excel that gives you the flexibility and analytical power that pivot tables can give you.

What You Will Learn from This Book

It is widely agreed that close to 50% of Excel users leave 80% of Excel untouched. That is, most users don't tap into the full potential of Excel's built-in utilities. Of these utilities, the most prolific by far is the pivot table. Despite the fact that pivot tables have been a cornerstone of Excel for more than 12 years now, they remain one of the most underutilized tools in the entire Microsoft Office Suite. If you have picked up this book, you are savvy enough to have heard of pivot tables or even have used them on occasion. You have a sense that pivot tables have a power that you are not using, and you want to learn how to leverage that power to quickly increase your productivity.

Within the first two chapters, you will be able to create basic pivot tables, increase your productivity, and produce reports in minutes instead of hours.

IN THIS INTRODUCTION

What You Will Learn from This Book 1

What Is New in Excel 2007's Pivot Tables 2

Skills Required to Use This Book 2

Case Study: Life Before Pivot Tables 2

The Invention of the Pivot Table 5

Case Study: Life After Pivot Tables 7

Sample Files Used in This Book 9

Conventions Used in This Book 9

Within the first seven chapters, you will be able to output complex pivot reports with drill-down capabilities accompanying charts. By the end of the book, you will be able to build a dynamic pivot table reporting system.

What Is New in Excel 2007's Pivot Tables

Microsoft streamlined the pivot table interface to make it easier to use. In the last six versions of Excel, you generally created and modified a pivot table by dragging field names around the worksheet. Excel provided subtle visual clues about where a dropped field would appear, but these clues were too subtle for most. If you accidentally dropped a text field in the data area instead of the row area, disaster would result. Now, in Excel 2007, you can build a pivot table by checking a few boxes. Excel's IntelliSense figures out the best location for the field. To modify the default, you can drag field names around the PivotTable Field List.

Also new in Excel 2007 is the easier interface for sorting and filtering fields in a pivot table. Whereas sorting was formerly hidden three levels deep in the menu system, it is now just one click away from the PivotTable Field List.

Formatting such as heat maps, data bars, banded rows, and columns are now available as icons on the Excel 2007 Ribbon.

Finally, Microsoft is pushing a high-end server product that allows many people to access data stored in pivot tables. It is no surprise that pivot tables play a key role in the interactivity of Excel Services for SharePoint.

Skills Required to Use This Book

We have created a reference that is comprehensive enough for hard-core analysts yet relevant to casual users of Excel. The bulk of the book covers how to use pivot tables in the Excel user interface. The final chapter describes how to create pivot tables in Excel's powerful VBA macro language. This means that any user who has a firm grasp of the basics (preparing data, copying, pasting, entering simple formulas) should have no problem understanding the concepts in this book.

CASE STUDY

Life Before Pivot Tables

Imagine that it is 1992. You are using Lotus 1-2-3 or Excel 4. You have thousands of rows of transactional data, as shown in Figure I.1. Your manager asks you to prepare a summary report showing revenue by region and product.

In 1992, preparing this report was a daunting task. It required superhuman spreadsheet skills that few could master. Here are the steps you needed to take:

Figure I.1

As a financial analyst in 1992, you are responsible for producing a summary from this dataset.

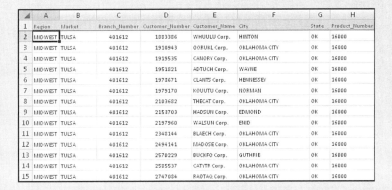

1. You need to get a list of the unique regions in the dataset. Use the Advanced Filter command with Unique Records Only (see Figure I.2) to extract a list of the unique regions.

Figure I.2

Even today, the Advanced Filter command is not a lot of fun to use.

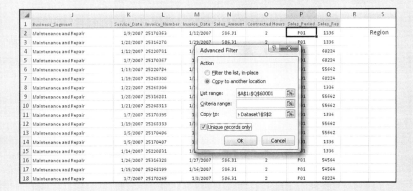

2. You need to get a list of the unique products in the dataset. Use the Advanced Filter command with Unique Records Only a second time to extract a list of the unique products.

3. You need to turn the list of products sideways so that it runs across the columns. Copy the list of unique models. Then choose Edit, Paste Special, Transpose to arrange the products as headings going across the report. You now have a skeleton of the report, as shown in Figure I.3.

4. You could use the DSUM function to total a column based on one criterion, but not based on two criteria. Therefore, you need to abandon typical functions and instead rely on an array formula. Before entering the array formula, set up two fields above the report to hold a sample region and sample model.

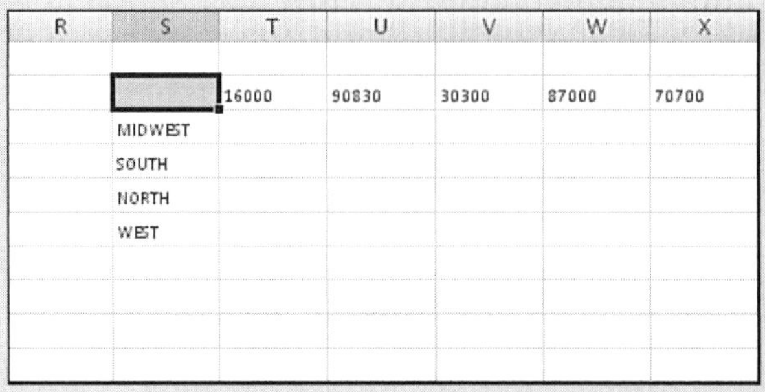

Figure I.3

After using a second Advanced Filter command and choosing Edit, Paste Special, Transpose, you have this skeleton of the final report. You still have a long way to go.

R	S	T	U	V	W	X
		16000	90830	30300	87000	70700
	MIDWEST					
	SOUTH					
	NORTH					
	WEST					

5. In the corner cell of the report, build an array formula to test whether the region column is North and the Model column is 4055T, and if so, add the corresponding row from the Revenue column. After typing this formula, remember to press Ctrl+Shift+Enter; otherwise, the formula will not work. The formula is shown in the formula bar in Figure I.4.

> **TIP** For a complete explanation of two-condition sums using array formulas, see http://www.MrExcel.com/tip031.shtml.

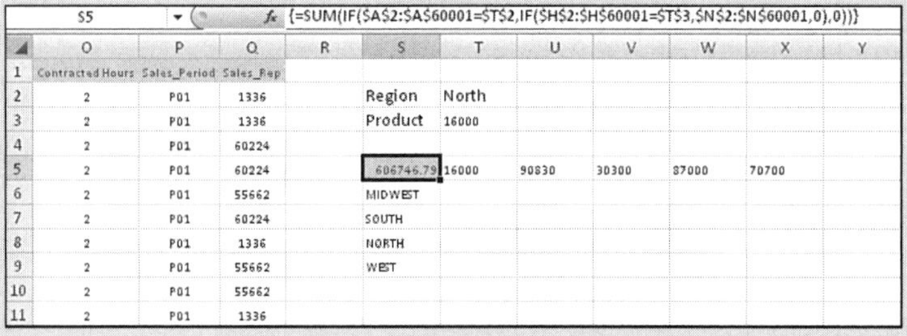

Figure I.4

With the array formula in the corner of the report, you are ready to use the not-so-intuitive Data Table 2 command.

S5 f_x {=SUM(IF($A$2:$A$60001=$T$2,IF($H$2:$H$60001=$T$3,$N$2:$N$60001,0),0))}

▲	O	P	Q	R	S	T	U	V	W	X	Y
1	Contracted Hours	Sales_Period	Sales_Rep								
2	2	P01	1336		Region	North					
3	2	P01	1336		Product	16000					
4	2	P01	60224								
5	2	P01	60224		606746.79	16000	90830	30300	87000	70700	
6	2	P01	55662		MIDWEST						
7	2	P01	60224		SOUTH						
8	2	P01	1336		NORTH						
9	2	P01	55662		WEST						
10	2	P01	55662								
11	2	P01	1336								

6. You know you're a hard-core data analyst if you can still imagine pressing the keystrokes for /`Data Table 2` in Lotus 1-2-3. Figure I.5 shows the equivalent function in Excel. In Excel 2007, this command is found in Data, Data Tools, What If Analysis, Data Table.

7. Finally, after using two advanced filters and a Paste Special command, writing the hardest formula in the world, and then using the Data Table command, you have the result your manager is looking for, as shown in Figure I.6. If you could pull off this analysis in 10 minutes, you were doing an amazing job.

Now, if your manager takes a look at the report and asks you to add Market to the analysis, you are nearly back at square one and are looking at an additional 15 minutes to produce the new report.

Figure I.5
The Data Table command replicates the formula in the top-left corner of the table but replaces two references in the formula with the headings at the top and left of the report.

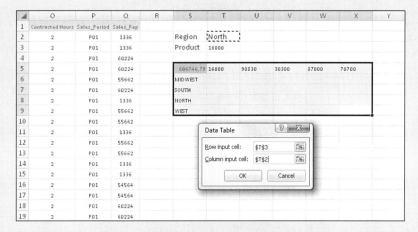

Figure I.6
After 10 minutes display-ing knowledge of obscure spreadsheet commands, you have produced the needed report.

{=TABLE(T3,T2)}

R	S	T	U	V	W	X	Y
	Region	North					
	Product	16000					
	606746.79	16000	90830	30300	87000	70700	
	MIDWEST	463076.5	93561.62	448800.4	76684.16	311416.6	
	SOUTH	846514.5	157821.09	1046231	184514.5	375218.9	
	NORTH	606746.8	151657.83	610790.5	143852.2	407311.6	
	WEST	444820.1	855022.28	521975.9	99519.52	526649.8	

The Invention of the Pivot Table

The concept that led to today's pivot table came from the halls of the Lotus Development Corporation with a revolutionary spreadsheet program called Lotus Improv. Improv was envisioned in 1986 by Pito Salas of the Advanced Technology Group at Lotus. Realizing that spreadsheets often have patterns of data, Pito concluded that if a user could build a tool that could recognize these patterns, then he could build enhanced data models. Lotus ran with the concept and started developing the next-generation spreadsheet.

Pito Salas, inventor of the pivot table concept, is always working on cutting-edge products at http://www.salas.com.

Throughout 1987, Lotus demonstrated its new program to a few companies. In 1988, Steve Jobs saw the program and immediately wanted it developed for his upcoming NeXT computer platform. The program, finally named Lotus Improv, was eventually shipped in 1991 for the NeXT platform. A version for Windows was introduced in 1993.

The core concept behind Improv was that data, data views, and formulas should be encapsulated as separate entities and treated as different animals. For the first time in a spreadsheet program, a dataset was given a name that could be grouped into larger categories. This naming and grouping capability paved the way for the most powerful feature in Improv: rearranging data. With Improv, a user could define and store a set of categories and then change the view by simply dragging the category names with the mouse. The user could also create totals and group summaries.

Microsoft eventually picked up on this concept in its pivot table functionality in Excel 5. Years later, with the release of Excel 97, Microsoft offered users an enhanced pivot table wizard and key improvements to pivot table functionality, such as the capability to add calculated fields. Excel 97 also opened the pivot cache to developers, fundamentally changing the way pivot tables are created and managed. Microsoft introduced the pivot chart with Excel 2000, providing users a way to represent pivot tables graphically. Since Excel 2000, changes made to pivot tables have been mainly cosmetic, much to the chagrin of pivot table fans everywhere.

Life After Pivot Tables

You have 600,000 rows of transactional data, as discussed in the previous case study. Your manager asks you to prepare a summary report showing revenue by Region and Model. Luckily, you have pivot tables at your disposal. Here are the steps you would follow today:

1. Select a single cell in your dataset. Choose PivotTable from the Insert tab. Click OK. You are given a blank pivot table, as shown in Figure I.7.

Figure I.7
After three mouse clicks, you have a blank pivot table report. Three more mouse clicks to go.

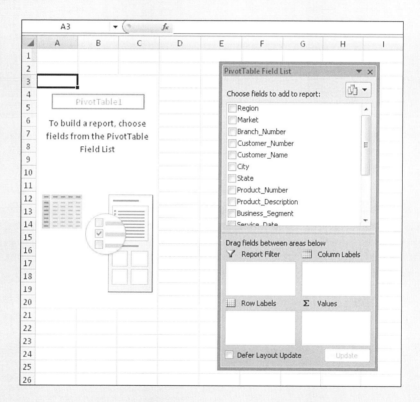

2. From the Pivot Table Field List, click the Region check box. Excel adds it to the left side of the pivot table. Click the check box next to Product_Number. In the lower portion of the dialog box, drag Product_Description from the Row Labels section to the Column Labels section. Click the Sales_Amount field in the top of the Pivot Table Field List. After a total of six mouse clicks, you have the required report, as shown in Figure I.8.

Figure I.8
Add three fields to the report.

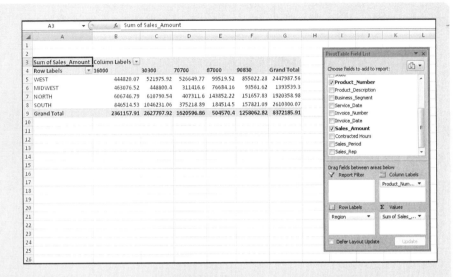

If you are racing, you can actually create the report shown in Figure I.8 in exactly 10 seconds. This is an amazing accomplishment. Realistically, it would take you about 50 seconds at normal speed to create the report. If you are a spreadsheet wizard and are instead following the steps in the previous case study, the non–pivot table solution would take you at least 12 times longer.

Further, when your manager comes back with the request to add Market to the analysis, you need just seconds to check the Market field in the PivotTable Field List to add it to the report, as shown in Figure I.9.

Figure I.9
Creating a new report with the Market field is as simple as choosing the field from the list.

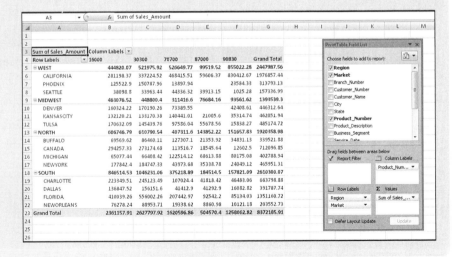

Sample Files Used in This Book

All data files used throughout this book are available for download from http://www. mrexcel.com/pivotbookdata2007.html.

Conventions Used in This Book

This book follows certain conventions:

- **Monospace**—Text messages you see onscreen or code appears in a `monospace` font.
- **Bold Monospace**—Text you type appears in a **`bold, monospace`** font.
- **Italic**—New and important terms appear in *italics*.
- **Initial Caps**—Ribbon names, dialog box names, and dialog box elements are presented with initial capital letters so that you can identify them easily.

Referring to Ribbon Commands

Office 2007 features a new interface called the *Ribbon*. The Ribbon in Excel 2007 is composed of several tabs labeled Home, Insert, Page Layout, and so on. When you click on the Page Layout tab, you see the icons available on the Page Layout tab.

When the active cell is inside a pivot table, two new tabs appear on the Ribbon. In the help files, Microsoft has been calling these tabs "PivotTable Tools | Options" and "PivotTable Tools | Design." For convenience, this book refers to these elements as the Options tab and the Design tab, respectively.

Within each Ribbon, the icons are arranged into logical groups. The name of each group is shown in a colored band at the bottom of the group. When referring to a specific icon, the book mentions the group name. To refer to the item in Figure I.10, this book says, "Click the Field Settings icon in the Active Field group of the Options tab."

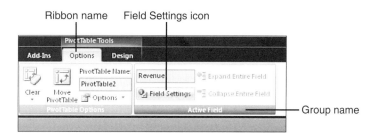

Ribbon name   Field Settings icon

Figure I.10
Icons are referred to by the ribbon tab, the group name, and then the icon name.

Group name

In some cases, the Ribbon icon leads to a drop-down with additional choices. In these cases, the book lists the hierarchy of Ribbon, Group, Icon, Menu Choice, Submenu Choice. For example, in Figure I.11, the shorthand specifies "Choose Design, Layout, Blank Rows, Remove Blank Line After Each Item."

Menu choice

Figure I.11
For shorthand, instructions might say Ribbon, Group, Icon, Menu Choice, Submenu Choice.

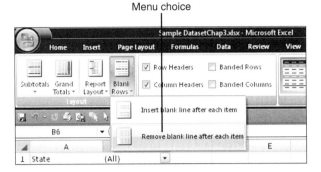

Special Elements

This book contains the following special elements:

NOTE

Notes provide additional information outside the main thread of the chapter discussion that might still be useful for you to know.

TIP

Tips provide you with quick workarounds and time-saving techniques to help you do your work more efficiently.

CAUTION

Cautions warn you about potential pitfalls you might encounter. Pay attention to them because they alert you to problems that otherwise could cause you hours of frustration.

CASE STUDY

Case studies provide a real-world look at topics previously introduced in the chapter.

Pivot Table Fundamentals

1

What Is a Pivot Table?

Imagine that Excel is a large toolbox that contains different tools at your disposal. The pivot table is essentially one tool in your Excel toolbox. If a pivot table were indeed a physical tool that you could hold in your hand, a kaleidoscope would most accurately represent it.

When you look through a kaleidoscope at an object, you see that object in a different way. You can turn the kaleidoscope to move around the details of the object. The object itself doesn't change, and it's not connected to the kaleidoscope. The kaleidoscope is simply a tool you use to create a unique perspective on an ordinary object.

Think of a pivot table as a kaleidoscope that is pointed at your dataset. When you look at your dataset through a pivot table, you have the opportunity to see details in your data you may not have noticed before. Furthermore, you can turn your pivot table to see your data from different perspectives. The dataset itself doesn't change, and it's not connected to the pivot table. The pivot table is simply a tool you are using to create a unique perspective on your data.

A pivot table allows you to create an interactive view of your dataset. We call this view a *pivot table report*. With a pivot table report, you can quickly and easily categorize your data into groups, summarize large amounts of data into meaningful information, and perform a wide variety of calculations in a fraction of the time it takes by hand. But the real power of a pivot table report is that you can interactively drag and drop fields within your report, dynamically changing your perspective and recalculating totals to fit your current view.

IN THIS CHAPTER

What Is a Pivot Table? 11

Why Should You Use a Pivot Table? 12

When Should You Use a Pivot Table? 13

The Anatomy of a Pivot Table 14

Pivot Tables Behind the Scenes 16

Limitations of Pivot Table Reports 17

Next Steps 19

Why Should You Use a Pivot Table?

As a rule, your dealings in Excel can be split into two categories: calculating data and shaping (formatting) data. Although many built-in tools and formulas facilitate both of these tasks, the pivot table is often the fastest and most efficient way to calculate and shape data.

Let's look at one simple scenario that illustrates this point. You have just given your manager some revenue information by month, and he has predictably asked for more information. He adds a note to the worksheet and emails it back to you. As you can see in Figure 1.1, he would like you to add a line that shows credits by month.

Figure 1.1
Your manager predictably changes his request after you provide the first pass of a report.

	A	B	C	D	E	F	G	H
1		Jan	Feb	Mar	Apr	May	Jun	Jul
2	Revenues	66,427,076	68,619,453	69,444,496	67,669,316	69,572,075	67,196,220	66,884,771
3		Please add a "credits" line and show the amount of credits for each month						
4								

To meet this new requirement, you run a query from your legacy system that will provide the needed data. As usual, the data is formatted specifically to make you suffer. Instead of data by month, the legacy system provides detailed transactional data by day, as shown in Figure 1.2.

Figure 1.2
The data from the legacy system is by day instead of by month.

	A	B	C
1	Document Number	In Balance Date	Credit Amount
2	D29210	01/03/03	(34.54)
3	D15775	01/03/03	(313.64)
4	D46035	01/03/03	(389.04)
5	D45826	01/03/03	(111.56)
6	D69172	01/03/03	(1,630.25)
7	D25388	01/03/03	(3,146.22)
8	D49302	01/03/03	(1,217.37)
9	D91669	01/03/03	(197.44)
10	D14289	01/03/03	(33.75)
11	D38471	01/03/03	(6,759.20)
12	D18645	01/03/03	(214.54)
13	D63807	01/03/03	(19.58)
14	D77943	01/03/03	(136.17)
15	D37446	01/03/03	(128.36)

Your challenge is to calculate the total dollar amount of credits by month and shape the results into an extract that fits the format of the original report. The final extract should look like the data shown in Figure 1.3.

Creating the extract manually would take 18 mouse clicks and three keystrokes:

Format dates to month: three clicks

Create subtotals: four clicks

Extract subtotals: six clicks, three keystrokes

Transpose vertical to horizontal: five clicks

Figure 1.3
Your goal is to produce a summary by month and transpose the data to a horizontal format.

	A	B	C	D	E	F	G
1							
2	-3,695,319	-3,698,537	-3,833,977	-3,624,967	-3,800,526	-3,603,367	-3,746,754
3							
4							

In contrast, creating the extract with a pivot table would take nine mouse clicks:

Create the pivot table report: five clicks

Group dates into months: three clicks

Transpose vertical to horizontal: one click

Both methods give you the same extract, which can be pasted into the final report, as shown in Figure 1.4.

Figure 1.4
After adding credits to the report, you can calculate net revenue.

	A	B	C	D	E	F	G	H
1		Jan	Feb	Mar	Apr	May	Jun	Jul
2	Revenues	66,427,076	68,619,453	69,444,496	67,669,316	69,572,075	67,196,220	66,884,771
3	Credits	-3,695,319	-3,698,537	-3,833,977	-3,624,967	-3,800,526	-3,603,367	-3,746,754
4	Adjusted Revenues	62,731,757	64,920,916	65,610,519	64,044,349	65,771,549	63,592,853	63,138,017
5								

Using a pivot table to accomplish this task not only cuts down the number of actions by more than half, but also reduces the possibility of human error. Over and above that, using a pivot table allows for the quick and easy shaping and formatting of the data.

What this example shows is that using a pivot table is not just about calculating and summarizing your data. Pivot tables can often help you do a number of tasks faster and better than conventional functions and formulas. For example, you can use pivot tables to instantly transpose large groups of data vertically or horizontally. You can use pivot tables to quickly find and count the unique values in your data. You can also use pivot tables to prepare your data to be used in charts.

The bottom line is that pivot tables can help you dramatically increase your efficiency and decrease your errors on a number of tasks you may have to accomplish with Excel. Pivot tables can't do everything for you, but knowing how to use just the basics of pivot table functionality can take your data analysis and productivity to a new level.

When Should You Use a Pivot Table?

Large datasets, ever-changing impromptu data requests, and multilayered reporting are absolute productivity killers if you have to tackle them by hand. Going hand-to-hand combat with one of these not only is time consuming, but also opens up the possibility of an untold number of errors in your analysis. So how do you recognize when to use a pivot table before it's too late?

Generally, a pivot table would serve you well in any of the following situations:

- You have a large amount of transactional data that has become increasingly difficult to analyze and summarize in a meaningful way.
- You need to find relationships and groupings within your data.
- You need to find a list of unique values for one field in your data.
- You need to find data trends using various time periods.
- You anticipate frequent requests for changes to your data analysis.
- You need to create subtotals that frequently include new additions.
- You need to organize your data into a format that's easy to chart.

The Anatomy of a Pivot Table

Because the anatomy of a pivot table is what gives it its flexibility and, indeed, its ultimate functionality, truly understanding pivot tables would be difficult without understanding their basic structure.

A pivot table is composed of four areas. The data you place in these areas defines both the utility and appearance of the pivot table. Keeping in mind that you will go through the process of creating a pivot table in the next chapter, let's prepare by taking a closer look at the four areas and the functionality around them.

Values Area

The *values area* is shown in Figure 1.5. It is a large rectangular area below and to the right of the headings. In this example, the values area contains a sum of the revenue field.

Values area

Figure 1.5
The heart of the pivot table is the values area. This area typically includes a total of one or more numeric fields.

	A	B	C	D	E	F
1	REGION	(All)				
2						
3	Sum of REVENUE	MONTH				
4	MODEL	January	February	March	April	May
5	2500P	$33,073	$29,104	$25,612	$22,538	$19,834
6	3002C	$35,880	$31,574	$27,785	$24,451	$21,517
7	3002P	$90,258	$79,427	$69,896	$61,508	$54,127
8	4055T	$13,250	$11,660	$10,261	$9,030	$7,946
9	4500C	$100,197	$88,173	$77,593	$68,281	$60,088
10						

The values area is the area that calculates. This area is required to have at least one field and one calculation on that field in it. The data fields that you drop here are those that you want to measure or calculate. The values area might include Sum of Revenue, Count of Units, and Average of Price.

It is also possible to have the same field dropped in the values area twice, but with different calculations. A marketing manager might want to see Minimum of Price, Average Price, and Maximum of Price.

Row Area

The *row area* is shown in Figure 1.6. It is composed of the headings that go down the left side of the pivot table.

Figure 1.6
The headings down the left side of the pivot table make up the row area of the pivot table.

	A	B	C	D	E	F
1	REGION	(All) ▾				
2						
3	REVENUE	MONTH				
4	MODEL ▾	January	February	March	April	May
5	2500P	$33,073	$29,104	$25,612	$22,538	$19,834
6	3002C	$35,880	$31,574	$27,785	$24,451	$21,517
7	3002P	$90,258	$79,427	$69,896	$61,508	$54,127
8	4055T	$13,250	$11,660	$10,261	$9,030	$7,946
9	4500C	$100,197	$88,173	$77,593	$68,281	$60,088
10						

Row area

Dropping a field into the row area displays the unique values from that field down the rows of the left side of the pivot table. The row area typically has at least one field, although it is possible to have no fields. The example earlier in the chapter where you needed to produce a one-line report of credits is an example where there are no row fields.

The types of data fields that you would drop here include those that you want to group and categorize—for example, Products, Names, and Locations.

Column Area

The *column area* is composed of headings that stretch across the top of columns in the pivot table. In the pivot table in Figure 1.7, the month field is in the column area.

Dropping fields into the column area would display your items in column-oriented perspective. The column area is ideal to show trending over time. The types of data fields that you would drop here include those you want to trend or show side by side—for example, Months, Periods, and Years.

Column area

Figure 1.7
The column area stretches across the top of the columns. In this example, it contains the unique list of months in your dataset.

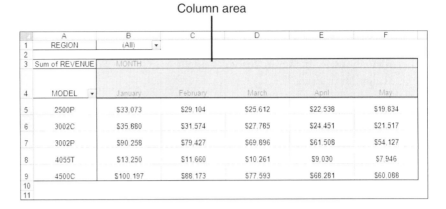

Report Filter Area

The *report filter area* is an optional set of one or more drop-downs at the top of the pivot table. In Figure 1.8, the report filter area contains the Region field, and the pivot table is set to show all regions.

Report filter area

Figure 1.8
Report filter fields are great for quickly filtering a report. The Region drop-down in cell B1 would allow you to print this report for one particular region manager.

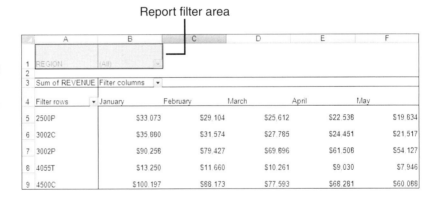

Dropping fields into the report filter area would allow you to filter the data items in your fields. The report filter area is optional and comes in handy when you need to filter your results dynamically. The types of data fields that you would drop here include those that you want to isolate and focus on—for example, Regions, Line of Business, and Employees.

Pivot Tables Behind the Scenes

It's important to know that pivot tables do come with a few file space and memory implications for your system. To get an idea of what this means, let's look at what happens behind the scenes when you create a pivot table.

When you initiate the creation of a pivot table report, Excel takes a snapshot of your dataset and stores it in a *pivot cache*. A pivot cache is nothing more than a special memory subsystem in which your data source is duplicated for quick access. Although the pivot cache is not a physical object that you can see, you can think of it as a container that stores the snapshot of the data source.

Each pivot table report you create from a separate data source creates its own pivot cache that increases your memory usage and file size. The increase in memory usage and file size depends on the size of the original data source that is being duplicated to create the pivot cache.

Your pivot table report is essentially a view that gets its data solely from the pivot cache. This means that your pivot table report and your data source are disconnected.

> **CAUTION**
>
> Any changes you make to your data source are not picked up by your pivot table report until you take another snapshot of the data source or "refresh" the pivot cache. Refreshing is easy: Simply right-click on the pivot table and click Refresh Data. You can also select the large Refresh button on the Options tab.

The benefit of working against the pivot cache and not your original data source is optimization. Any changes you make to the pivot table report, such as rearranging fields, adding new fields, or hiding items, are made rapidly and with minimal overhead.

Limitations of Pivot Table Reports

Before discussing the limitations of pivot table reports, we should note that Excel 2007 offers a dramatic increase in the number of rows and columns allowed in one worksheet. Indeed, you may have upgraded specifically *because* Excel 2007 offers over 1 million rows and 16,384 columns per worksheet.

This increase in limits has a ripple effect on several of the tools and functions in Excel, forcing limitation increases in many areas including pivot tables. Table 1.1 highlights the changes in pivot table limits from Excel 2000 to Excel 2007. Whereas some of these limitations remain constant, others are highly dependent on available system memory.

Table 1.1   Pivot Table Limitations

Category	Excel 2000	Excel 2002/2003	Excel 2007
Number of Row Fields (could be limited by available memory)	Limited by available memory	Limited by available memory	1,048,576
Number of Column Fields	256	256	16,384

continues

Table 1.1   Continued

Category	Excel 2000	Excel 2002/2003	Excel 2007
Number of Page Fields	256	256	16,384
Number of Data Fields	256	256	16,384
Number of Unique Items in a Single Pivot Field (could be limited by available memory)	8,000	32,500	1,048,576
Number of Calculated Items	Limited by available memory	Limited by available memory	Limited by available memory
Number of Pivot Table Reports on One Worksheet	Limited by available memory	Limited by available memory	Limited by available memory

A Word About Compatibility

As you can imagine, the extraordinary increases in pivot table limitations lead to some serious compatibility questions. For instance, what if you create a pivot table that contains more than 256 column fields and more than 32,500 unique data items? How are users with previous versions of Excel affected? Luckily, Excel 2007 comes with some precautionary measures that can help you avoid compatibility issues.

The first precautionary measure is Compatibility mode. Compatibility mode is a state that Excel 2007 automatically enters when opening an .xls file. When Excel 2007 is in Compatibility mode, it artificially takes on the limitations of Excel 2003. This means while you are working with an .xls file, you cannot exceed any of the Excel 2003 pivot table limitations shown in Table 1.1. This effectively prevents you from unwittingly creating a pivot table that is not compatible with previous versions of Excel. If you want to get out of Compatibility mode, you have to save the .xls file as one of Excel's new file formats (.xlsx or .xlsm).

> **CAUTION**
>
> Beware of the upgrade option on the Office Icon menu. Although this command is designed to convert a file from Excel 2003 to Excel 2007, it actually deletes the Excel 2003 copy of the file.

The second precautionary measure is Excel's Compatibility Checker. The Compatibility Checker is a built-in tool that checks for any compatibility issues when you try to save an Excel 2007 workbook as an .xls file. If your pivot table exceeds the bounds of Excel 2003 limitations, the Compatibility Checker alerts you with a dialog box similar to the one shown in Figure 1.9.

Figure 1.9
The Compatibility Checker alerts you of any compatibility issues before you save to a previous version of Excel.

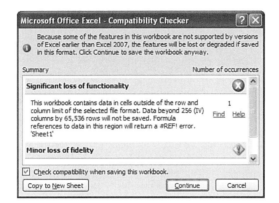

With this dialog box, Excel gives you the option of saving your pivot data as hard values in the new .xls file. If you choose to do so, the data from your pivot table is saved as hard values, but the pivot table object and the pivot cache are lost.

> **NOTE**
> For information on Excel 2007's compatibility tools, pick up Que Publishing's *Special Edition Using Microsoft Excel 2007* by Bill Jelen.

Next Steps

In the next chapter, you learn how to prepare your data to be used by a pivot table and walk through creating your first pivot table report with the Pivot Table Wizard.

Creating a Basic Pivot Table

2

Preparing Your Data for Pivot Table Reporting

When you have a family portrait taken, the photographer takes time to make sure that the lighting is right, the poses are natural, and everyone smiles his or her best smile. This preparation ensures that the resulting photo is effective in its purpose.

When you create a pivot table report, you're the photographer, taking a snapshot of your data. Taking time to make sure your data looks its best ensures that your pivot table report is effective in accomplishing the task at hand.

One of the benefits of working in a spreadsheet is that you have the flexibility of laying out your data to suit your needs. Indeed, the layout you choose depends heavily on the task at hand. However, many of the data layouts used for presentations are not appropriate when used as the source data for a pivot table report.

As you read the next section that goes into preparing your data, keep in mind that pivot tables have only one hard rule as it pertains to your data source: Your data source must have column headings, which are labels in the first row of your data describing the information in each column. If this is not the case, your pivot table report cannot be created.

However, just because your pivot table report is created successfully does not mean that it's effective. A host of things can go wrong as a result of bad data preparation—from inaccurate reporting to problems with grouping and sorting.

Let's look at a few of the steps you can take to ensure you end up with a viable pivot table report.

IN THIS CHAPTER

Preparing Your Data for Pivot
Table Reporting 21

Case Study: Cleaning Up Data for Pivot
Table Analysis 25

Creating a Basic Pivot Table 26

Case Study: Analyzing Activity
by Market 35

Keeping Up with Changes in Your
Data Source 39

Sharing the Pivot Cache 41

Saving Time with New Pivot Table Tools 42

Next Steps 44

Ensure Your Data Is in a Tabular Layout

A perfect layout for the source data in a pivot table is a tabular layout. In tabular layout, there are no blank rows or columns. Every column has a heading. Every field has a value in every row. Columns do not contain repeating groups of data.

Figure 2.1 shows an example of data structured properly for a pivot table. There are headings for each column. Even though the values in D2:D6 are all the same model, the model number appears in each cell. Month data is organized down the page instead of across the columns.

Tabular layouts are *database-centric*, meaning that you would most commonly find these types of layouts in databases. These layouts are designed to store and maintain large amounts of data in a well-structured, scalable format.

Figure 2.1
This data is structured properly for use as a pivot table source.

	A	B	C	D	E	F
1	REGION	MARKET	STORE	MODEL	MONTH	REVENUE
2	North	Great Lakes	65061011	4055T	April	$2,354
3	North	Great Lakes	65061011	4055T	February	$3,040
4	North	Great Lakes	65061011	4055T	January	$3,454
5	North	Great Lakes	65061011	4055T	March	$2,675
6	North	Great Lakes	65061011	4055T	May	$2,071
7	North	New England	2105015	2500P	April	$11,851
8	North	New England	2105015	2500P	February	$15,304
9	North	New England	2105015	2500P	January	$17,391
10	North	New England	2105015	2500P	March	$13,468
11	North	New England	2105015	2500P	May	$10,429
12	North	New England	22022012	3002C	April	$256
13	North	New England	22022012	3002C	February	$330
14	North	New England	22022012	3002C	January	$375
15	North	New England	22022012	3002C	March	$290

> **TIP**
> You might work for a manager who demands that the column labels be split into two rows. For example, he may want the heading Gross Margin to be split with Gross in row 1 and Margin in row 2. Because pivot tables require a unique heading one row high, your manager's preference can be problematic. To overcome this problem, start typing your heading; for example, type `Gross`. Before leaving the cell, press Alt+Enter and then type `Margin`. The result is a single cell that contains two lines of data.

Avoid Storing Data in Section Headings

Examine the data in Figure 2.2. This spreadsheet shows a report of sales by month and model for the North region of a company. Because the data in rows 2 through 24 pertains to the North region, the author of the worksheet put a single cell with North in B1. This approach is effective for display of the data, but not effective when used as a pivot table data source.

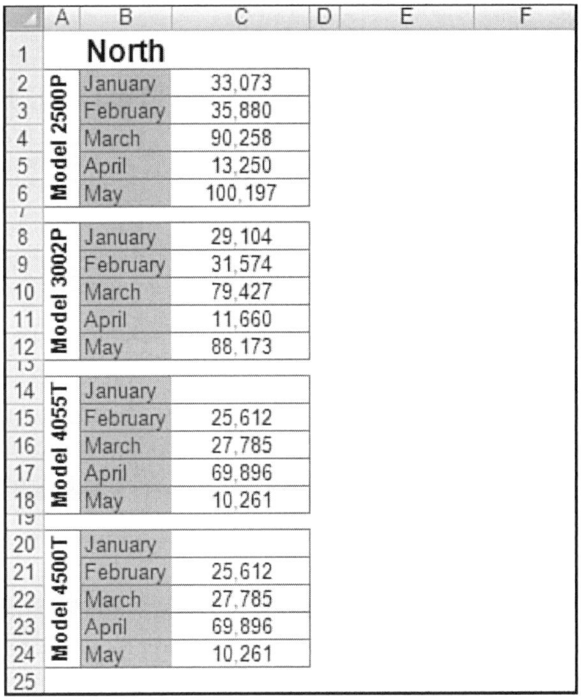

Figure 2.2
Region and model data are not formatted properly in this dataset.

Also in Figure 2.2, the author was very creative with the model information. The data in rows 2 through 6 applies to Model 2500P, so the author entered this value once in A2 and then applied a fancy vertical format combined with Merge Cells to create an interesting look for the report. Again, although this is a cool format, it is not useful for pivot table reporting.

Also, the worksheet in Figure 2.2 is missing column headings. You can guess that column A is Model, column B is Month, and column C is Sales, but for Excel to create a pivot table, this information must be included in the first row of the data.

Avoid Repeating Groups as Columns

The format shown in Figure 2.3 is common. A time dimension is presented across several columns. Although it is possible to create a pivot table from this data, this format is not ideal.

The problem is that the headings spread across the top of the table pull double duty as column labels and actual data values. In a pivot table, this format would force you to manage and maintain six fields, each representing a different month.

Eliminate Gaps and Blank Cells in Your Data Source

Delete all empty columns within your data source. An empty column in the middle of your data source causes your pivot table to fail on creation because the blank column, in most cases, does not have a column name.

Figure 2.3
This matrix format is common but not effective for pivot tables. The Month field is spread across several columns of the report.

	A	B	C	D	E	F	G	H
1	North							
2								
3	MODEL	JANUARY	FEBRUARY	MARCH	APRIL	MAY	JUNE	
4	4054T	$2,789	$2,454	$2,160	$1,901	$1,673	$1,472	
5	4500C	$32,605	$28,692	$25,249	$22,219	$19,553	$17,207	
6	3002P	$52,437	$46,145	$40,607	$35,734	$31,446	$27,673	
7	2500P	$17,391	$15,304	$13,468	$11,851	$10,429	$9,178	
8	4055T	$2,468	$2,172	$1,911	$1,682	$1,480	$1,302	
9	3002C	$375	$330	$290	$256	$225	$198	
10								

Delete all empty rows within your data source. Empty rows may cause you to inadvertently leave out a large portion of your data range, making your pivot table report incomplete.

Fill in as many blank cells in your data source as possible. Although filling in cells is not required to create a workable pivot table, blank cells in and of themselves are generally errors waiting to happen. So a good practice is to represent missing values with some logical missing value code wherever possible.

> **NOTE**
> Although this may seem like a step backwards for those of you who are trying to create a nicely formatted report, it will pay off in the end. Once you are able to create a pivot table, there will be plenty of opportunity to apply some pleasant formatting. In Chapter 3, you will discover how to apply styles formatting to your pivot tables.

Apply Appropriate Type Formatting to Your Fields

Formatting your fields appropriately helps you avoid a whole host of possible issues from inaccurate reporting to problems with grouping and sorting.

Make certain that any fields to be used in calculations are explicitly formatted as a number, currency, or any other format appropriate for use in mathematical functions. Fields containing dates should also be formatted as any one of the available date formats.

Summary of Good Data Source Design

The attributes of an effective tabular design are as follows:

- The first row of your data source is made up of field labels or headings that describe the information in each column.
- Each column in your data source represents a unique category of data.
- Each row in your data source represents individual items in each column.
- None of the column names in your data source double as data items that will be used as filters or query criteria (that is, names of months, dates, years, names of locations, names of employees).

Cleaning Up Data for Pivot Table Analysis

The worksheet shown in Figure 2.4 is a great-looking report. However, it cannot be effectively used as a data source for a pivot table. Can you identify the problems with this dataset?

Figure 2.4
Someone spent a lot of time formatting this report to look good, but what problems prevent it from being used as a data source for a pivot table?

	A	B	C	D	E	F	G	H	I
1	REGION	MARKET	STORE		JANUARY	FEBRUARY	MARCH	APRIL	MAY
2	MODEL 2500C								
3		Tulsa	32139049		$12,968	$11,412	$10,042	$8,837	$7,777
4	South	Gulf Coast	36133013		$3,703	$3,259	$2,868	$2,523	$2,221
5	North	Shenandoah Valley	62067017		$15,682	$13,800	$12,144	$10,687	$9,404
6	North	New England	2105015		$17,391	$15,304	$13,468	$11,851	$10,429
7									
8	MODEL 3002C								
9	North	New England	22022012		$375	$330	$290	$256	$225
10	North		12118068		$21,454	$18,880	$16,614	$14,620	$12,866
11			44040030		$979	$862	$758	$667	$587
12	North	South Carolina	53154014		$14,051	$12,365	$10,881	$9,575	$8,426
13	South	Indiana	65060010		$20,586	$18,116	$15,942	$14,029	$12,345
14	South	Tennessee	74075025		$19,217	$16,911	$14,882	$13,096	$11,524
15									
16	MODEL 3002P								
17	North	New England	12011011		$52,437	$46,145	$40,607	$35,734	$31,446
18	North	Ohio	44040020		$3,209	$2,824	$2,485	$2,187	$1,924
19	North	Ohio	34037017		$34,612	$30,459	$26,804	$23,587	$20,757
20	West	California	33130010		$157,434	$138,542	$121,917	$107,287	$94,412
21	West	California	33130010		$19,087	$16,797	$14,781	$13,007	$11,446
22	South	Texas	46049049		$40,950	$36,036	$31,712	$27,906	$24,558
23	South	Gulf Coast	3106026		$38,088	$33,517	$29,495	$25,956	$22,841
24									

1. The model information does not have its own column. Model information appears in the Region column. To correct this problem, insert a new column for Model and include the model number on every row.

2. There are blank columns and rows in the data. Column D should be deleted. The blank rows between models (such as rows 7 and 15) also should be deleted.

3. Blank cells present the data in an outline format. The person reading this worksheet would probably assume that cells B10:B11 are in the New England market and cell A11 is in the North region. These blank cells need to be filled in with the values from above.

> **TIP**
> Here's a trick for filling in the blank cells. Select the entire range of data. Then select the Home tab on the Ribbon and choose the Find & Select icon from the Editing group. This brings up a menu from which you select Go To Special. In the Go To Special dialog box, select Blanks. With all the blank cells selected, start a formula by typing the equal sign (=), press the up arrow on your keyboard, and then press Ctrl+Enter to fill this formula in all blank cells. Remember to copy and paste special values to convert the formulas to values.

4. The worksheet presents one data column—the data containing month—as several columns in the worksheet. Columns E through I need to be reformatted as two columns. Place the month name in one column and the sales for that month in the next column. This step either requires a fair amount of copying and pasting or a few lines of VBA macro code.

> **TIP**
>
> For a great book on learning VBA macro programming, read Que Publishing's *VBA and Macros for Microsoft Excel* by Bill Jelen and Tracy Syrstad. It is another book in this *Business Solutions* series.

After you make the four changes described here, the data is ready for use as a pivot table data source. As you can see in Figure 2.5, every column has a heading. There are no blank cells, rows, or columns in the data. The monthly data is now presented down column E instead of across several columns.

Figure 2.5
Although this data will take up six times as many rows, it is perfectly formatted for pivot table analysis.

	A	B	C	D	E	F
1	REGION	MARKET	STORE	MODEL	MONTH	REVENUE
2	North	Great Lakes	65061011	4055T	April	$2,354
3	North	Great Lakes	65061011	4055T	February	$3,040
4	North	Great Lakes	65061011	4055T	January	$3,454
5	North	Great Lakes	65061011	4055T	March	$2,675
6	North	Great Lakes	65061011	4055T	May	$2,071
7	North	New England	2105015	2500P	April	$11,851
8	North	New England	2105015	2500P	February	$15,304
9	North	New England	2105015	2500P	January	$17,391
10	North	New England	2105015	2500P	March	$13,468
11	North	New England	2105015	2500P	May	$10,429
12	North	New England	22022012	3002C	April	$256
13	North	New England	22022012	3002C	February	$330
14	North	New England	22022012	3002C	January	$375
15	North	New England	22022012	3002C	March	$290

Creating a Basic Pivot Table

Now that you have a good understanding of the importance of a well-structured data source, let's walk through creating a basic pivot table.

> **TIP**
>
> The sample dataset used throughout this book is available for download at www.MrExcel.com/pivotbookdata2007.html.

To start, click on any single cell in your data source. This ensures that the pivot table captures the range of your data source by default. Next, select the Insert tab and find the Tables group. In the Tables group, select PivotTable and then choose PivotTable from the drop-down list. Figure 2.6 demonstrates how to start a pivot table.

Figure 2.6
Start a pivot table by
selecting PivotTable from
the Insert tab.

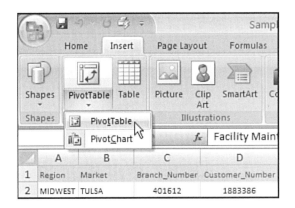

Choosing these options activates the Create PivotTable dialog box, shown in Figure 2.7.

Figure 2.7
The Create PivotTable
dialog box replaces the
classic PivotTable and
PivotChart Wizard.

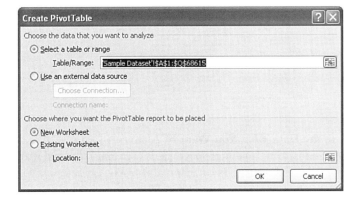

NOTE

There are other ways to activate the Create PivotTable dialog box. Clicking the PivotTable icon on the Insert tab activates the Create PivotTable dialog box. You can also press the hotkeys Alt+N+V+T to start a pivot table.

A more roundabout way is to format your dataset as a table and then choose the Summarize with Pivot command. To do this, place your cursor inside your dataset and select Format as Table from the Styles group in the Home tab. After your table has been formatted, place your cursor anywhere inside your dataset to activate the Table Tools tab. There you can select the Summarize with Pivot option in the Tools group.

Where Have All the Wizards Gone?
As you look at Figure 2.7, you may notice that it doesn't look like the old PivotTable and PivotChart Wizard found in the previous versions of Excel. The reason is that it's not a wizard at all. Microsoft has actually abandoned the classic multi-step wizard for a more streamlined one-step dialog box.

The problem with the classic wizard was that, by the time most first-time users reached step 2, they were either confused or intimidated. Although each subsequent version of Excel has tried to simplify the process of creating a pivot table, the multistep wizard itself ultimately introduced too much complexity for many users. In contrast, Excel 2007's one-step dialog box presents you with only the minimum requirements necessary to create the pivot table, making for a far less intimidating process.

As you can see in Figure 2.8, the Create PivotTable dialog box asks you only two questions: where's the data that you want to analyze, and where do you want to put the pivot table?

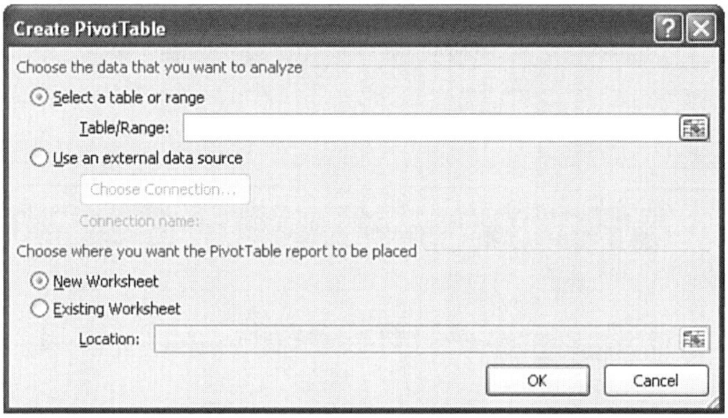

Figure 2.8
The Create PivotTable dialog box asks you only two questions.

- **Choose the Data That You Want to Analyze**—In this section, you tell Excel where your dataset is. You can either specify a dataset that is located within your workbook, or you can tell Excel to look for an external dataset. As you can see in Figure 2.8, Excel is smart enough to read your dataset and fill in the range for you. However, you always should take note of this to ensure you are capturing all your data.

- **Choose Where You Want the PivotTable Report to Be Placed**—In this section, you tell Excel where you want your pivot table to be placed. This is set to New Worksheet by default, meaning your pivot table will be placed in a new worksheet within the current workbook. You will rarely change this setting because there are relatively few times you'll need your pivot table to be placed in a specific location.

After you have answered the two questions in the Create PivotTable dialog box, simply click the OK button. At this point, Excel adds a new worksheet that contains an empty pivot table report. Next to that is the PivotTable Field List dialog box, illustrated in Figure 2.9. This dialog box helps you build your pivot table.

Finding the PivotTable Field List
The PivotTable Field List dialog box is your main work area in Excel 2007. This is the place where you add fields and make changes to your pivot table report. By default, this dialog box pops up when you place your cursor anywhere inside your pivot table. However, if you explicitly close this dialog box, you override the default and essentially tell the dialog box not to activate when you are in the pivot table.

If clicking on the pivot table does not activate the PivotTable Field List dialog box, you can manually activate it by right-clicking anywhere inside the pivot table and selecting Show Field List. You can also click on the large Field List icon on the Options ribbon.

Figure 2.9
You use the PivotTable Field List dialog box to build your pivot table.

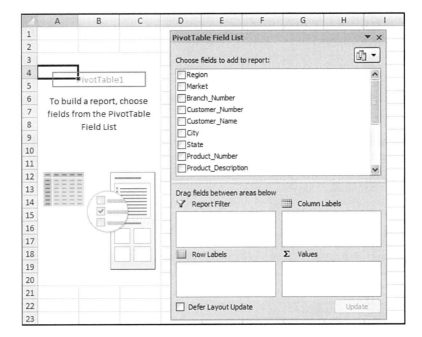

Adding Fields to the Report

The idea here is to add the fields you need into the pivot table by using the four "drop zones" found in the PivotTable Field List: Report Filter, Column Labels, Row Labels, and Values. These drop zones, which correspond to the four areas of the pivot table, are used to populate your pivot table with data.

> **TIP**
> Review Chapter 1, "Pivot Table Fundamentals," for a refresher on the four areas of a pivot table.

- **Report Filter**—Adding a field to the Report Filter drop zone includes that field in the filter area of your pivot table, allowing you to filter on its unique data items.
- **Column Labels**—Adding a field into the Column Labels drop zone displays the unique values from that field across the top of the pivot table.
- **Row Labels**—Adding a field into the Row Labels drop zone displays the unique values from that field down the left side of the pivot table.

■ **Values**—Adding a field into the Values drop zone includes that field in the values area of your pivot table, allowing you to perform a specified calculation using the values in the field.

Now let's pause a moment and go over some fundamentals of laying out your pivot table report. This is generally the point where most new users get stuck. How do you know which field goes where?

Before you start dropping fields into the various drop zones, ask yourself two questions: What am I measuring? and How do I want to see it? The answer to the first question tells you which fields in your data source you need to work with, and the answer to the second question tells you where to place the fields.

For your first pivot table report, you want to measure the dollar sales by region. This automatically tells you that you need to work with the Sales_Amount field and the Region field. How do you want to see it? You want regions to go down the left side of the report and the sales amount to be calculated next to each region.

To achieve this effect, you need to add the Region field to the Row Labels drop zone and add the Sales_Amount field to the Values drop zone.

Find the Region field in the field list, as shown in Figure 2.10.

Figure 2.10
Find the field you want to add to your pivot table.

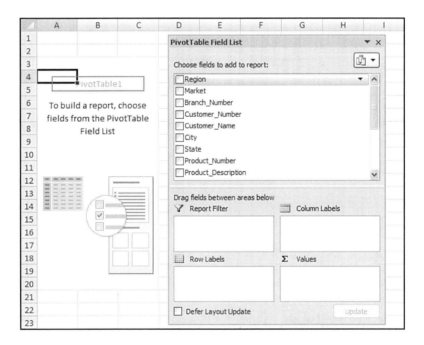

Place a check in the check box next to the field. As you can see in Figure 2.11, not only is the field automatically added to the Row Labels drop zone, but your pivot table is updated to show the unique region names.

Figure 2.11
Place a check next to the
Region field to automati-
cally add that field to
your pivot table.

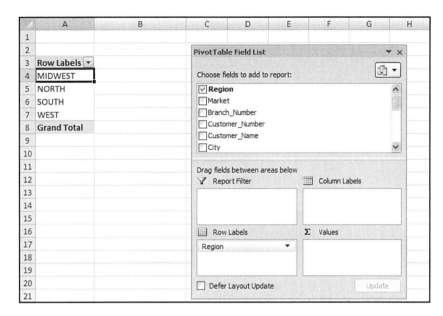

Now that you have regions in your pivot table, it's time to add in the dollar sales. To do that, simply find the Sales_Amount field and place a check next to it. As Figure 2.12 illustrates, the Sales_Amount field is automatically added to the Values drop zone, and your pivot table report now shows the total dollar sales for each region.

Figure 2.12
Place a check next to the
Sales_Amount field to
add data to your pivot
table report.

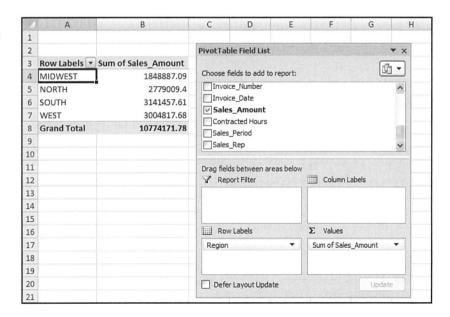

At this point, you have created your first pivot table report!

How Does Excel Know Where Your Fields Go?

As you've just experienced, the new PivotTable Field List interface allows you to add the fields to your pivot table by simply placing a check next to the field name. Excel automatically adds the checked fields to the pivot table. The question is how Excel knows in which drop zone to put the fields you check. The answer is that Excel doesn't really know which drop zone to use; it makes a decision based on data type. Here's how it works. When you place a check next to a field, Excel evaluates the data type for that field. If the data type is numeric, Excel places the field into the Values drop zone; otherwise, Excel places the field into the Row Labels drop zone. This placement obviously underlines the importance of correctly assigning the data types for your fields.

—— C A U T I O N ——————————————

Watch out for blanks in your numeric fields. If you have even one blank cell in a numeric field, Excel reads that cell as a Text field.

Adding Layers to Your Pivot Table

Now you can add another layer of analysis to your report. This time you want to measure the amount of dollar sales each region earned by business segment. Because your pivot table already contains the Region and Sales_Amount fields, all you have to do is place a check next to the Business_Segment field. As you can see in Figure 2.13, your pivot table automatically added a layer for Business Segment and refreshed the calculations to include subtotals for each region. Because the data is stored efficiently in the pivot cache, this change took less than a second.

Figure 2.13
Before pivot tables, adding layers to analyses would have required hours of work and complex formulas.

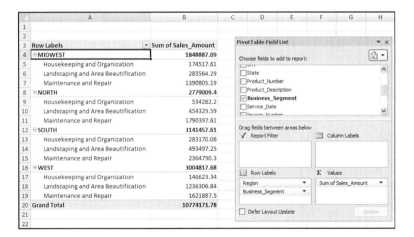

Rearranging Your Pivot Table

Suppose this view doesn't work for your manager. He wants to see business segments across the top of the pivot table report. To rearrange them, simply drag the Business_Segment field from the Row Labels drop zone to the Column Labels drop zone, as illustrated in Figure 2.14.

Figure 2.14
Rearranging a pivot table is as simple as dragging fields from one drop zone to another.

> **NOTE**
> You don't have to move your fields into a drop zone to be able to drag them around. You can actually drag fields directly from the field list into the desired drop zone. You can also move a field into a drop zone by using that field's context menu: Click the black triangle next to the field name and then select the desired drop zone.

Instantly, the report is restructured, as shown in Figure 2.15.

Creating a Report Filter

Often, you may be asked to produce reports for one particular region, market, or product. Instead of building separate pivot table reports for every possible analysis scenario, you can use the Filter field to create a report filter. For example, you can create a region filter by simply dragging the Region field to the Report Filter drop zone. This way, you can analyze one particular region. Figure 2.16 shows the totals for just the North region.

Figure 2.15
Your business segments are now column oriented.

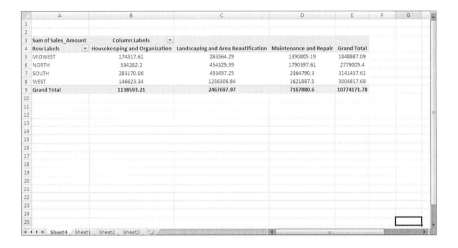

Figure 2.16
With this setup, you not only can see revenues by line of business clearly, but also can click on the Region drop-down to focus on one region.

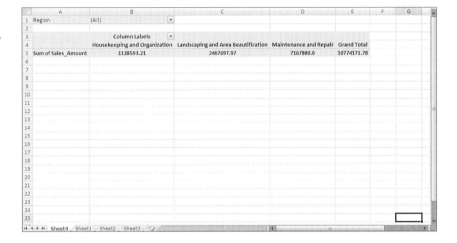

Longing for Drag-and-Drop Functionality?

One of the major complaints long-time Excellers will undoubtedly have with Excel 2007 is that you can no longer drag and drop fields directly onto the pivot table layout. This functionality is allowed only within the PivotTable Field List dialog box (dragging into drop zones). The good news, however, is that Microsoft has provided the option of working with a classic pivot table layout, which enables the drag-and-drop functionality.

To activate the classic pivot table layout, right-click anywhere inside the pivot table and select Table Options. In the Table Options dialog box, select the Display tab and place a check next to Classic PivotTable Layout, as demonstrated in Figure 2.17. Click the OK button to apply the change.

Figure 2.17
Place a check next to
Classic PivotTable Layout.

At this point, you can drag and drop fields directly onto your pivot table layout.

Unfortunately, this setting is not global. That is, you have to go through the same steps to apply the classic layout to each new pivot table you create. However, this setting persists when a pivot table is copied.

CASE STUDY

Analyzing Activity by Market

Your organization has 14 markets that sell products revolving around six types of facility services. You have been asked to build a report that breaks out each market, highlighting the dollar sales by each product. You are starting with an intimidating transaction table that contains more than 68,000 rows of data. To start your report, do the following:

1. Place your cursor inside your dataset, select the Insert tab, click PivotTable, and then choose PivotTable from the drop-down list.

2. When the Create PivotTable dialog box activates, simply click the OK button.

    At this point, you should see an empty pivot table with the field list, as shown in Figure 2.18.

3. Find the Market field in the PivotTable Field List and place a check in the box next to it. The Market field immediately appears in the Row Labels area, as illustrated in Figure 2.19.

    Now that you have your market names, it's time to calculate the total dollar sales for each market.

4. Find the Sales_Amount field in the PivotTable Field List and place a check in the box next to it. The Sales_Amount field automatically appears in the Values drop zone, as illustrated in Figure 2.20.

5. To get the product breakouts, find the Product_Description field in the PivotTable Field List and drag it into the Column Labels drop zone, as demonstrated here in Figure 2.21.

Figure 2.18
The beginnings of your pivot table report.

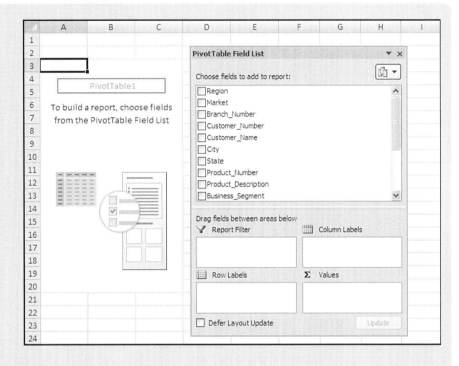

Figure 2.19
With one click, you get a list of the unique markets in your 68,000 rows of data.

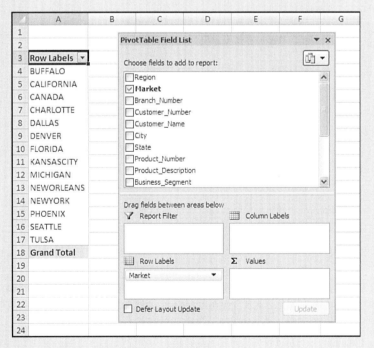

Figure 2.20
Add the Sales_Amount field.

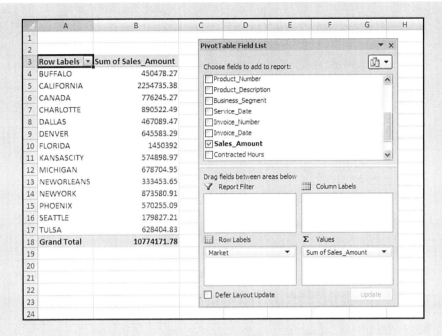

Figure 2.21
Drag the Product_Description field into the Column Labels drop zone.

In five easy steps, you have calculated and designed a report that satisfies the requirements given to you. After a little formatting, your pivot table report should look similar to the one shown in Figure 2.22.

You can go the extra mile and add one more dimension to your pivot table report to allow for analysis by region.

Choose any cell in your pivot table report to redisplay the PivotTable Field List. Drag the Region field into the Report Filter drop zone, as shown in Figure 2.23.

> **TIP**
>
> If clicking on the pivot table does not activate the PivotTable Field List dialog box, right-click anywhere inside the pivot table and select Show Field List.

With the Region field placed into the filter area, you can now create separate reports by region if needed. Figure 2.24 demonstrates how selecting the drop-down in the pivot table filter area allows you to select a region by which to filter.

Lest you lose sight of the analytical power you just displayed, keep in mind that your data source has more than 68,000 rows and 17 columns, which is a hefty set of data by Excel standards. Despite the amount of data, you produced a relatively robust analysis in a matter of minutes.

Figure 2.22
This summary can be created in less than a minute.

	A	B	C
1			
2			
3	Sum of Sales_Amount	Column Labels	
4	Row Labels	Cleaning & Housekeeping Services	Facility Maintenance and Repair
5	BUFFALO	$66,845	$69,570
6	CALIFORNIA	$37,401	$281,198
7	CANADA		$294,257
8	CHARLOTTE	$170,341	$223,350
9	DALLAS	$18,807	$136,848
10	DENVER	$12,564	$160,324
11	FLORIDA	$20,449	$410,039
12	KANSASCITY	$65,439	$132,120
13	MICHIGAN	$243,449	$65,077
14	NEWORLEANS	$73,573	$76,278
15	NEWYORK	$223,988	$177,842
16	PHOENIX	$96,686	$125,523
17	SEATTLE	$12,536	$38,099
18	TULSA	$96,515	$170,632
19	Grand Total	$1,138,593	$2,361,158
20			

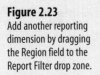

Figure 2.23
Add another reporting
dimension by dragging
the Region field to the
Report Filter drop zone.

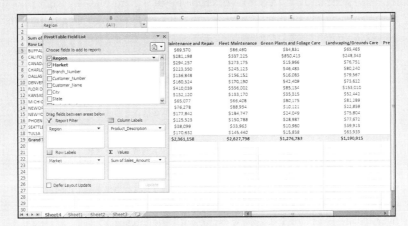

Figure 2.24
Select any region from
the filter area drop-down
to filter the data in the
pivot table for just that
region.

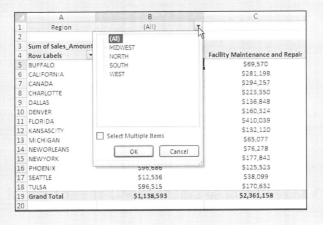

Keeping Up with Changes in Your Data Source

Let's go back to the family portrait analogy. As years go by, your family will change in appearance and may even grow to include some new members. The family portrait that was taken years ago remains static and no longer represents the family today. So another portrait will have to be taken.

As time goes by, your data may change and grow with newly added rows and columns. However, the pivot cache that feeds your pivot table report is disconnected from your data source, so it cannot represent any of the changes you make to your date source until you take another snapshot.

2

The action of updating your pivot cache by taking another snapshot of your data source is called *refreshing* your data. There are two reasons you may have to refresh your pivot table report:

■ Changes have been made to your existing data source.

■ Your data source's range has been expanded with the addition of rows or columns.

These two scenarios are handled in different ways.

Changes Have Been Made to Your Existing Data Source

If a few cells in your pivot table's source data have changed due to edits or updates, your pivot table report can be refreshed with a few clicks. Simply right-click inside your pivot table report and select Refresh Data. This selection takes another snapshot of your dataset, overwriting your previous pivot cache with the latest data.

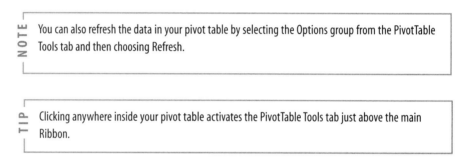

> **NOTE**
> You can also refresh the data in your pivot table by selecting the Options group from the PivotTable Tools tab and then choosing Refresh.

> **TIP**
> Clicking anywhere inside your pivot table activates the PivotTable Tools tab just above the main Ribbon.

Your Data Source's Range Has Been Expanded with the Addition of Rows or Columns

When changes have been made to your data source that affect its range (for example, you've added rows or columns), you have to update the range being captured by the pivot cache.

To do this, click anywhere inside your pivot table and then select Options from the PivotTable Tools tab. From here, select Change PivotTable Data Source. This selection triggers the dialog box shown in Figure 2.25.

All you have to do here is update the range to include new rows and columns. After you have specified the appropriate range, click the OK button.

Figure 2.25
The Change PivotTable Data Source dialog box enables you to redefine the source data for your pivot table.

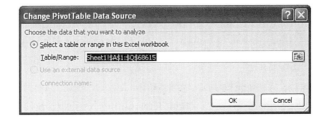

Sharing the Pivot Cache

Many times, you may have to analyze the same dataset in multiple ways. In most cases, this process requires you to create separate pivot tables from the same data source. You might remember that each time you create a pivot table, you are storing a snapshot of your entire dataset in a pivot cache. Every pivot cache that is created increases your memory usage and file size. Because of this increase in file size, you should consider sharing your pivot cache. That is, in those situations in which you need to create multiple pivot tables from the same data source, use the same pivot cache to feed multiple pivot tables. By using the same pivot cache for multiple pivot tables, you gain a certain level of efficiency when it comes to memory usage and files size.

In previous versions of Excel, when you created a pivot table using a dataset already being used in another pivot table, Excel actually gave you the option of using the same pivot cache. In Excel 2007, Excel gives you no such option. Each time you create a new pivot table in Excel 2007, a new pivot cache is automatically created even though one may already exist for the dataset being used. The side effect of this behavior is that your spreadsheet bloats with redundant data each time you create a new pivot table using the same dataset.

You can easily work around this potential problem by employing copy and paste. That's right. By simply copying a pivot table and pasting it somewhere else, you create another pivot table, *without* duplicating the pivot cache. This allows you to link as many pivot tables as you want to the same pivot cache, with a negligible increase in memory and file size.

Side Effects of Sharing a Pivot Cache

It's important to note that there are a few side effects to sharing a pivot cache. For example, suppose you have two pivot tables using the same pivot cache. Certain actions affect both pivot tables. They include

- **Refreshing Your Data**—You cannot refresh one pivot table and not the other. Refreshing affects both tables.

- **Adding a Calculated Field**—If you create a calculated field in one pivot table, your newly created calculated field shows up in the other pivot table's field list.

- **Adding a Calculated Item**—If you create a calculated item in one pivot table, it shows in the other as well.

- **Grouping or Ungrouping Fields**—Any grouping or ungrouping you perform affects both pivot tables. For instance, suppose you group a date field in one pivot table to show months. The same date field in the other pivot table is also grouped to show months.

Although none of these side effects are critical flaws in the concept of sharing a pivot cache, it is important to keep them in mind when determining if using a pivot table as your data source is the best option for your situation.

Saving Time with New Pivot Table Tools

Microsoft has invested a lot of time and effort in the overall pivot table experience. The results of these efforts are tools that make pivot table functionality more accessible and easier to use. Let's take a moment to look at a few of the tools that help you save time when managing your pivot tables.

Deferring Layout Updates

The frustrating part of building a pivot table from a large data source is that each time you add a field to a pivot area, you are left waiting while Excel crunches through all that data. This can become a maddeningly time-consuming process if you have to add several fields to your pivot table.

Excel 2007 offers some relief for this problem by providing a way to defer layout changes until you are ready to apply them. You can activate this option by clicking the relatively inconspicuous Defer Layout Update check box on the PivotTable Field List dialog box, as shown in Figure 2.26.

Here's how this feature works. When you place a check in the Defer Layout Update check box, you prevent your pivot table from making real-time updates as you move your fields around without your pivot table. In Figure 2.26, notice that fields in the drop zones are not in the pivot table yet. The reason is that the Defer Layout Update check box is active. When you are ready to apply your changes, simply click the Update button on the lower-right corner of the PivotTable Field List dialog box.

> **NOTE**
> Remember to remove the check from the Defer Layout Update check box when you are done building your pivot table. Leaving it checked results in your pivot table remaining in a state of manual updates, preventing you from using the other features of the pivot table (that is, sorting, filtering, grouping).

Starting Over with One Click

Often you might want to start from scratch when working with your pivot table layouts. Excel 2007 provides a simple way to essentially start over without deleting your pivot cache. Select Options under the PivotTable Tools tab and select the Clear dropdown.

Figure 2.26
Click the Defer Layout
Update check box to pre-
vent your pivot table
from updating while you
add fields.

As you can see in Figure 2.27, this command allows you to either clear your entire pivot
table layout or remove any existing filters you may have applied in your pivot table.

Figure 2.27
The Clear command
allows you to clear your
pivot table fields or
remove the applied fil-
ters in your pivot table.

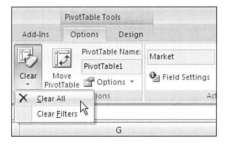

Relocating Your Pivot Table

You may find that, after you have created your pivot table, you need to move it to another
location. It may be in the way of other analyses on the worksheet, or you may simply need
to move it to another worksheet. Although there are several ways to move your pivot table,
Excel 2007 provides a no-frills way to easily change the location of your pivot table.

Select Options under the PivotTable Tools tab and select Move PivotTable. This icon activates the Move PivotTable dialog box illustrated in Figure 2.28. All you have to do here is specify where you want your pivot table moved.

Figure 2.28
The Move PivotTable dialog box allows you to quickly move your pivot table to another location.

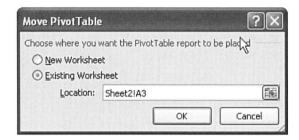

Next Steps

In the next chapter, you learn how to enhance your pivot table reports by customizing your fields, changing field names, changing summary calculations, applying formats to data fields, adding and removing subtotals, and using the Show As setting.

Customizing a Pivot Table

Although pivot tables provide an extremely fast way to summarize data, sometimes the pivot table defaults aren't exactly what you need. You can use many powerful settings to tweak the information in your pivot table. These tweaks range from making cosmetic changes to changing the underlying calculation used in the pivot table.

In Excel 2007, controls to customize the pivot table are found in a myriad of places: the Options ribbon, the Design ribbon, the Field Settings dialog box, the Data Field Settings dialog box, the PivotTable Options dialog box, and context menus. Rather than cover each set of controls sequentially, this chapter seeks to cover functional areas in customizing pivot table customization:

- **Minor Cosmetic Changes**—Changing blanks to zeros, adjusting the number format, renaming a field. Although these changes are minor, they are annoying and affect almost every pivot table that you create.

- **Layout Changes**—Comparing three possible layouts, showing/hiding subtotals and totals.

- **Major Cosmetic Changes**—Using table styles to quickly format your table.

- **Summary Calculation**—Changing from Sum to Count, Min, Max, and more. If you have a table that defaults to Count of Revenue instead of Sum of Revenue, you need to visit this section.

- **Advanced Calculation**—Using settings to show data as a running total, % of total, and more.

- **Other Options**—Quickly reviewing more obscure options found throughout the Excel interface.

IN THIS CHAPTER

Making Common Cosmetic Changes 46

Making Layout Changes 52

Case Study: Converting a Pivot Table
to Values 56

Customizing the Pivot Table Appearance
with Styles and Themes 61

Changing Summary Calculations 65

Adding and Removing Subtotals 68

Using Running Total Options 70

Case Study: Producing Revenue by Line of
Business Report 77

Next Steps 81

Making Common Cosmetic Changes

A few changes need to be made to almost every pivot table. These changes make your pivot table easier to understand and interpret.

Figure 3.1 shows a typical pivot table. This pivot table has two fields in the Row Labels area and one field in the Column Labels area.

Figure 3.1
A default pivot table.

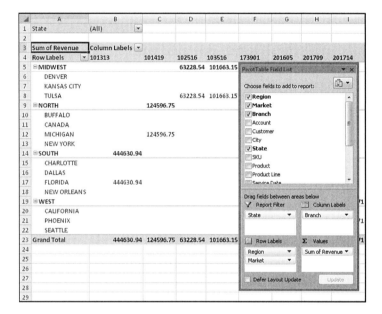

This pivot table contains several annoying items that you might want to change quickly:

- The default table style uses no gridlines. This makes it difficult to follow the rows and columns across.

- Numbers in the values area are in a general number format. There are no commas, currency symbols, and so on.

- For sparse datasets, there are many blanks in the values area. The blank cell in B6 indicates that there were no sales in Denver for branch 101313. Most people would prefer to see a zero instead of blanks.

- Excel renames fields in the values area with the unimaginative name Sum of Revenue. You can change this name.

You can correct each of these annoyances with just a few mouse clicks. The following sections address each issue.

Applying a Table Style to Restore Gridlines

The default pivot table layout contains no gridlines. This format is annoying and a giant step backward. Luckily, you can easily apply a table style. Any table style that you choose will be better than the default.

Follow these steps to apply a table style:

1. Make sure that the active cell is in the pivot table.
2. From the Ribbon, choose the Design tab.
3. Three arrows appear at the right side of the PivotTable Style gallery. Click the bottom arrow to open the complete gallery, as shown in Figure 3.2.
4. Choose any style other than the first style from the drop-down. Styles toward the bottom of the gallery tend to have more formatting.

Figure 3.2
The gallery contains 75 styles to choose from.

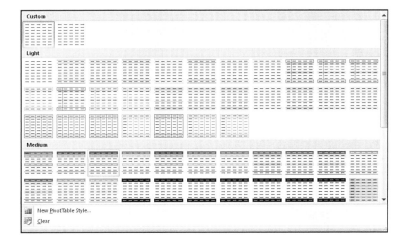

It doesn't matter which style you choose from the gallery; any of the 74 other styles are better than the default style.

➡ For more details about customizing styles, **see** "Customizing the Pivot Table Appearance with Styles and Themes," **p. 61**.

Changing the Number Format to Add Thousands Separators

If you've gone to the trouble of formatting your underlying data, you might expect that the pivot table would capture some of this formatting. Unfortunately, it does not.

Even if your underlying data fields were formatted with a certain numeric format, the default pivot table presents values formatted with a general format.

For example, in the figures in this chapter, the numbers are in the hundreds of thousands. At this level of sales, you would normally have a thousands separator and probably no decimal places. Although the original data had a numeric format applied, the pivot table routinely formats your numbers in an ugly general style.

You access the numeric format for a field in the Data Field Settings dialog box. There are four ways to display this dialog box:

- Right-click a number in the values area of the pivot table and choose Value Field Settings.

- Double-click the Sum of Revenue cell in cell A3 of Figure 3.3.

- Click the drop-down arrow on the Sum of Revenue field in the drop zones of the PivotTable Field List. Then choose Field Settings from the context menu.

- Select any cell in the values area of the pivot table. From the Options ribbon, choose Field Settings from the Active Field group.

As shown in Figure 3.3, the Data Field Settings dialog box is displayed. To change the numeric format, click the Number Format button in the lower-left corner.

Figure 3.3
Display the Data Field Settings dialog box and then click Number Format.

In the Format Cells dialog box, you can choose any built-in number format or choose a custom format. The custom number format shown in Figure 3.4 displays numbers in thousands with a *K* abbreviation after the number.

> **NOTE** Although Excel 2007 offers a Live Preview feature for many dialog boxes, the Format Cells dialog box does not offer one. You must assign the number format and then click OK twice to see the changes.

Figure 3.4
Choose an easier-to-read number format from the Format Cells dialog box.

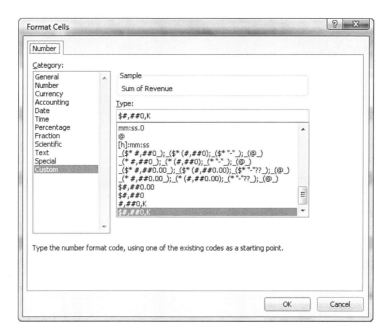

Replacing Blanks with Zeros

One of the elements of good spreadsheet design is that you should never leave blank cells in a numeric section of the worksheet. Even Microsoft believes in this rule; if your source data for a pivot table contains 1 million numeric cells and 1 blank cell, Excel 2007 treats the entire column as if it were text. This is why it is incredibly annoying that the default setting for a pivot table leaves many blanks in the values area of some pivot tables.

The blank tells you that there were no sales for that particular combination of labels. In the default view, an actual zero is used to indicate that there was activity, but the total sales were zero. This value might mean that a customer bought something and then returned it, resulting in net sales of zero. Although there are limited applications in which you would want to differentiate between having no sales and having net zero sales, this seems rare. In 99% of the cases, you should fill in the blank cells with zeros.

Follow these steps to change this setting for the current pivot table:

1. Select a cell inside the pivot table.
2. On the Options ribbon, choose the Options icon from the Pivot Table Options group to display the PivotTable Options dialog box.
3. On the Layout & Format tab, in the Format section, type **0** next to the field labeled For Empty Cells Show (see Figure 3.5).
4. Click OK to accept the change.

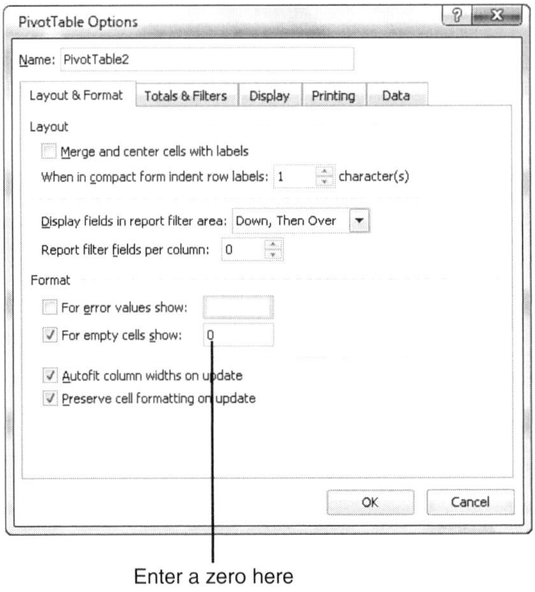

Figure 3.5
Enter a zero here to
replace the blank cells
with zero.

Enter a zero here

The result is that the pivot table is filled with zeros instead of blanks, as shown in
Figure 3.6.

Figure 3.6
Your report is now a solid
contiguous block of non-
blank cells.

Changing a Field Name

Every field in the final pivot table has a name. Fields in the row, column, and filter areas inherit their names from the heading in the source data. Fields in the data section are given names such as Sum of Revenue. In some instances, you may prefer to print a different name in the pivot table. You might prefer Total Revenue instead of the default name. In these situations, the capability to change your field names comes in quite handy.

Although many of the names are inherited from headings in the original dataset, when your data is from an external data source, you might not have control over field names. In these cases, you might want to change the names of the fields as well.

To change a field name in the values area, follow these steps:

1. Select a cell in the pivot table that contains the appropriate value. In Figure 3.7, the values area contains both hours and revenue. If you want to rename Sum of Revenue, select any cell from B5:B24.

2. On the Options ribbon, select the Field Settings icon from the Active Field group.

3. In the Data Field Settings dialog box, type a new name in the Custom Name field. You can enter any unique name you like. One common frustration occurs when you would like to rename Sum of Revenue to Revenue. The problem is that this name is not allowed because it is not unique; you already have a Revenue field in the source data. To work around this limitation, you can name the field and add a space to the end of the name. Excel considers "Revenue " (with a space) to be different from "Revenue" (with no space). Because this change is cosmetic, the readers of your spreadsheet will not notice the space after the name.

The new name appears in the pivot table. Now look at cell B5 in Figure 3.7. The name Revenue (with a space) is less awkward than the default Sum of Revenue.

Figure 3.7
The name typed in the Custom Name box appears in the pivot table. Although names should be unique, you can trick Excel into accepting a similar name by adding a space to the end of it.

Making Layout Changes

Excel 2007 offers three layout styles instead of the two styles available in previous versions of Excel. The new style—Compact Layout—is promoted to be the default layout for your pivot tables.

Layout changes are controlled in the Layout group of the Design ribbon, as shown in Figure 3.8. This group offers four icons:

- **Subtotals**—Moves subtotals to the top or bottom of each group, or turns them off.
- **Grand Totals**—Turns the grand totals on or off for rows and columns.
- **Report Layout**—Uses the Compact, Outline, or Tabular forms.
- **Blank Rows**—Inserts or removes blank lines after each group.

Figure 3.8
The Layout group on the Design ribbon offers different layouts and options for totals.

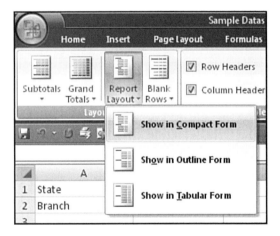

Using the New Compact Layout

By default, all new pivot tables use the compact layout shown in Figure 3.6. In this layout, multiple fields in the row area are stacked up in column A. Note in the figure that the Denver market and Midwest region are both in column A.

The compact form is suited for using the Expand and Collapse icons. Select one of the market cells—A7 as an example—and click the Collapse Entire Field icon on the Options ribbon. Excel hides all the detail below this field and shows only the regions, as shown in Figure 3.9.

Collapse icon

Figure 3.9
Click the Collapse Entire
Field icon to hide levels
of detail.

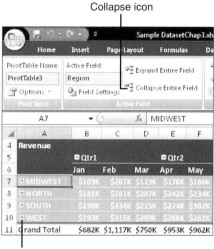

Plus icon

After a field is collapsed, you can show detail for individual regions by using the plus icons
in column A, or you can click Expand Entire Field on the Options ribbon to see the detail
again.

> TIP If you select a cell in the innermost row field and click Expand Entire Field, Excel displays the Show
> Detail dialog box, as shown in Figure 3.10, to allow you to add a new innermost row field.

Figure 3.10
When you attempt to
expand the innermost
field, Excel offers to add a
new innermost field.

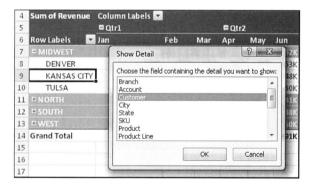

Using the Outline Form Layout

When you select Design, Layout, Report Layout, Show in Outline Form, Excel fills column A with the outermost row field. Additional row fields occupy columns B, C, and so on.

Figure 3.11 shows the pivot table in Outline form.

Figure 3.11
The Outline layout puts each row field in a separate column.

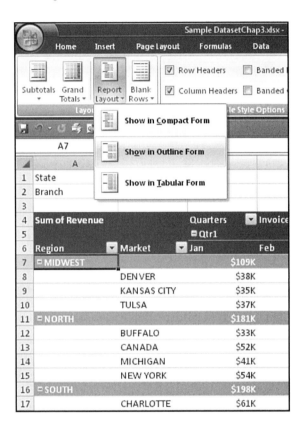

This layout is better suited if you plan to copy the values from the pivot table to a new location for further analysis. Although the Compact layout offers a clever approach by squeezing multiple fields in one column, it is not ideal for reusing the data later.

By default, both the Compact and Outline layouts put the subtotals at the top of each group. You can use the Subtotals drop-down on the Design ribbon to move the totals to the bottom of each group, as shown in Figure 3.12.

Using the Traditional Tabular Layout

Pivot table veterans will recognize the tabular layout shown in Figure 3.13. This layout is similar to the one that has been used in pivot tables since their invention. In this layout, the subtotals can never appear at the top of the group.

Figure 3.12
With subtotals at the
bottom of each group,
the pivot table occupies
several more rows.

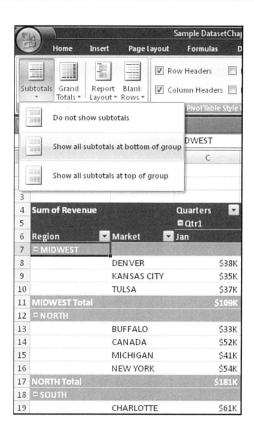

The tabular layout is probably the best layout if you hope to later use the resulting summary data in a subsequent analysis.

Figure 3.13
The tabular layout is similar to pivot tables in prior versions of Excel.

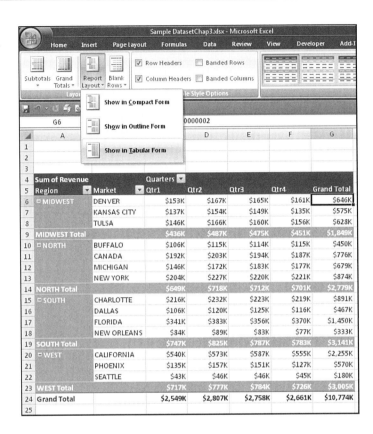

Sum of Revenue		Quarters ▼				
Region ▼	Market ▼	Qtr1	Qtr2	Qtr3	Qtr4	Grand Total
⊟ MIDWEST	DENVER	$153K	$167K	$165K	$161K	$646K
	KANSAS CITY	$137K	$154K	$149K	$135K	$575K
	TULSA	$146K	$166K	$160K	$156K	$628K
MIDWEST Total		$436K	$487K	$475K	$451K	$1,849K
⊟ NORTH	BUFFALO	$106K	$115K	$114K	$115K	$450K
	CANADA	$192K	$203K	$194K	$187K	$776K
	MICHIGAN	$146K	$172K	$183K	$177K	$679K
	NEW YORK	$204K	$227K	$220K	$221K	$874K
NORTH Total		$649K	$718K	$712K	$701K	$2,779K
⊟ SOUTH	CHARLOTTE	$216K	$232K	$223K	$219K	$891K
	DALLAS	$106K	$120K	$125K	$116K	$467K
	FLORIDA	$341K	$383K	$356K	$370K	$1,450K
	NEW ORLEANS	$84K	$89K	$83K	$77K	$333K
SOUTH Total		$747K	$825K	$787K	$783K	$3,141K
⊟ WEST	CALIFORNIA	$540K	$573K	$587K	$555K	$2,255K
	PHOENIX	$135K	$157K	$151K	$127K	$570K
	SEATTLE	$43K	$46K	$46K	$45K	$180K
WEST Total		$717K	$777K	$784K	$726K	$3,005K
Grand Total		$2,549K	$2,807K	$2,758K	$2,661K	$10,774K

CASE STUDY

Converting a Pivot Table to Values

Say that you want to summarize your dataset to show sales by Region, Market, and Quarter. Your goal is to export this data for use by another system.

The result in Figure 3.13 is close to the desired output, with a few exceptions:

- The subtotals in rows 9, 14, 19, and 23 should be removed.
- The blank cells in A7:A8, A11:A13, A16:A18, and A21:A22 should be filled in.
- The grand total should be removed from row 24 and column G.
- The pivot table should be converted from a live pivot table to static values.

To make these changes, follow these steps:

1. Select any cell in the pivot table.
2. From the Design ribbon, choose Grand Totals, Off for Rows and Columns.

3. Select Design, Subtotals, Do Not Show Subtotals.

4. Select A5:F19, as shown in Figure 3.14.

Figure 3.14
After removing the total and subtotal information, select the data and one row of headings.

Sum of Revenue		Quarters			
Region	Market	Qtr1	Qtr2	Qtr3	Qtr4
MIDWEST	DENVER		$153K	$167K	$165K	$161K
	KANSAS CITY		$137K	$154K	$149K	$135K
	TULSA		$146K	$166K	$160K	$156K
NORTH	BUFFALO		$106K	$115K	$114K	$115K
	CANADA		$192K	$203K	$194K	$187K
	MICHIGAN		$146K	$172K	$183K	$177K
	NEW YORK		$204K	$227K	$220K	$221K
SOUTH	CHARLOTTE		$216K	$232K	$223K	$219K
	DALLAS		$106K	$120K	$125K	$116K
	FLORIDA		$341K	$383K	$356K	$370K
	NEW ORLEANS		$84K	$89K	$83K	$77K
WEST	CALIFORNIA		$540K	$573K	$587K	$555K
	PHOENIX		$135K	$157K	$151K	$127K
	SEATTLE		$43K	$46K	$46K	$45K

5. Press Ctrl+C to copy the data from the pivot table.

6. In a blank section of the workbook, choose Home, Clipboard, Paste, Paste Values to make a static copy of the data. The final step is filling in the blank cells in the first column of the table.

7. Select column A of the dataset.

8. In the Editing group of the Home ribbon, choose the Find & Select drop-down and then choose Go To Special.

9. In the Go To Special dialog box, as shown in Figure 3.15, select Blanks and click OK.

10. Type the equal sign (=), press the up-arrow key, and then press Ctrl+Enter to accept this formula for all the blank cells. This combination enters a formula in which each blank cell inherits the value from the cell above it, as shown in Figure 3.16.

> CAUTION
>
> If you attempt to choose Copy and then Paste Values, Excel complains that you cannot use this command on nonadjacent cells. Instead, follow steps 11–13.

11. Reselect the cells in column A.

12. Click the Copy icon in the Clipboard group on the Home ribbon.

13. Choose Paste Values from the Paste drop-down on the Home ribbon.

Figure 3.15
Choosing Blanks from
the Go To Special dialog
box selects only the
blank cells in column A.

Figure 3.16
The last step is changing
the formulas in column A
to values.

	A	B	C	D	E	F
1	Region	Market	Qtr1	Qtr2	Qtr3	Qtr4
2	MIDWEST	DENVER	152765.3	166664.4	165395.1	160758.5
3	MIDWEST	KANSAS CITY	136665.2	154095.8	149462	134676
4	MIDWEST	TULSA	146153.9	166451.2	159978.8	155821
5	NORTH	BUFFALO	106007.1	114995.1	114101.4	115374.7
6	NORTH	CANADA	192128.2	203268.4	194148.3	186700.4
7	NORTH	MICHIGAN	146055.7	172088.1	183393.4	177167.7
8	NORTH	NEW YORK	204326.6	227364.4	220464.5	221425.4
9	SOUTH	CHARLOTTE	215948.3	232195.5	223124.8	219253.9
10	SOUTH	DALLAS	105561.7	120483.6	124672.2	116371.9
11	SOUTH	FLORIDA	341442.1	382833.5	355618.1	370498.4
12	SOUTH	NEW ORLEANS	84270.91	89273.93	83194.94	76713.87
13	WEST	CALIFORNIA	539932.3	573288.1	586729.8	554785.2
14	WEST	PHOENIX	134711.2	157080.3	151470.6	126993
15	WEST	SEATTLE	42662.6	46484.11	46151.79	44528.71
16						

The result is a solid block of summary data, as shown in Figure 3.17. These 90 cells are a summary of the 1.1 million cells in the original dataset, but they also are suitable for exporting to other systems.

Figure 3.17
The final dataset is suitable for exporting to another system.

▲	A	B	C	D	E	F
1	Region	Market	Qtr1	Qtr2	Qtr3	Qtr4
2	MIDWEST	DENVER	152765.3	166664.4	165395.1	160758.5
3	MIDWEST	KANSAS CITY	136665.2	154095.8	149462	134676
4	MIDWEST	TULSA	146153.9	166451.2	159978.8	155821
5	NORTH	BUFFALO	106007.1	114995.1	114101.4	115374.7
6	NORTH	CANADA	192128.2	203268.4	194148.3	186700.4
7	NORTH	MICHIGAN	146055.7	172088.1	183393.4	177167.7
8	NORTH	NEW YORK	204326.6	227364.4	220464.5	221425.4
9	SOUTH	CHARLOTTE	215948.3	232195.5	223124.8	219253.9
10	SOUTH	DALLAS	105561.7	120483.6	124672.2	116371.9
11	SOUTH	FLORIDA	341442.1	382833.5	355618.1	370498.4
12	SOUTH	NEW ORLEANS	84270.91	89273.93	83194.94	76713.87
13	WEST	CALIFORNIA	539932.3	573288.1	586729.8	554785.2
14	WEST	PHOENIX	134711.2	157080.3	151470.6	126993
15	WEST	SEATTLE	42662.6	46484.11	46151.79	44528.71
16						

3

Controlling Blank Lines, Grand Totals, Subtotals, and Other Settings

Additional settings in the pivot table allow you to toggle various elements.

Subtotals can be moved to the top or bottom of the group or turned off entirely. As noted previously, moving the subtotals to the top of the group saves a few rows in the pivot table. However, top subtotals are available only when the layout is set to Compact or Outline. Use the Subtotals icon on the Design ribbon to choose the subtotals option. Figure 3.18 shows the subtotals at the top of each group.

Grand totals can appear at the bottom of each column and/or at the end of each row, or they can be turned off altogether. Settings for grand totals appear in the Grand Totals drop-down of the Layout group on the Design ribbon. The wording in this drop-down seems just a bit confusing.

If you would like a grand total column on the right side of the table, you need to select On for Rows only. Even though it is a grand total column, each total is totaling a single row.

Similarly, to add a grand total row, you need to select On for Rows Columns only. Each individual grand total in the total row is totaling the cells in a column.

In Figure 3.18, the grand total column appears because the Grand Totals drop-down is set to On For Rows Only.

The Blank Rows drop-down allows you to insert blank lines between groups. In Figure 3.18, the blank lines in rows 13, 19, and 25 appear because Insert Blank Line After Each Item was selected in the Blank Rows drop-down.

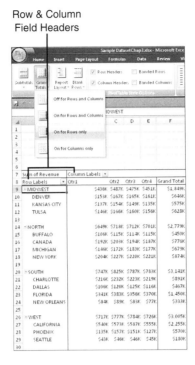

Figure 3.18
Subtotals at the top, grand totals for the rows, and blank lines between groups are controlled through icons in the Layout group on the Design ribbon.

As you examine the pivot table in Figure 3.18, you might think the area around B8:B9 appears strange. Whereas the sales figures for columns C, D, and E are closely aligned with the headings, the Qtr1 heading in B8 appears far away from the sales figures in B9:B29. This happens because all the headings in B8:E8 are left-aligned. Something is causing column B to be too wide. That something is the text Column Labels in B7. This text, plus Row Labels in A8, is a new feature in Excel 2007. Although this feature might have been designed to improve readability, it is annoying that the text makes column B too wide.

To remove these text entries, click the Field Headers icon in the Show/Hide group on the Options ribbon. This group also has icons to turn off the plus and minus buttons or to hide the PivotTable Field List. Figure 3.19 shows this section of the Ribbon, as well as the pivot table with all three items turned off.

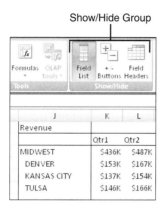

Figure 3.19
In Excel 2007, field headers serve little purpose.

Customizing the Pivot Table Appearance with Styles and Themes

The PivotTable Styles gallery on the Design ribbon offers 84 built-in styles. Grouped into 28 styles each of Light, Medium, and Dark, the gallery offers variations on the accent colors used in the current theme.

Note that you can modify the thumbnails for the 84 styles shown in the gallery by using the four check boxes in the PivotTable Style Options group. In Figure 3.20, the 84 styles are shown with all four of the option buttons unchecked.

In Figure 3.21, the 84 styles are shown with accents for row headers, column headers, and alternating colors in the columns.

The PivotTable Style Options group appears to the left of the PivotTable Styles gallery. If you want banded rows or columns, it is best to choose this option before opening the gallery. Some of the 84 themes do not support banded columns or banded rows.

> **TIP**
> By checking the Banded Columns check box prior to opening the gallery, you can see which styles support the banded columns. If the Banded Columns or Rows check box is selected and the thumbnail in the gallery does not show the effect, you know to avoid that style.

Excel 2007's Live Preview feature works in the styles gallery. As you hover your mouse cursor over style thumbnails, the worksheet shows a preview of the style.

Figure 3.20
The 84 thumbnails appear one way when no style options are checked.

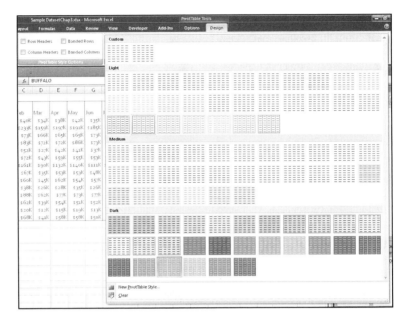

Figure 3.21
The 84 thumbnails appear differently with three style options checked. You can see that many of the styles do not support banded columns, even though this option is chosen.

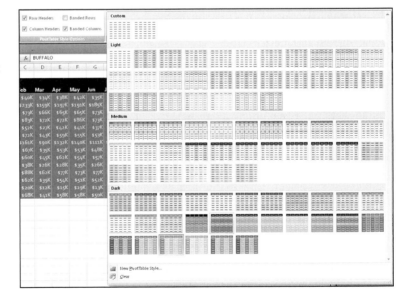

Customizing a Style

You can create your own pivot table styles. The new styles are added to the gallery and will be available on every new pivot table created on your computer.

Say that you want to create a pivot table style in which the banded colors are two rows high. Follow these steps to create the new style:

1. Find an existing style in the PivotTable Styles gallery that supports banded rows. Right-click the style in the gallery and choose Duplicate. Excel displays the Modify Table Quick Style dialog box.

2. Choose a new name for the style. Excel initially appends a *2* to the existing style name, so you have a name like PivotStyleMedium16 2.

3. In the Table Element list, click on First Row Stripe. A new section called Stripe Size appears in the dialog box.

4. Choose 2 from the Stripe Size drop-down, as shown in Figure 3.22.

Figure 3.22
Customize the style in the Modify Table Quick Style dialog box.

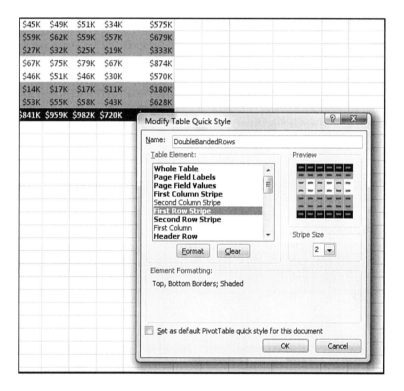

5. If you want to change the stripe color, click the Format button. The Format Cells dialog box appears. Here, click the Fill tab and then choose a fill color. Click OK to accept the color and return to the Modify Table Quick Style dialog box.

6. In the Table Element List, click on Second Row Stripe. Change the Stripe Size drop-down to 2.

7. Click OK. Prepare to be disappointed that the change didn't work. It's okay, though. When you modified table style Medium 16, you actually created a brand new style. The pivot table is still formatted in the original style.

8. Open the PivotTable Styles gallery. Your new style is added to the top of the gallery in the Custom section. Choose the style to apply the formatting, as shown in Figure 3.23.

Figure 3.23
Your new style is available at the top of the gallery.

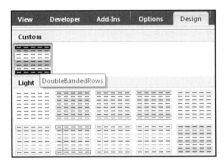

Choosing a Default Style for Future Pivot Tables

You can control which style is the default style to use for all future pivot tables on the computer. The default can either be one of the built-in styles or a new custom style that you modified.

In the PivotTable Styles gallery on the Design ribbon, right-click the style and choose Set as Default.

Modifying Styles with Document Themes

The formatting options for pivot tables in Excel 2007 are impressive. The 84 styles, combined with 8 combinations of the Style options, make for hundreds of possible format combinations.

In case you ever become tired of these combinations, you can visit the Themes drop-down on the Page Layout ribbon. Twenty built-in themes are available here. Each theme has a new combination of accent colors, fonts, and shape effects. Choosing a new theme affects the fonts and colors in your pivot table styles.

To change a document theme, open the Themes drop-down on the Page Layout ribbon. As you hover the mouse cursor over the themes in the drop-down, Live Preview shows you the colors and fonts in your table, as shown in Figure 3.24. To select a theme, click on it.

> **CAUTION**
>
> Changing the theme affects the entire workbook. It changes the colors, fonts, and effects of all charts, shapes, tables, and pivot tables on all worksheets of the active workbook.

> **TIP**
>
> Some of the themes have contemporary fonts. You can apply the colors from a new theme without changing the fonts in your document by using the Colors drop-down in the Themes group on the Page Layout ribbon.

Figure 3.24
Choose a document theme to modify the colors and fonts in the built-in styles.

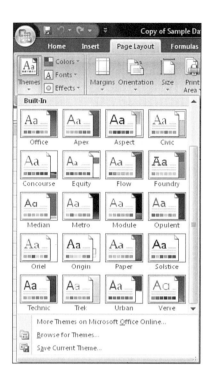

Changing Summary Calculations

When creating your pivot table report, Excel , by default, summarizes your data by either counting or summing the items. Instead of Sum or Count, you might want to choose functions such as Min, Max, and Count Numeric. In all, 11 options are available. However, the common reason to change a summary calculation is that Excel incorrectly chose to count instead of sum your data.

Understanding Why One Blank Cell Causes a Count

If all the cells in a column contain numeric data, Excel chooses to sum. If just one cell is either blank or contains text, Excel chooses to count.

In Figure 3.25, the worksheet contains more than 60,000 numeric entries in column N and a single blank cell in N2. The one blank cell is enough to cause Excel to count the data instead of summing.

In Excel 2007, the first clue that you have a problem appears when you click the check box for Revenue in the Fields section of the PivotTable Field List. If Excel moves the Revenue field to the Row Labels drop zone, you know that Excel considers the field to be text instead of numeric.

Figure 3.25
The single blank cell in N2 causes problems in the default pivot table.

▲	K	L	M	N	O
1	Service Date	Invoice	Invoice Date	Revenue	Hours
2	1/14/2007	25207118	1/15/2007		3
3	2/11/2007	25405302	2/12/2007	$157.52	3
4	3/9/2007	25606405	3/10/2007	$157.52	3
5	4/27/2007	26027333	4/28/2007	$157.52	3
6	4/27/2007	26027497	4/28/2007	$157.52	3
7	6/18/2007	26454936	6/18/2007	$157.52	3

Be vigilant while dragging fields into the Values drop zone. If a calculation appears to be dramatically too low, check to see whether the field name reads Count of Revenue instead of Sum of Revenue. When you created the pivot table in Figure 3.26, you should have noticed that your company had only $68,613 in revenue instead of $10 million. This should be a hint to notice that the heading in B3 reads Count of Revenue instead of Sum of Revenue. In fact, 68,613 is the number of records in the dataset.

Figure 3.26
Your revenue numbers look anemic. Notice in cell B3 that Excel chose to count instead of sum the revenue. This often happens if you inadvertently have one blank cell in your Revenue column.

▲	A	B	C
1			
2			
3	Row Labels ▼	Count of Revenue	
4	MIDWEST	12432	
5	NORTH	16103	
6	SOUTH	22186	
7	WEST	17892	
8	Grand Total	68613	
9			
10			

You can easily override the incorrect Count calculation. Activate the Data Field Settings dialog box by double-clicking on Count of Revenue and then change the Summarize Value Field By setting from Count to Sum, as shown in Figure 3.27.

Using Functions Other Than Count or Sum

Excel offers a total of 11 functions in the Summarize By section of the PivotTable Field dialog box. The options available are as follows:

- **Sum**—Provides a total of all numeric data.
- **Count**—Counts all cells, including numeric, text, and error cells. This is equivalent to the Excel function =COUNTA().
- **Average**—Provides an average. Figure 3.28 shows a report detailing average sales per region and product line. An analyst might wonder why the average housekeeping sale in the West is $152 higher than in the Midwest.

Figure 3.27
Change the function from Count to Sum in the Data Field Settings dialog box.

Figure 3.28
Average sales per region and product line.

Average of Revenue	MIDWEST	NORTH	SOUTH	WEST	Grand Total
Housekeeping	401	417	512	553	449
Landscaping	180	161	174	172	171
Maintenance	133	149	126	156	139
Grand Total	149	173	142	168	157

- **Max**—Shows the largest value.

- **Min**—Shows the smallest value.

- **Product**—Multiplies all the cells together. For example, if your dataset has cells with values of 3, 4, and 5, the product would be 60.

- **Count Nums**—Counts only the numeric cells. This is equivalent to the Excel function =COUNT().

- **StdDev** and **StdDevP**—Calculate the standard deviation. Use StdDevP if your dataset contains the complete population. Use StdDev if your dataset contains a sample of the population. Figure 3.29 shows the results of two tests. Although the students averaged 87% on both tests, the math test had a higher standard deviation. Standard deviations explain how tightly results are grouped around the mean.

- **Var** and **VarP**—Calculate the statistical variance. Use VarP if your data contains a complete population. If your data contains only a sampling of the complete population, use Var to estimate the variance.

Figure 3.29
A low standard deviation
on the science test
means that all the stu-
dents understand the
concepts equally well. A
higher standard devia-
tion on the math test
indicates that student
scores were spread over
a wider range.

	Average of Grade	StdDevp of Grade2
Math	87.0%	3.7%
Science	87.0%	0.6%
Grand Total	**87.0%**	**2.7%**

Adding and Removing Subtotals

Subtotals are undeniably an essential feature of pivot table reporting. Sometimes you may want to suppress the display of subtotals, and other times you may want to show more than one subtotal per field.

Suppress Subtotals When You Have Many Row Fields

When you have many row fields in your report, subtotals can mire your view. Take the example in Figure 3.30. You might want to suppress the subtotals for the Market and Product Line fields.

Figure 3.30
Sometimes you don't
need subtotals at every
level.

Region	Market	Product Line	Product	Sum of Revenue
MIDWEST	DENVER	Housekeepin	Cleaning & Housekeeping Services	12,564
		Housekeeping Total		12,564
		Landscaping	Green Plants and Foliage Care	42,409
			Landscaping/Grounds Care	73,622
		Landscaping Total		116,030
		Maintenance	Facility Maintenance and Repair	160,324
			Fleet Maintenance	170,190
			Predictive Maintenance/Preventative Maintenance	186,475
		Maintenance Total		516,989
	DENVER Total			**645,583**
	KANSAS CITY	Housekeepin	Cleaning & Housekeeping Services	65,439
		Housekeeping Total		65,439
		Landscaping	Green Plants and Foliage Care	35,315
			Landscaping/Grounds Care	52,442
		Landscaping Total		87,757
		Maintenance	Facility Maintenance and Repair	132,120
			Fleet Maintenance	133,170
			Predictive Maintenance/Preventative Maintenance	156,412
		Maintenance Total		421,703
	KANSAS CITY Total			**574,899**
	TULSA	Housekeepin	Cleaning & Housekeeping Services	96,515

To remove subtotals for the Product Line field, click on the Product Line field in the drop zone section of the PivotTable Field List. Choose Field Settings. In the Field Settings dialog box, choose None under Subtotals, as shown in Figure 3.31.

Repeat this step for other row fields. After repeating these steps for Market, you'll find the report in Figure 3.32 to be much easier on the eyes.

Figure 3.31
Choose None to remove subtotals at the Product Line level.

Figure 3.32
After specifying None for two fields, you give the report a cleaner look.

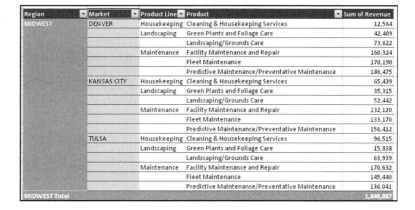

> **TIP**
> If you want to suppress the subtotals for all the row fields, it is easier to choose Design, Layout, Subtotals, Do Not Show Subtotals.

Adding Multiple Subtotals for One Field

You can add customized subtotals to a row or column label field. Select the Region field in the drop zone of the PivotTable Field List and choose Field Settings.

In the Field Settings dialog box, choose Custom and select the types of subtotals you would like to see. The dialog box in Figure 3.33 shows five subtotals selected for the Region field.

Figure 3.33
By selecting the Custom option in the Subtotals section, you can specify multiple subtotals for one field.

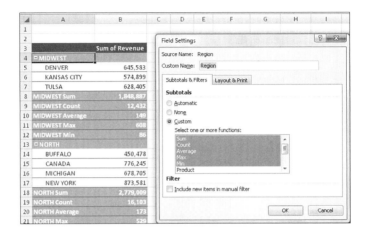

Using Running Total Options

So far, every pivot table created has used the Normal option. When you want to create running totals or compare an item to another item, you have eight choices other than Normal.

The nine options are on the second tab of the Data Field Settings dialog box. To access them, follow these steps:

1. Select a cell in the values area of your pivot table. Or, select the Sum of Revenue cell.

2. On the Options ribbon, click the Field Settings icon in the Active Group field.

3. Click the Show Values As tab in the Data Field Settings dialog box.

Initially, the Show Values As drop-down is set to Normal, and the Base Field and Base Item list boxes are grayed out, as shown in Figure 3.34.

The capability to create custom calculations is another example of the unique flexibility of pivot table reports. With the Show Data As setting, you can change the calculation for a particular data field to be based on other cells in the values area.

When you click the Show Values As drop-down, you have eight choices other than Normal. The choices are

- **% of Row**—Shows percentages that total across the pivot table to 100%.

- **% of Column**—Shows percentages that total up and down the pivot table to 100%.

- **% of Total**—Shows percentages such that all the detail cells in the pivot table total to 100%.

- **Difference From**—Shows the difference of one item compared to another item or to the previous item.

- **% of**—Expresses the values for one item as a percentage of another item.
- **% Difference From**—Expresses the percentage change from one item to another item.
- **Running Total In**—Calculates a running total.
- **Index**—Calculates the relative importance of items.

The following sections illustrate a number of these options.

Figure 3.34
Access the second tab of the Data Field Settings dialog box to see the running total options.

Display Change from Year to Year with Difference From

Companies always want to know how they are doing this month compared to last month. Or, if their business is seasonal, they want to know how they are doing this month versus the same month of last year.

To set up such a report, double-click the Sum of Revenue field and click the Show Values As tab. In the Show Data As drop-down list, select Difference From. Because you want to compare one year to another, select Years from the Base Field option. In the Base Item field are several viable options. If you always want to compare one year to the prior year, select the (Previous) option, as shown in Figure 3.35. If you have several years' worth of data and want to always compare to a base year of 2007, you could select 2007.

Figure 3.35 shows both the dialog box settings and the report that results from the settings. The report shows that January 2008 revenue was $55K higher than the same month in 2007.

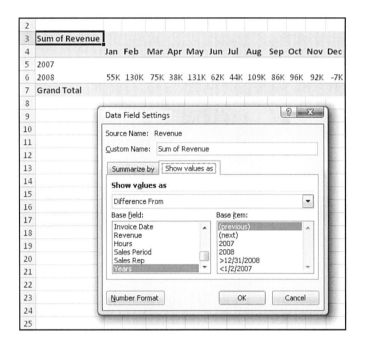

2														
3	Sum of Revenue													
4		Jan	Feb	Mar	Apr	May	Jun	Jul	Aug	Sep	Oct	Nov	Dec
5	2007												
6	2008	55K	130K	75K	38K	131K	62K	44K	109K	86K	96K	92K	-7K
7	Grand Total												

NOTE When you use an option from the Show Data As drop-down list, Excel does not change the headings in any way to indicate that the data is in something other than normal view. It is helpful to manually add a title above the pivot table to inform the readers what they are looking at.

Compare One Year to a Prior Year with % Difference From

The % Difference From option is similar to Difference From. This option displays the change as a percentage of the base item. In Figure 3.36, the report shows 2008 as a percentage change from 2007.

Track YTD Numbers with Running Total In

If you need to compare a year-to-date (YTD) total revenue by month, you can do so with the Running Total In option. In Figure 3.37, the Revenue field is set up to show a Running Total In with a base field of Invoice Date. With this report, you can see that the company earned a total of $2.6 million through March 2007.

Determine How Much Each Line of Business Contributes to the Total

The head of the company is often interested in what percentage of the revenue each division of the company is contributing. You can use the % of Row option, as in Figure 3.38, to show such a report. Each row totals to 100%. You can see that Maintenance contributed 70.97% of the revenue in February, but only 59.82% in December.

Figure 3.36
The % Difference From option shows that revenue from January 2008 is up 8.02% over January 2007.

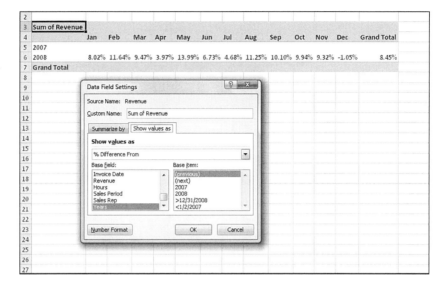

Figure 3.37
The Running Total In option is great for calculating YTD totals.

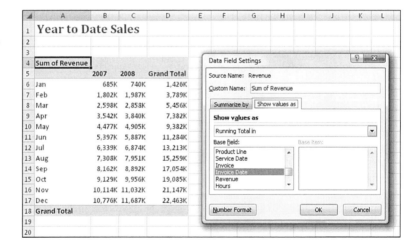

Create Seasonality Reports

A seasonality report is great for seeing the seasonality of your business. The % of Column option produces percentages that total to 100% in each column. Figure 3.39 shows a report in which Jan+Feb+Mar+…+Dec add to 100% for each year.

Measure Percentage for Two Fields with % of Total

The option % of Total can be used for a myriad of reports. Figure 3.40 shows a report by Region and Product Line. The values in each cell show the percentage of revenue contribution from that region and line. Cell F8 shows that sales from Maintenance account for 66.53% of the total revenue. The South region's sales of Maintenance account for 21.95% of total sales.

Figure 3.38
The % of Row option produces percentages that total to 100% in each row.

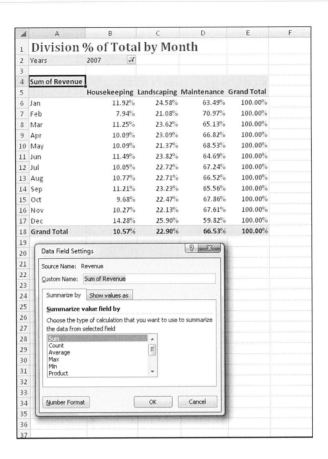

Figure 3.39
The % of Column option produces percentages that total to 100% in each column. This option is great for measuring seasonality.

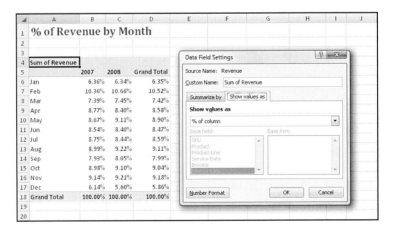

Figure 3.40
The % of Total option produces a report in which every cell is a percentage of total sales. The manager of the South Region Maintenance department can use this report to explain why his department should get a raise this year.

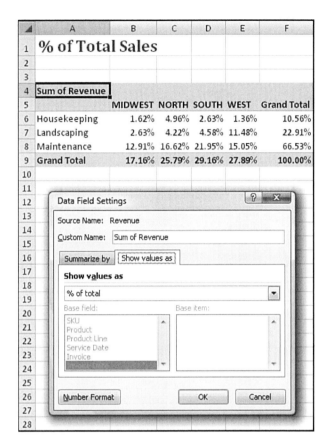

Compare One Line to Another Line Using % Of

The % Of option allows you to compare one item to another item. This comparison might be relevant if you believe that housekeeping and landscaping should be related. You can set up a pivot table that compares each product line to landscaping revenue. The result is shown in Figure 3.41.

Track Relative Importance with the Index Option

The final option, Index, creates a fairly obscure calculation. Microsoft claims that this calculation describes the relative importance of a cell within a column.

Look at the normal data at the top of Figure 3.42. To calculate the index for Georgia Peaches, Excel first calculates Georgia Peaches x Grand Total Sales. This would be $180 x $848. Next, Excel calculates Georgia Sales x Peach Sales. This would be $210 x $290. It then divides the first result by the second result to come up with a relative importance index of 2.51.

Figure 3.41
This report is created using the % Of option with Landscaping as the base item.

Figure 3.42
Using the Index function, Excel shows that peach sales are more important in Georgia than in Tennessee.

The index report is shown at the bottom of Figure 3.42. Excel explains that peaches are more important to Georgia (with an index of 2.51) than they are to California (with an index of 0.49).

Even though Georgia sold more apples than Tennessee, apples are more important to Tennessee (index of 1.51) than to Georgia (index of 0.34). Relatively, an apple shortage will cause more problems in Tennessee than in Georgia.

CASE STUDY

Producing Revenue by Line of Business Report

You have been asked to produce a report that provides a comprehensive look at revenue by product line. This analysis needs to include revenue dollars by product line for each market, the percent of revenue that each product line represents within the markets, and the percent total company dollars that each market represents within the product lines. Here are the steps to follow:

1. Place your cursor inside your data source. Choose the Insert ribbon and then click the Pivot Table icon.

2. When the Create PivotTable dialog box appears, simply choose OK. A new worksheet is created with the beginnings of a pivot table report and the PivotTable Field List, as shown in Figure 3.43.

Figure 3.43
After clicking OK, you get this blank pivot table report.

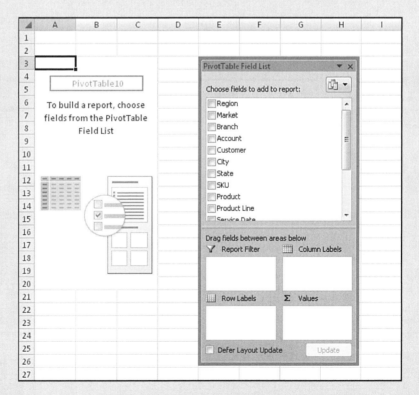

3. Click the Market field in the fields section of the PivotTable Field List to automatically move Market to the Row Labels drop zone. Then drag the Product Line field into the Column Labels drop zone, as shown in Figure 3.44.

Figure 3.44
Setting up the row and column fields.

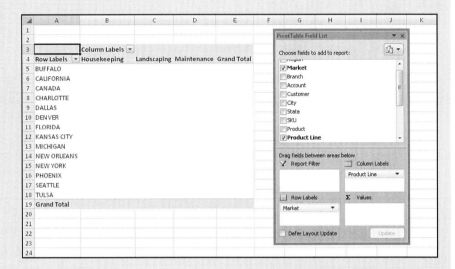

4. Drag the Revenue field into the Values drop zone three times to create three separate revenue data items. There is a new Sum Values item in the Column Labels drop zone. Move this to the Row Labels drop zone, as shown in Figure 3.45.

Figure 3.45
Having three copies of Sum of Revenue doesn't look useful…yet.

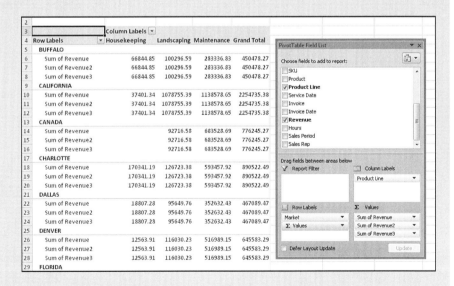

5. In the Values drop zone, click on the first Sum of Revenue field and select Field Settings, as shown in Figure 3.46.

Figure 3.46
Use the drop-down in the Values drop zone to access Field Settings for a particular data field.

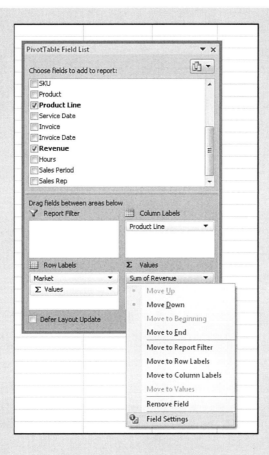

6. Change the name of the data field to `Total Revenue`, as shown in Figure 3.47. Then click the Number Format button to open the Format Cells dialog box. Change the format of the data item to Currency and then close both dialog boxes by clicking OK.

Figure 3.47
Set up the first Revenue item as normal.

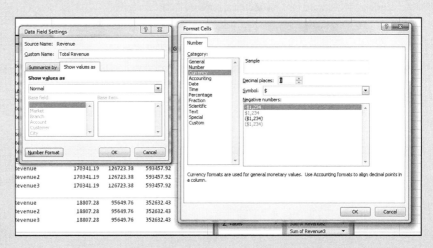

7. Open the Data Field Settings for the Sum of Revenue2 field.

8. Change the name of the data field to `Percent of Market`. On the Show Values As tab, in the Show Values As drop-down, select the % of Row option. After you do that, choose the Number Format button to open the Format Cells dialog box. Change the format of the cells to Percentage, as shown in Figure 3.48. Close both dialog boxes by clicking OK twice.

Figure 3.48
Use % of Row to get the Percentage of Market.

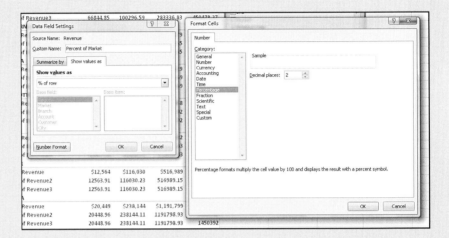

9. Open the Date Field Settings dialog box for Sum of Revenue3.

10. Change the name of the data field to `Percent of Company`. On the Show Values As tab, choose the % of Column option. After you do that, choose the Number button to open the Format Cells dialog box. Change the format of the cells to Percentage and then close both dialog boxes by clicking OK.

As shown in Figure 3.49, your product line analysis is complete! You have the Total Revenue field, which gives you the revenue dollars by product line for each market. Then you have the Percent of Market field, which shows you the percent of revenue that each line represents within the markets. Finally, you have the Percent of Company field, which shows line of business revenue as a percentage of total company dollars.

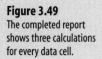

Figure 3.49
The completed report
shows three calculations
for every data cell.

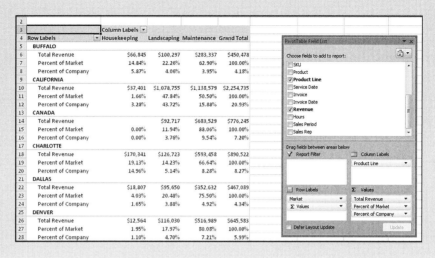

Next Steps

Note that other pivot table customizations are covered in subsequent chapters:

- Sorting a pivot table is covered in Chapter 4.
- Filtering records in a pivot table is covered in Chapter 4.
- Grouping daily dates up to months or years is covered in Chapter 4.
- Adding new calculated fields is covered in Chapter 5.
- Using data visualizations and conditional formatting in a pivot table is covered in Chapter 4.

In the next chapter, we discuss the filtering, sorting, and data visualization options available in Excel 2007. Using these tools is a great way to focus your pivot table on the largest drivers of success for your business.

Controlling the Way You View Your Pivot Data

4

Microsoft added some excellent new features to Excel 2007's pivot tables:

- Whenever Mike or Bill entertained an audience with one of his seminars, they could be sure to "wow" the audience with obscure features like the Top 10 AutoShow feature that was buried four menus deep in prior versions of Excel. Microsoft has exposed the AutoSort and AutoShow options so that they are now just two clicks away from any pivot table.

- Grouping features go from being buried three levels deep in Excel 2003 to a button right on the Ribbon in Excel 2007.

- The Pivot Table Options dialog box has been expanded in Excel 2007.

This chapter covers grouping, sorting, filtering, data visualizations, and pivot table options.

IN THIS CHAPTER

Grouping Pivot Fields .83

Case Study: Creating an Order Lead-
Time Report 88

Case Study: Grouping Text Fields 90

Looking at the PivotTable Field List 93

Sorting in a Pivot Table 96

Filtering the Pivot Table 102

Case Study: Creating a Top 10 Report 113

Next Steps 116

Grouping Pivot Fields

Although most of your summarization and calculation needs can be accomplished with standard pivot table settings, in special situations you might want your report to be summarized even further.

For example, transactional data is typically stored with a transaction date. You commonly want to report this data by month, quarter, or year. The Group option allows you to quickly and easily consolidate transactional dates into a larger group such as month or quarter. Then you can summarize the data in those groups just as you would with any other field in your pivot table.

As you learn in the next section, grouping is not limited to date fields. You can also group nondate fields to consolidate specific pivot items into a single item.

Grouping Date Fields

Figure 4.1 shows a pivot report by date. With two years' worth of transactional data, the report spans 500+ columns. These 500 columns are a summary of the original 68,615 rows, but managers often want detail by month instead of detail by day.

Figure 4.1
When reported by day, the summary report spans 500+ columns. It would be meaningful to report by month, quarter, or year instead.

	B4	▼	f_x	1/5/2007		
▲	A	B	C	D	E	F
1						
2						
3	**Total Revenue**	Column Labels ▼				
4	**Row Labels** ▼	1/5/2007	1/6/2007	1/7/2007	1/8/2007	1/9/2007 1
5	ACASCO Corp.	$0	$0	$0	$0	$0
6	ACECUL Corp.	$0	$0	$0	$0	$0
7	ACEHUA Corp.	$0	$0	$0	$0	$0
8	ACOPUL Corp.	$0	$0	$0	$0	$0
9	ACORAR Corp.	$0	$0	$0	$0	$0
10	ACSBUR Corp.	$0	$0	$0	$0	$0
11	ADACEC Corp.	$0	$0	$0	$0	$0
12	ADADUL Corp.	$0	$0	$0	$0	$0
13	ADANAS Corp.	$0	$0	$0	$0	$0
14	ADCOMP Corp.	$0	$0	$0	$0	$0
15	ADDATI Corp.	$0	$0	$0	$0	$0

Excel makes it easy to group date fields. Select any date heading such as cell B4 in Figure 4.1. On the Options ribbon, click Group Field in the Group group.

Figure 4.2
Business users of Excel usually group by months, quarters, and years.

When your field contains date information, the Grouping dialog box appears. By default, the Months option is selected. You have choices to group by Seconds, Minutes, Hours, Days, Months, Quarters, and Years. It is possible and usually advisable to select more than one field in the Grouping dialog box. In this case, you want to select Months, Quarters, and Years, as shown in Figure 4.2.

There are several interesting points to note about the resulting pivot table. First, notice that Quarters and Years have been added to your Field List. Don't let this fool you. Your source data is not changed to include these new fields; instead, these fields are now part of your pivot cache in memory. Another interesting point to note is that, by default, the Years and Quarters fields are automatically added to the same area as the original date field in the pivot table layout, as shown in Figure 4.3.

Figure 4.3
By default, Excel adds the new grouped date fields to your pivot table layout.

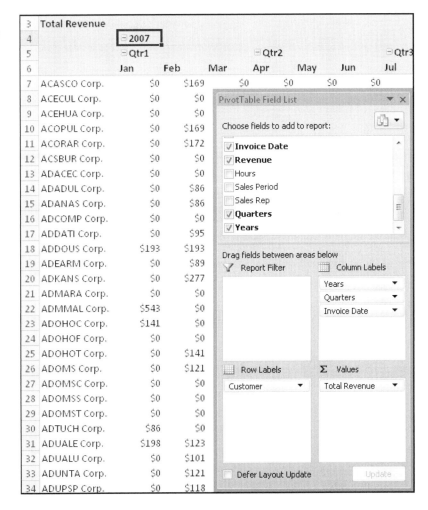

Including Years When Grouping by Months

Although this point is not immediately obvious, it is important if you group a date field by month that you also include the year in the grouping.

Examine the pivot table shown in Figure 4.4. This table has a date field that has been grouped by month and year. The months in column A use the generic abbreviations Jan, Feb, and so on. The sales for January 2007 are $339,689.

Figure 4.4
This table has a date field that is grouped by both month and year.

Total Revenue			
	2007	2008	Grand Total
Jan	$339,689	$342,176	$681,865
Feb	$571,162	$545,934	$1,117,096
Mar	$375,814	$391,879	$767,693
Apr	$470,817	$464,133	$934,950
May	$480,326	$486,771	$967,097
Jun	$444,156	$458,654	$902,810
Jul	$467,175	$445,152	$912,327
Aug	$490,895	$511,890	$1,002,785
Sep	$429,654	$421,199	$850,853
Oct	$468,895	$491,119	$960,014
Nov	$492,393	$491,028	$983,421
Dec	$357,572	$335,689	$693,261
Grand Total	$5,388,548	$5,385,624	$10,774,172

If, instead, you choose to group the date field only by month, Excel still continues to report the date field using the generic Jan abbreviation. The problem is that dates from January 2007 and January 2008 are both rolled up and reported together as "Jan." Having a report that totals Jan 2007 and Jan 2008 might be useful only if you are performing a seasonality analysis. Under any other circumstance, the report of $681,865 in January sales is too ambiguous and is likely to be interpreted wrong. To avoid ambiguous reports like the one shown in Figure 4.5, always include a year in the Group dialog box when you are grouping by month.

Grouping Date Fields by Week

The Grouping dialog box offers the choices to group by Second, Minute, Hour, Day, Month, Quarter, or Year. What if you need to group on a weekly or biweekly basis? This can be done.

The first step is to find an actual paper calendar for the year in question. Your data might start on January 5, 2007, so it is helpful to know that January 5 was a Friday in that year. You are going to have to decide if weeks should start on Sunday or Monday or any other day. Check the paper calendar to learn that the nearest starting Monday is January 1, 2007.

Figure 4.5
If you fail to include the Year field in the grouping, the report mixes sales from Jan 2007 and Jan 2008 in the same number.

3		Total Revenue
4	Jan	$681,865
5	Feb	$1,117,096
6	Mar	$767,693
7	Apr	$934,950
8	May	$967,097
9	Jun	$902,810
10	Jul	$912,327
11	Aug	$1,002,785
12	Sep	$850,853
13	Oct	$960,014
14	Nov	$983,421
15	Dec	$693,261
16	Grand Total	$10,774,172

Select any date heading in your pivot table. Then choose Group Field from the Options ribbon. In the Grouping dialog box, unselect all the By options and choose only the Days field. This enables the spin button for Number of Days. To produce a report by week, increase the number of days from 1 to 7.

Finally, you have to set up the Starting At date. If you were to accept the default of starting at January 5, 2007, all your weekly periods would run from Friday through Thursday. By checking a calendar before you begin, you know that you want the first group to start on January 1, 2007. Change this setting as shown in Figure 4.6.

4

Figure 4.6
The key to being able to access the Number of Days spin button is to select only Days from the By field.

The result is a report showing sales by week, as shown in Figure 4.7.

Figure 4.7
You've produced a report
showing sales by week.

	A	B
1		
2		
3		Total Revenue
4	1/1/2007 - 1/7/2007	$30,279
5	1/8/2007 - 1/14/2007	$92,522
6	1/15/2007 - 1/21/2007	$80,952
7	1/22/2007 - 1/28/2007	$81,745
8	1/29/2007 - 2/4/2007	$96,813
9	2/5/2007 - 2/11/2007	$142,908
10	2/12/2007 - 2/18/2007	$150,969
11	2/19/2007 - 2/25/2007	$143,122
12	2/26/2007 - 3/4/2007	$144,677
13	3/5/2007 - 3/11/2007	$85,248

CAUTION

If you choose to group by week, none of the other grouping options can be selected. You cannot group this or any other field by month or quarter.

Grouping Two Date Fields in One Report

When you group a date field by months and years, Excel repurposes the original date field to show months and adds a new field to show years. The new field is called Years. This is simple enough if you have only one date field in the report.

If you need to produce a report that has two date fields, and you attempt to group both date fields by months and years, Excel arbitrarily names the first grouped field "Years" and the second grouped field "Years2." This naming convention inevitably leads to confusion. In this case, it is important to rename the fields with a meaningful name.

CASE STUDY

Creating an Order Lead-Time Report

The material schedulers at a manufacturing plant are usually concerned with the lead time from when an order arrives to when it needs to ship. The schedulers may know that it takes 60 business days to procure material, schedule production, and build the product. In a perfect world, if all their customers would order 61 or more days in advance, the manufacturing plant would not have to keep any excess raw material inventory on hand.

But, in the real world, the plant always receives orders in which the customer wants the product faster. In these cases, the manufacturing plant may purchase extra inventory of the components with the longest lead time to accommodate rush orders.

If your transactional data source includes a field for date shipped and another field for date ordered, you can easily produce a report showing the normal order lead time by product. This is a valuable report for the master schedulers in the manufacturing plant. Here are the steps to follow:

1. Build a report with **Ship Date** going across the column area of the report.

2. Group the Ship Date field by month and year.

3. In the PivotTable Field List, drag the Years field to the Report Filter drop zone area of the pivot table. Use the drop-down in B1 to select one year from the data.

4. Drag the Order Date field to the row area of the pivot table.

5. Group the Order Date field by months and years.

6. Excel arbitrarily names the years field for Order Date as Years2, so rename the field **Order Year**.

7. Double-click the Sum of Revenue label in cell A3. Choose the Show Values As tab. In the Show Values As drop-down, choose % of Column.

8. In the Data Field Settings dialog box, change the Custom Name box from Sum of Revenue to Percent of Sales.

9. While you are in the PivotTable Field Options dialog box, click the Number Format button. Give the Revenue field a custom number format of **0.0%;;**. The semicolons suppress the display of negative and zero values.

The resulting table is shown in Figure 4.8. Cell C11 indicates that 15.62% of the orders shipped in January 2009 were ordered during the month of January. Another 34.92% of those orders were received in December 2008. This means that 50.54% of the sales from January were received within the manufacturing lead time. This fact dictates that your manufacturing facility needs to keep a whole lot of inventory on hand to meet these short lead-time orders.

4

Figure 4.8
The order lead-time report makes use of two fields grouped by month and year.

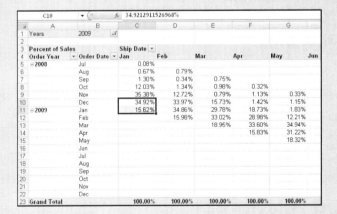

Grouping Numeric Fields

The Grouping dialog box for numeric fields allows you to group items into equal ranges.

In Figure 4.9, the Row Labels field contains a numeric age. Currently, the data shows ages from 20 through 75.

Select any age in column A and choose Group Field from the Options dialog box. Excel displays the Grouping dialog box.

In the Grouping dialog box, choose parameters for the group. In Figure 4.9, the dialog is suggesting groups from 20 to 75 in increments of 10 years.

Figure 4.9
Select an age and choose Group Field to display the Grouping dialog box.

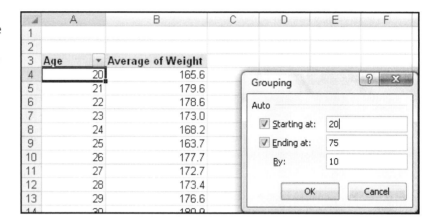

The result, shown in Figure 4.10, summarizes the various ages in groups.

Figure 4.10
The numeric row field has been grouped into ranges.

	A	B
1		
2		
3	Age	Average of Weight
4	20-29	172.7
5	30-39	186.8
6	40-49	206.4
7	50-59	207.9
8	60-69	165.6
9	70-79	158.1
10	Grand Total	184.9

CASE STUDY

Grouping Text Fields

You get a call from the VP of Sales. Secretly, the Sales department is considering a massive reorganization of the sales regions. The VP would like to see a report showing sales for last year by the new proposed regions. You've been around long enough to know that the proposed regions will change several times before the reorganization happens, so you are not willing to change the Region field in your source data just yet.

First, build a report showing revenue by market. The VP of Sales is proposing building a North region composed of Canada, Buffalo, Michigan, New York, and Seattle. Using the Ctrl key, highlight the five markets that make up the proposed North region. Figure 4.11 shows the pivot table before the first group is created.

Figure 4.11
Use the Ctrl key to select the noncontiguous cells that will make up the new North region.

3	Row Labels ▼	Sum of Revenue
4	BUFFALO	450,478
5	CALIFORNIA	2,254,735
6	CANADA	776,245
7	CHARLOTTE	890,522
8	DALLAS	467,089
9	DENVER	645,583
10	FLORIDA	1,450,392
11	KANSAS CITY	574,899
12	MICHIGAN	678,705
13	NEW ORLEANS	333,454
14	NEW YORK	873,581
15	PHOENIX	570,255
16	SEATTLE	179,827
17	TULSA	628,405
18	Grand Total	10,774,172

From the Options ribbon, click Group Selection. Excel adds a new field called Market2. The five selected cells are sequenced together and belong to a Market2 grouping that is arbitrarily called Group1, as shown in Figure 4.12.

4

Figure 4.12
Excel arbitrarily calls the first grouping Group1.

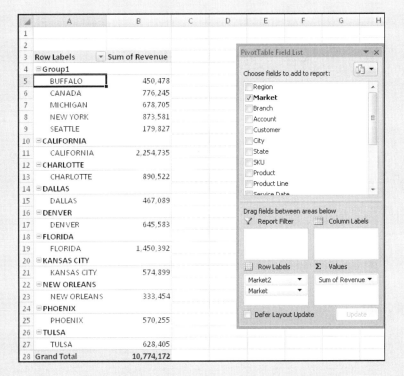

Select Group1 in A4. Click the Field Settings icon on the Options ribbon. Give the field a name such as **New Region**.

Click in cell A4 and type a meaningful name instead of Group1.

As you repeat these steps to build other regions, Excel continues to assign names such as Group2, Group3, and so on. After creating each region, simply type a meaningful name over the cell containing the arbitrary group name.

You will find that the New Region field is a real field. You can use the sorting feature (discussed later in this chapter) to sequence it alphabetically.

By default, Excel does not add subtotals for the New Region field. Use the Subtotals drop-down on the Design ribbon to add subtotals.

Figure 4.13 shows the report as it is ready for the VP of Sales. You can probably already predict that the Sales department will need to shuffle markets from the Central region to balance the regions.

Figure 4.13
After you group all the markets into new regions, the report is ready for review.

	A	B
1		
2		
3	Row Labels ▼	Sum of Revenue
4	⊟Central	4,103,622
5	CALIFORNIA	2,254,735
6	DENVER	645,583
7	KANSAS CITY	574,899
8	TULSA	628,405
9	⊟North	2,958,837
10	BUFFALO	450,478
11	CANADA	776,245
12	MICHIGAN	678,705
13	NEW YORK	873,581
14	SEATTLE	179,827
15	⊟South	3,711,713
16	CHARLOTTE	890,522
17	DALLAS	467,089
18	FLORIDA	1,450,392
19	NEW ORLEANS	333,454
20	PHOENIX	570,255
21	Grand Total	10,774,172

Ungrouping

After you have established groups, you can undo the groups by using the Ungroup icon on the Options ribbon. Simply select one of the grouped cells and then click the Ungroup icon.

Looking at the PivotTable Field List

The next topics in this chapter involve sorting and filtering your pivot table. Both of these tasks involve subtleties in the PivotTable Field List.

The following sections take you through a quick tour of the PivotTable Field List.

Docking and Undocking the PivotTable Field List

The PivotTable Field List starts out docked on the right side of the Excel window.

Grab the gray title bar for the pane and drag to the left to allow the pane to float anywhere in your Excel window.

After you have undocked the PivotTable Field List, you might find that it is difficult to redock it on either side of the screen. To redock the Field List, you must grab the title bar and drag until at least 80% of the Field List is off the edge of the window. Pretend that you are trying to completely remove the floating Field List from the screen. Eventually, Excel will get the hint and redock the Field List. Note that the PivotTable Field List can be docked on either the right or left side of the screen.

Rearranging the PivotTable Field List

As shown in Figure 4.14, a small drop-down appears near the top right of the PivotTable Field List. Select this drop-down to see the five possible arrangements of the PivotTable Field List. Although the default is to have the Fields section at the top of the list and the areas section at the bottom of the list, four other arrangements are possible.

Figure 4.14
Use this drop-down to rearrange the PivotTable Field List.

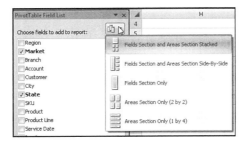

The final three arrangements offered in the drop-down are rather confusing. If someone changes the PivotTable Field List to show only the areas section, you could not see new fields to add to the pivot table.

If you ever encounter a version of the PivotTable Field List with only the areas sections (see Figure 4.15) or only the fields, remember that you can return to a less confusing view of the data by using the arrangement drop-down.

Figure 4.15
If you encounter this confusing arrangement of the PivotTable Field List, use the drop-down to return to an arrangement showing fields and areas.

Using the Areas Section Drop-Downs

As shown in Figure 4.16, every field in the areas section has a visible drop-down arrow. When you select this drop-down arrow, you see four categories of choices:

- The first four choices allow you to rearrange the field within the list of fields in that area of the pivot table.
- The next four choices allow you to move the field to a new area. (However, this could easily be accomplished by dragging the field to a new area.)
- The next choice allows you to remove the field from the pivot table.
- The final choice displays the Field Settings dialog box for the field.

Because these drop-down arrows are always visible, you might be more likely to open these drop-downs. However, they are far less powerful than the hidden drop-downs in the Fields section of the list.

Using the Fields Drop-Down

A second set of drop-downs is available in the PivotTable Field List. Hover the mouse cursor over any field in the Fields section of the PivotTable Field List, and a hidden drop-down arrow appears, as shown in Figure 4.17.

After you open the drop-down in the Fields section, you can see that all the really useful sorting and filtering options are behind the hidden drop-down.

Figure 4.18 shows the drop-down menu for the Product Line field in the top of the PivotTable Field List. Both the Label Filters and Value Filters options open to a flyout menu with many powerful filter choices.

Figure 4.16
The drop-downs in the areas section of the PivotTable Field List are not very useful.

Figure 4.17
You have to hover your mouse cursor over a field before you realize that a drop-down is available.

4

CAUTION

Microsoft has created a catch-22 for anyone trying to teach pivot tables. If this book suggests that you use the Product Line drop-down in the PivotTable Field List, most people would tend to use the drop-down visible in the areas section of the PivotTable Field List. For the rest of this chapter, when the text refers to the "Product drop-down in the Fields section of the PivotTable Field List," you should use the hidden drop-down shown in Figure 4.18.

Figure 4.18
You shouldn't be surprised that all the powerful features are in the drop-down that Microsoft hides from view.

Sorting in a Pivot Table

By default, items in each pivot field are sorted in ascending sequence based on the item name.

Microsoft has dramatically simplified pivot table sorting in Excel 2007. You have the freedom to sort your data fields to suit your needs. You can use one of several methods to apply sorting to your pivot table:

- Using the Sorting buttons on the Options ribbon
- Using the hidden drop-down in the Fields section of the PivotTable Field List
- Using the manual method

Sorting Using the Sort Icons on the Options Ribbon

Three icons appear in the Sort group of the Options ribbon. The AZ button sorts ascending. The ZA button sorts descending. The Sort icon brings up a dialog box with more options.

To successfully use the Sort icons, you need to pay attention to where you place the cell pointer before clicking on the icon.

In Figure 4.19, the pivot table is in the default sort order. The regions are sorted alphabetically (Midwest, North, South, West). Within each region, the markets are sorted alphabetically (Denver, Kansas City, Tulsa).

Figure 4.19
This pivot table is in the default sequence.

	Row Labels	▾	Sum of Revenue
3	Row Labels		Sum of Revenue
4	⊟MIDWEST		$1,848,887
5	DENVER		$645,583
6	KANSAS CITY		$574,899
7	TULSA		$628,405
8	⊟NORTH		$2,779,009
9	BUFFALO		$450,478
10	CANADA		$776,245
11	MICHIGAN		$678,705
12	NEW YORK		$873,581
13	⊟SOUTH		$3,141,458
14	CHARLOTTE		$890,522
15	DALLAS		$467,089
16	FLORIDA		$1,450,392
17	NEW ORLEANS		$333,454
18	⊟WEST		$3,004,818
19	CALIFORNIA		$2,254,735
20	PHOENIX		$570,255
21	SEATTLE		$179,827
22	Grand Total		$10,774,172

There are eight ways to sort this data. You get a different sort depending on whether you've selected A4, B4, A5, or B5 when you click the AZ or ZA buttons. Refer to Figure 4.19 when you read these options:

- If you select cell A4 and click ZA, the regions are sorted in descending order. The West region appears first. Within the West region, the markets are still sorted in ascending sequence (California, Phoenix, Seattle).

- If you select cell A5 and click ZA, the markets are sorted in descending order within each region. The markets in the West region appear in descending sequence (Seattle, Phoenix, California).

- If you select cell B4 and click ZA, the regions are sorted so that the largest region appears first. This is the South region with $3.1 million, followed by the West region with $3 million. The markets retain their previous sequence.

- If you select cell B5 and click ZA, the markets are sorted within each region so that the largest market appears first. In the South region, the Florida market appears first, with $1.5 million, followed by the Charlotte market with $891K.

In Figure 4.20, the regions are sorted in descending alphabetical order, and the markets are sorted in descending revenue order within the regions.

Figure 4.20
After two sorts, the regions are in descending order alphabetically, and the markets are in descending order by region.

	A	B
1		
2		
3	Row Labels ▾	Sum of Revenue
4	⊟WEST	$3,004,818
5	CALIFORNIA	$2,254,735
6	PHOENIX	$570,255
7	SEATTLE	$179,827
8	⊟SOUTH	$3,141,458
9	FLORIDA	$1,450,392
10	CHARLOTTE	$890,522
11	DALLAS	$467,089
12	NEW ORLEANS	$333,454
13	⊟NORTH	$2,779,009
14	NEW YORK	$873,581
15	CANADA	$776,245
16	MICHIGAN	$678,705
17	BUFFALO	$450,478
18	⊟MIDWEST	$1,848,887
19	DENVER	$645,583
20	TULSA	$628,405
21	KANSAS CITY	$574,899
22	Grand Total	$10,774,172

Think about sorting using the Data or Home ribbon; the sort is a one-time event. If data changes, you must manually choose to sort the data again.

Pivot table sorts are more powerful. When you sort using the pivot table sorting options, Excel sets up a rule for the field. If you change the order of the pivot fields, Excel continues to apply the rule. In Figure 4.21, the Region field was removed from the report. Excel remembered that the Market field should be sorted by descending revenue. Excel properly re-sorted the data, moving Phoenix from row 6 to row 13.

Sorting Using the Field List Hidden Drop-Down

An alternative method for sorting is to use the hidden drop-down in the Fields section of the PivotTable Field List.

Hover the mouse cursor over any field in the top half of the PivotTable Field List, and a drop-down appears. Choose this drop-down to access AZ and ZA options, as well as a More Sort Options menu choice, as shown in Figure 4.22.

You can use the More Sort Options choice to access the Sort dialog box, as shown in Figure 4.23. In this pivot table version of the Sort dialog box, you can choose to sort the specific field based on another field. In the figure, you can see that the customer field should be sorted into descending revenue sequence.

Figure 4.21
Sort rules applied to a pivot table cause the data to be re-sorted after every pivot or refresh.

3	Row Labels ▼	Sum of Revenue
4	CALIFORNIA	$2,254,735
5	FLORIDA	$1,450,392
6	CHARLOTTE	$890,522
7	NEW YORK	$873,581
8	CANADA	$776,245
9	MICHIGAN	$678,705
10	DENVER	$645,583
11	TULSA	$628,405
12	KANSAS CITY	$574,899
13	PHOENIX	$570,255
14	DALLAS	$467,089
15	BUFFALO	$450,478
16	NEW ORLEANS	$333,454
17	SEATTLE	$179,827
18	**Grand Total**	**$10,774,172**

Figure 4.22
Use the drop-down in the Fields section of the PivotTable Field List to access sort options for a specific field.

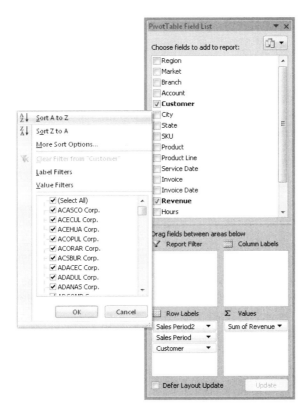

4

Figure 4.23
You can specify complex sort criteria by using this Sort dialog box.

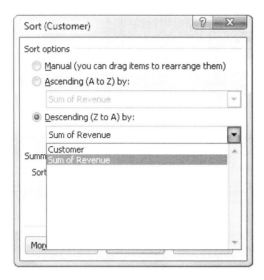

Understanding the Effect of Layout Changes on AutoSort

If you change the report filter, the report automatically re-sorts. Different customers might appear at the top of the list based on their purchases of the filtered items.

If you drop a new field on the report, the pivot table remembers the AutoSort option for the sorted field and does its best to present the data in that order. This may not be in the spirit of your report focusing on the best customers. Say that you add the Market field as the outer row field. The Market field is sorted alphabetically by name, but within each region, the customers are arranged in descending order by revenue.

Using a Manual Sort Sequence

Note that the dialog box in Figure 4.23 offers something called a *manual sort*. Rather than using the dialog box, you can invoke a manual sort in a surprising way.

Note that the regions in Figure 4.23 are in the order West, South, North, Midwest. If this company is based in New York, company traditions might dictate that the North region should be shown first, followed by South, West, and Midwest. On the face of it, there is no easy way to sort the Region field into this sequence. An ascending sort would cause the Midwest region to be first. A descending sort would cause the West region to be first. Neither sort will be in the proper sequence to match the company's standard reporting.

You might try to convince your company to change a decades-long tradition of reporting in the North, South, West, Midwest sequence, or even change the region names to accommodate sorting in your pivot table. Both of these concepts would be tough to sell and are not viable options. Luckily, Microsoft offers a simple solution to this problem.

Place the cell pointer in cell B4 and type the word **North**. Excel figures out that you want to move the North column to be first and moves all the North values to column B. West is moved to column C, South moves to column D, and Midwest stays in column E. Next, type **South** in cell C4. The values in C and D switch places.

This behavior is completely unintuitive. You should never try this behavior with a regular (nonpivot table) dataset in Excel. You would never expect Excel to change the column sequence just by moving the columns.

Figure 4.24 shows the pivot table after typing new column headings in cells B4 and C4.

Figure 4.24

Simply type a heading in B4 to move a new region to be first.

	Sum of Revenue	Column Labels					
	Row Labels	WEST	SOUTH	NORTH	MIDWEST	CANADA	Grand Total
4	CATYOF Corp.	$36,827	$27,001	$3,867	$19,687		$87,382
5	NYCTRA Corp.			$74,152			$74,152
6	OMUSAC Corp.	$16,557	$28,499	$18,644	$9,674		$73,373
7	CALTRA Corp.	$71,684					$71,684
8	SANFRA Corp.	$48,997					$48,997
9	SUASHU Corp.	$14,466	$28,353	$536	$4,232		$47,587
10	TAREKA Corp.		$43,963		$2,774		$46,737

CAUTION

After you use this technique, any new regions you add to the data source are added at the end of the list. Figure 4.24 shows the pivot table after a region named Canada is added. Because Excel does not know where to add Canada, it automatically goes to the end of the list.

Using a Custom List for Sorting

The other solution to the North, South, West, Midwest sequence problem is to set up a custom list. Custom lists are maintained in the Excel Options dialog box.

Follow these steps to set up a custom list:

1. In an out-of-the-way section of the worksheet, type the regions in their proper sequence. Type one region per cell, going down a column.
2. Select the cells containing the list of regions in the proper sequence.
3. Select the Office Icon menu. Choose Excel Options from the bottom of the menu.
4. On the Popular category, click the Edit Custom Lists button.
5. In the Custom Lists dialog box, your selection address is entered in the Import text box. Click Import to bring the regions in as a new list, as shown in Figure 4.25. The new list appears at the bottom of the Custom Lists box.
6. Click OK to close the Custom Lists dialog box. Then click OK to close the Excel Options dialog box.

The custom list is now stored on your computer and will be available for all future Excel sessions.

Figure 4.25
Import a new custom list to enable custom sorts.

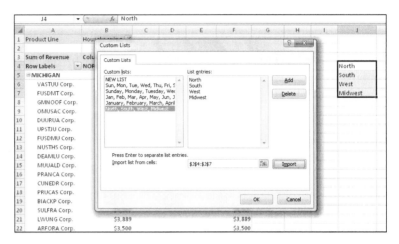

To sort the pivot table by the custom list, follow these steps:

1. Select one of the Region cells in the pivot table.
2. From the Options ribbon, click on the Sort icon.
3. In the Sort (Region) dialog box, choose Ascending by Region.
4. In the Sort (Region) dialog box, click the More Options button in the lower-left corner.
5. In the More Sort Options dialog box, uncheck the AutoSort checkbox.
6. As shown in Figure 4.26, in the More Sort Options dialog box, open the First Key Sort Order drop-down and choose North, South, West, Midwest.
7. Click OK twice.

Filtering the Pivot Table

Pivot table veterans will remember the old page area section of a pivot table. This area has been renamed the report filter area and still operates basically the same as in previous versions. Microsoft did add the capability to select multiple items from the report filter area.

However, Microsoft has added fantastic new filtering options that can be applied to fields in the column or row areas of a pivot table. It is a bit of a mystery why Microsoft did not rewrite the report filter area to have the same powerful options.

As described in the following sections, you can choose items from fields in the report filter area. The new filtering options are accessed from the hidden drop-down in the Fields section of the PivotTable Field List.

> **CAUTION**
>
> Although you can apply a filter to any field in the PivotTable Field List, the filter is active only if that field is in the row or column area of the pivot table!

Figure 4.26
Choose to sort by the custom list.

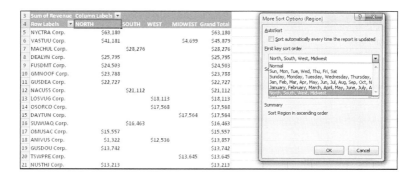

Adding Fields to the Report Filter Area

The pivot table in Figure 4.27 is a perfect ad hoc reporting tool to give to a high-level executive. You can use the drop-downs in B1:B5 to quickly find revenue for any combination of region, market, state, customer, or invoice date. This is a typical use of report filters.

Figure 4.27
With multiple fields in the Report Filter drop zone, this pivot table can answer many ad hoc queries.

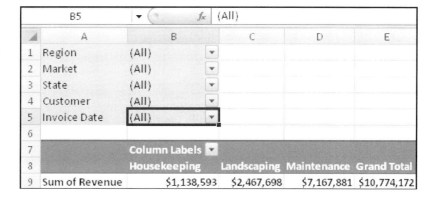

To set up the report, drag revenue to the Values drop zone and then drag as many fields as desired to the Report Filter drop zone.

> TIP
>
> If you add many fields to the report filter area, you might want to make use of one of the obscure pivot table options settings. Click Options on the Options ribbon. On the Layout & Format tab of the PivotTable Options dialog box, change the Report Filter Fields Per Column from 0 to a positive number. Excel rearranges the filter fields into multiple columns, as shown in Figure 4.28. You can also change Down, Then Over to Over, Then Down to rearrange the sequence of the filter fields.

Figure 4.28
To show the filter fields in multiple columns, change this setting to be nonzero.

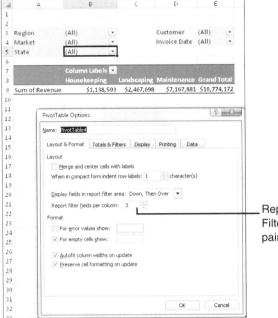

Report Filter Fields Per Column
Filters arranged in multiple pairs of columns

Choosing One Item from a Report Filter

To filter the pivot table, click on any drop-down in the report filter area of the pivot table. The drop-down always starts with (All), but then lists the complete unique set of items available in that field.

To filter to a single item, click that item in the list, as shown in Figure 4.29.

Choosing Multiple Items from a Report Filter

At the bottom of the report filter drop-down is a check box labeled Select Multiple Items. If you choose this box, Excel adds a check box next to each item in the drop-down. You can now check multiple items from the list.

In Figure 4.30, the pivot table is filtered to show revenue from three markets.

> **CAUTION**
>
> Using the Select Multiple Items filter leads to a situation in which the report consumer may not know what items are included in the report. In Figure 4.31, you can see that B2 reports the somewhat cryptic (Multiple Items) label. You should add a title to identify which markets are included in the report.

Figure 4.29
After you select this option, the report shows the revenue from the Kansas City market.

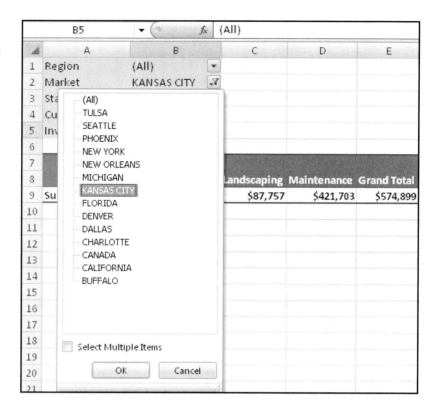

Figure 4.30
Use the Select Multiple Items check box to enable combination filters.

Figure 4.31
This report includes multiple markets, but which ones?

⃟	A	B	C	D	E
1	Region	(All) ▾			
2	Market	(Multiple Items) 𝗬			
3	State	(All) ▾			
4	Customer	(All) ▾			
5	Invoice Date	(All) ▾			
6					
7		Column Labels ▾			
8		Housekeeping	Landscaping	Maintenance	Grand Total
9	Sum of Revenue	$258,640	$274,193	$1,240,726	$1,773,559

Quickly Selecting or Clearing All Items from a Filter

The (All) check box at the top of the Market drop-down in Figure 4.30 is powerful. Choosing the (All) check box represents a quick way to select or unselect all the items in the drop-down.

If the (All) check box is unchecked, check it to select all items. If the (All) check box is checked, uncheck it to rapidly uncheck all items.

Using the Field List Filters

Hover your mouse cursor over the Market field in the Fields section of the PivotTable Field List, and a drop-down appears.

As shown in Figure 4.32, the bottom section of the drop-down is identical to the report filter drop-down after you've checked Select Multiple Items. You can use these check boxes as discussed previously to exclude certain items from the pivot table report.

However, the drop-down shown in Figure 4.32 includes two additional powerful options: Label Filters and Value Filters. If Excel detects that your column contains dates, the Label Filters option is replaced with a Date Filters option.

These options lead to a flyout menu with many powerful filtering options. These options are new in Excel 2007 and dramatically increase the efficiency of using pivot tables.

> **NOTE** You can access this drop-down either by hovering the mouse cursor over the item in the PivotTable Field List or by accessing the Column Labels or Row Labels drop-down in the pivot table. In Figure 4.33, there is only one field—Invoice Date—in the Row Labels drop zone, so using the Row Labels drop-down in cell A8 leads to a simple drop-down with the appropriate Date Filters and Value Filters entries.

Figure 4.32
The drop-down associated with the PivotTable Field List offers the same check box items as in the report filter fields.

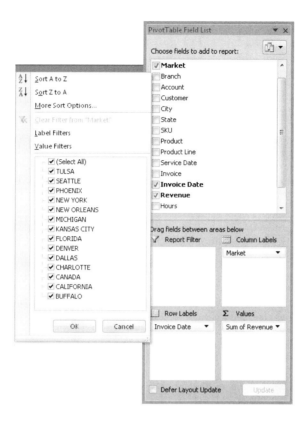

Figure 4.33
If you have only one field in the row area, using the Row Labels drop-down is a suitable way to access the filter options.

However, if you have two fields in the Row Labels drop zone of the report, the Row Labels drop-down is a bit more confusing. In Figure 4.34, both a date field and a text field occupy the row area of the pivot table. In this case, to use the Row Labels drop-down, you first have to use the Select Field drop-down at the top of the Row Labels drop-down. It is confusing to write this, but perhaps not as confusing to use it! You can use either the Field List drop-down or the Row Labels drop-down as you prefer.

Figure 4.34
When you have two Row Labels fields, you first have to use the Select Field drop-down within the first drop-down.

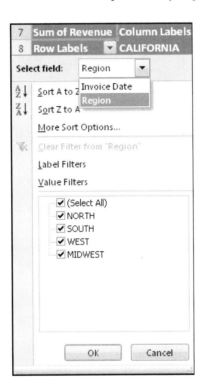

The next three sections discuss the various options available in the flyout menus in detail.

Using Label Filters

The Label Filters flyout menu offers 14 different filter rules, as shown in Figure 4.35.

When you choose one of the filter items from the menu, Excel displays the Label Filter dialog box. In this dialog box, you can use wildcard characters. Use an * to match any series of characters or use ? to match a single character. Figure 4.36 shows the Label Filter dialog box that appears after selecting Does Not End With.

The options available in the Label Filters flyout menu include

- Equals
- Does Not Equal
- Begins With

- Does Not Begin With
- Ends With
- Does Not End With
- Contains
- Does Not Contain
- Greater Than
- Greater Than or Equal To
- Less Than
- Less Than or Equal To
- Between
- Not Between

Figure 4.35
Choose from the Label Filters rules in the flyout menu.

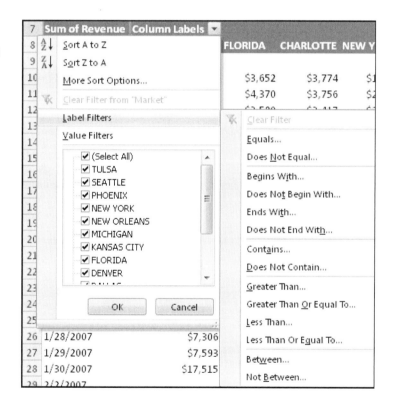

Using Date Filters

If you select the drop-down for a field that contains predominantly dates, the Date Filters flyout menu offers many canned date periods, as shown in Figure 4.37.

If you select Equals, Before, After, or Between, you can specify a date or a range of dates.

Figure 4.36
After you choose a label filter, you complete the filter in this dialog box.

Figure 4.37
Microsoft offers a fantastic but not all-inclusive list of date filters.

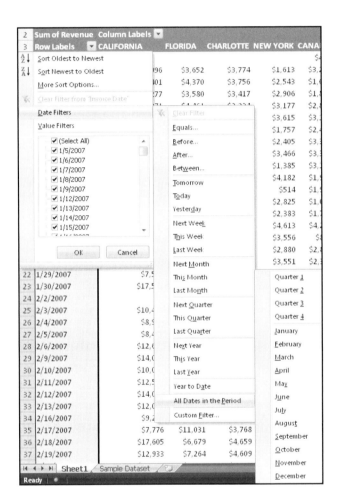

Options for the current, past, or next day; week; month; quarter; or year occupy 15 options. Combined with Year to Date, these options change day after day. You could pivot a list of projects by due date and always see the projects that are due in the next week using this option. When you open the workbook on another day, the report will recalculate.

> **TIP**
> In Microsoft's world, a week runs from Sunday through Saturday. If you select Next Week, the report always shows a period from the next Sunday through the following Saturday.

When you choose All Dates in the Period, a new flyout menu offers options such as Each Month and Each Quarter.

> **NOTE**
> People who use QuickBooks will recognize that this list is reminiscent of the reporting options that have been available in QuickBooks for several versions. Unfortunately, Microsoft left out a few key choices such as This Month to Date, Last Week to Date, and Next 4 weeks.

If you are frustrated that there is not a Last Week to Date option, you might have some hope that the Custom choice in the filter will solve the problem. Unfortunately, this hope is unfounded because the Custom date filter leads to a dialog box offering only a subset of the choices already on the menu.

Using Value Filters

The value filter is a powerful feature. It allows you to filter one of your row or column fields based on the numbers that appear in the values area of the pivot table.

Figure 4.38 shows a pivot table with revenue and hours by market.

Figure 4.38
The row field contains market names.

	A	B	C
1			
2		Values	
3	Row Labels	Sum of Revenue	Sum of Hours
4	CALIFORNIA	$2,254,735	33014
5	FLORIDA	$1,450,392	22640
6	CHARLOTTE	$890,522	14525
7	NEW YORK	$873,581	14213
8	CANADA	$776,245	12103
9	MICHIGAN	$678,705	10744
10	DENVER	$645,583	8641
11	TULSA	$628,405	9583
12	KANSAS CITY	$574,899	8547
13	PHOENIX	$570,255	10167
14	DALLAS	$467,089	6393
15	BUFFALO	$450,478	6864
16	NEW ORLEANS	$333,454	5057
17	SEATTLE	$179,827	2889
18	Grand Total	$10,774,172	165380

Can you filter the markets based on the revenue values in column B? To do so, select the Row Labels drop-down. Then choose Value Filters to see the flyout menu shown in Figure 4.39.

Figure 4.39
Even though you are fil-
tering the Market field,
these menu choices do
not refer to values in the
Market column.

When you access the Value Filter dialog box, you can specify that the Market field should
be filtered based on the numeric values in a particular value field. In Figure 4.40, you are
specifying that the report should show only markets with more than 10,000 billable hours.

Figure 4.40
In this dialog box, you
choose a numeric field
name and then specify
the filter.

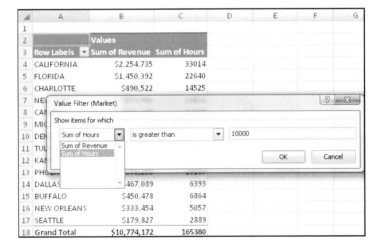

The resulting pivot table, shown in Figure 4.41, shows all the markets with more than
10,000 billable hours.

Figure 4.41
The report is limited to states that match the 10,000-hour threshold.

▲	A	B	C
1			
2		**Values**	
3	Row Labels ▼	Sum of Revenue	Sum of Hours
4	CALIFORNIA	$2,254,735	33014
5	FLORIDA	$1,450,392	22640
6	CHARLOTTE	$890,522	14525
7	NEW YORK	$873,581	14213
8	CANADA	$776,245	12103
9	MICHIGAN	$678,705	10744
10	PHOENIX	$570,255	10167
11	Grand Total	$7,494,436	117406

CASE STUDY

Creating a Top 10 Report

One of the cool value filters is the Top 10 filter. This choice can be used to select the Top *N*, Bottom *N*, Top *N*%, or Bottom *N*%.

For a value filter, you can select text row fields where the corresponding value fields are in the top 10, top 20, and so on.

In Figure 4.42, the pivot table shows revenue by customer.

Because there are more than 6,000 customers, your hope of getting any sales manager to read this report is slim. It would be much better to show a report of the top 20 customers.

Figure 4.42
There are too many customers to read the whole report.

▲	A	B
2	Row Labels ▼	Sum of Revenue
3	ACASCO Corp.	$675
4	ACECUL Corp.	$593
5	ACEHUA Corp.	$580
6	ACOPUL Corp.	$675
7	ACORAR Corp.	$2,232
8	ACSBUR Corp.	$720
9	ADACEC Corp.	$345
10	ADADUL Corp.	$690
11	ADANAS Corp.	$345
12	ADCOMP Corp.	$553
13	ADDATI Corp.	$379
14	ADDOUS Corp.	$5,209
15	ADEARM Corp.	$357

4

Follow these steps to filter the report:

1. Select the Row Labels drop-down in cell A2.

2. Choose Value Filters from the drop-down.

3. Choose Top 10 from the flyout menu. Excel displays the Top 10 Filter (Customer) dialog box, as shown in Figure 4.43.

Figure 4.43
Initially, the Top 10 Filter offers to find the top 10 customers.

4. Change the settings in the dialog box to specify that the report should filter to the top 20 items based on Sum of Revenue, as shown in Figure 4.44.

Figure 4.44
Change the dialog box to choose the top 20 customers.

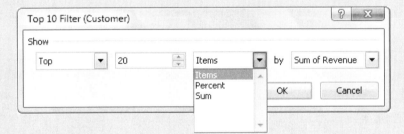

5. Click OK to close the dialog box. Your pivot table then shows only the top 20 customers.

6. If you wish the customers to be listed high to low, choose More Sort Options from the Row Labels drop-down. Excel displays the Sort dialog box.

7. Specify that the customers should be sorted in descending order based on the Sum of Revenue field, as shown in Figure 4.45.

As shown in Figure 4.46, the result is a compact pivot table showing the largest customers in descending order by revenue.

Figure 4.45
Specify that the cus-
tomers should be sorted
high to low.

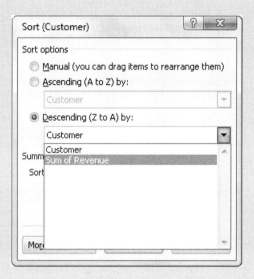

Figure 4.46
A top 20 customer report
is easy to create using
the Top 10 filter.

	A	B
2	**Row Labels**	**Sum of Revenue**
3	CATYOF Corp.	$87,382
4	NYCTRA Corp.	$74,152
5	OMUSAC Corp.	$73,373
6	CALTRA Corp.	$71,684
7	SANFRA Corp.	$48,997
8	SUASHU Corp.	$47,587
9	TAREKA Corp.	$46,737
10	VASTUU Corp.	$46,075
11	DEAMLU Corp.	$43,461
12	ANATUD Corp.	$39,943
13	FUSDMT Corp.	$33,689
14	ANIVUS Corp.	$31,566
15	WUTTUS Corp.	$30,951
16	MACHUL Corp.	$30,443
17	NATAUN Corp.	$29,241
18	SAOUSA Corp.	$28,818
19	LOSVUG Corp.	$26,002
20	DEALYN Corp.	$25,795
21	PRUCAS Corp.	$25,015
22	GMNOOF Corp.	$23,788
23	**Grand Total**	**$864,698**

4

Next Steps

In the next chapter, you learn how to use pivot table formulas to add entire new virtual fields to your pivot table.

4

Performing Calculations Within Your Pivot Tables

Introducing Calculated Fields and Calculated Items

When analyzing data with pivot tables, you will often find the need to expand your analysis to include data based on calculations that are not in your original dataset. Excel provides a way to perform calculations within your pivot table through *calculated fields* and *calculated items*.

A calculated field is a data field you create by executing a calculation against existing fields in the pivot table. Think of a calculated field as adding a virtual column to your dataset. This column takes up no space in your source data, contains the data you define with a formula, and interacts with your pivot data as a field—just like all the other fields in your pivot table.

A calculated item is a data item you create by executing a calculation against existing items within a data field. Think of a calculated item as adding a virtual row of data to your dataset. This virtual row takes up no space in your source data and contains summarized values based on calculations performed on other rows in the same field. Calculated items interact with your pivot data as a data item—just like all the other items in your pivot table.

With calculated fields and calculated items, you can insert a formula into your pivot table to create your own custom field or data item. Your newly created data becomes a part of your pivot table, interacting with other pivot data, recalculating when you refresh and supplying you with a calculated metric that does not exist in your source data.

The example in Figure 5.1 demonstrates how a basic calculated field can add another perspective on your data. Your pivot table shows total sales

IN THIS CHAPTER

Introducing Calculated Fields and Calculated Items 117

Creating Your First Calculated Field 121

Case Study: Summarizing Next Year's Forecast 124

Creating Your First Calculated Item 129

Understanding Rules and Shortcomings of Pivot Table Calculations 133

Managing and Maintaining Your Pivot Table Calculations 137

Next Steps 140

5

amount and contracted hours for each market. A calculated field that shows you average dollar per hour enhances this analysis and adds another dimension to your data.

Figure 5.1
Avg Dollar per Hour is a calculated field that adds another perspective to your data analysis.

	Sales_Amount	Contracted Hours	Avg Dollar Per Hour
Data			
Filter rows ▼			
BUFFALO	$450,478	6,864	$66
CALIFORNIA	$2,254,735	33,014	$68
CANADA	$776,245	12,103	$64
CHARLOTTE	$890,522	14,525	$61
DALLAS	$467,089	6,393	$73
DENVER	$645,583	8,641	$75
FLORIDA	$1,450,392	22,640	$64
KANSASCITY	$574,899	8,547	$67
MICHIGAN	$678,705	10,744	$63
NEWORLEANS	$333,454	5,057	$66
NEWYORK	$873,581	14,213	$61
PHOENIX	$570,255	10,167	$56
SEATTLE	$179,827	2,889	$62
TULSA	$628,405	9,583	$66
Grand Total	$10,774,172	165,380	$65

Now, you may look at Figure 5.1 and ask yourself: Why go through all the trouble of creating calculated fields or calculated items? Why not just use formulas in surrounding cells or even add your calculation directly into the source table to get the information you need?

To answer these questions, look at the different methods you could use to create the calculated field in Figure 5.1.

Method 1: Manually Add the Calculated Field to Your Data Source

You can manually add a calculated field to your data source, as shown in Figure 5.2, allowing the pivot table to pick up the field as a regular data field.

On the surface, this option looks simple, but this method of precalculating metrics and incorporating them into your data source is impractical on several levels.

If the definitions of your calculated fields change, you will have to go back to the data source, recalculate the metric for each row, and refresh your pivot table. If you have to add a metric, you will have go back to the data source, add a new calculated field, and then change the range of your pivot table to capture the new field.

Method 2: Use a Formula Outside Your Pivot Table to Create the Calculated Field

You can add a calculated field by performing the calculation in an external cell with a formula. In the example shown in Figure 5.3, the Average Dollar Per Hour column was created with formulas referencing the pivot table.

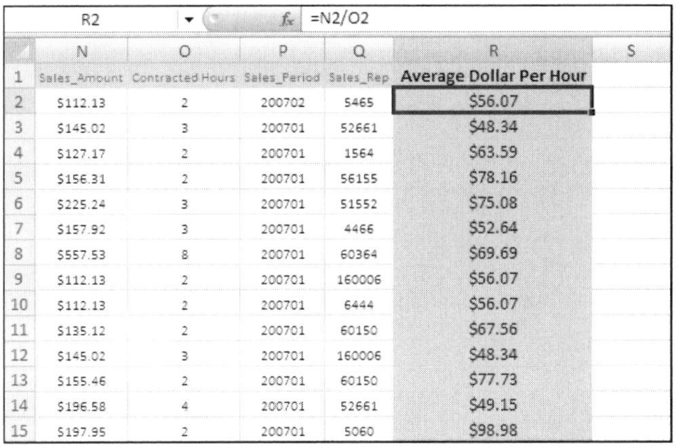

Figure 5.2
Precalculating calculated fields in your data source is both cumbersome and impractical.

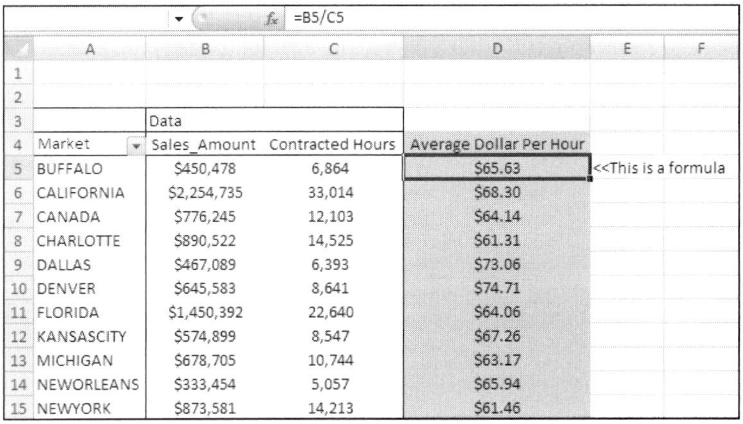

	N	O	P	Q	R	S
	Sales_Amount	Contracted Hours	Sales_Period	Sales_Rep	**Average Dollar Per Hour**	
1						
2	$112.13	2	200702	5465	$56.07	
3	$145.02	3	200701	52661	$48.34	
4	$127.17	2	200701	1564	$63.59	
5	$156.31	2	200701	56155	$78.16	
6	$225.24	3	200701	51552	$75.08	
7	$157.92	3	200701	4466	$52.64	
8	$557.53	8	200701	60364	$69.69	
9	$112.13	2	200701	160006	$56.07	
10	$112.13	2	200701	6444	$56.07	
11	$135.12	2	200701	60150	$67.56	
12	$145.02	3	200701	160006	$48.34	
13	$155.46	2	200701	60150	$77.73	
14	$196.58	4	200701	52661	$49.15	
15	$197.95	2	200701	5060	$98.98	

R2 f_x =N2/O2

Figure 5.3
Typing a formula next to your pivot table essentially gives you a calculated field that refreshes when your pivot table is refreshed.

f_x =B5/C5

	A	B	C	D	E	F
1						
2						
3		Data				
4	Market	Sales_Amount	Contracted Hours	Average Dollar Per Hour		
5	BUFFALO	$450,478	6,864	$65.63	<<This is a formula	
6	CALIFORNIA	$2,254,735	33,014	$68.30		
7	CANADA	$776,245	12,103	$64.14		
8	CHARLOTTE	$890,522	14,525	$61.31		
9	DALLAS	$467,089	6,393	$73.06		
10	DENVER	$645,583	8,641	$74.71		
11	FLORIDA	$1,450,392	22,640	$64.06		
12	KANSASCITY	$574,899	8,547	$67.26		
13	MICHIGAN	$678,705	10,744	$63.17		
14	NEWORLEANS	$333,454	5,057	$65.94		
15	NEWYORK	$873,581	14,213	$61.46		

Although this method gives you a calculated field that updates when your pivot table is refreshed, any changes in the structure of your pivot table have the potential of rendering your formula useless.

As you can see in Figure 5.4, moving the Market field to the report filter area changes the structure of your pivot table, exposing the weakness of makeshift calculated fields that use external formulas.

Method 3: Insert a Calculated Field Directly into Your Pivot Table

Inserting the calculated field directly into your pivot table is the best option, eliminating the need to manage formulas, providing for scalability when your data source grows or changes, and allowing for flexibility in the event that your metric definitions change.

Another huge advantage of this method is that you can alter your pivot table's structure and even measure different data fields against your calculated field without worrying about errors in your formulas or losing cell references.

5

Figure 5.4
External formulas run the risk of errors when the pivot table structure is changed.

	A	B	C	D	E	F
	D5	▼		f_x =B5/C5		
1	Market	(All)	▼			
2						
3	Data					
4	Sales_Amount	Contracted Hours		Average Dollar Per Hour		
5	$10,774,172	165,380		#DIV/0!	<<This is a formula	
6				#DIV/0!		
7				#DIV/0!		
8				#DIV/0!		
9				#DIV/0!		
10				#DIV/0!		
11				#DIV/0!		
12				#DIV/0!		
13				#DIV/0!		
14				#DIV/0!		
15				#DIV/0!		

The pivot table report shown in Figure 5.5 is the same one you see in Figure 5.1, except it has been restructured so that you get the average dollar per hour by market and product.

Figure 5.5
Your calculated field remains viable even when your pivot table's structure changes to accommodate new dimensions.

	A	B	C	D	E
1					
2					
3			Data		
4	Market ▼	Product_Description ▼	Sales_Amount	Contracted Hours	Avg Dollar Per Hour
5	⊟ TULSA	Cleaning & Housekeeping Services	$96,515	1,545	$62.47
6		Facility Maintenance and Repair	$170,632	3,000	$56.88
7		Fleet Maintenance	$145,440	1,942	$74.89
8		Green Plants and Foliage Care	$15,838	214	$74.01
9		Landscaping/Grounds Care	$63,939	778	$82.18
10		Predictive Maintenance/Preventative Maintenance	$136,041	2,104	$64.66
11	TULSA Total		$628,405	9,583	$65.57
12	⊟ SEATTLE	Cleaning & Housekeeping Services	$12,536	182	$68.88
13		Facility Maintenance and Repair	$38,099	672	$56.69
14		Fleet Maintenance	$33,963	564	$60.22
15		Green Plants and Foliage Care	$10,980	159	$69.05
16		Landscaping/Grounds Care	$39,913	800	$49.89
17		Predictive Maintenance/Preventative Maintenance	$44,336	512	$86.59
18	SEATTLE Total		$179,827	2,889	$62.25

The bottom line is that there are significant benefits in integrating your custom calculations into your pivot table, including

- The elimination of potential formula and cell reference errors
- The ability to add and remove data from your pivot table without affecting your calculations
- The ability to auto-recalculate when your pivot table is changed or refreshed
- The flexibility to change calculations easily when your metric definitions change
- The ability to manage and maintain your calculations effectively

Creating Your First Calculated Field

Before you create a calculated field, you must first have a pivot table. Build the pivot table you see here in Figure 5.6.

Figure 5.6
Create the pivot table shown here.

	A	B	C
1			
2			
3		Data	
4	Market ▼	Sales_Amount	Contracted Hours
5	TULSA	$628,405	9,583
6	SEATTLE	$179,827	2,889
7	PHOENIX	$570,255	10,167
8	NEWYORK	$873,581	14,213
9	NEWORLEANS	$333,454	5,057
10	MICHIGAN	$678,705	10,744
11	KANSASCITY	$574,899	8,547
12	FLORIDA	$1,450,392	22,640
13	DENVER	$645,583	8,641
14	DALLAS	$467,089	6,393
15	CHARLOTTE	$890,522	14,525
16	CANADA	$776,245	12,103
17	CALIFORNIA	$2,254,735	33,014
18	BUFFALO	$450,478	6,864
19	Grand Total	$10,774,172	165,380
20			

Now that you have a pivot table, it's time to create your first calculated field. To do this, you must activate the Insert Calculated Field dialog box. Select Options under the PivotTable Tools tab and then select Formulas from the Tools group. Selecting this option activates a drop-down menu from which you can select Calculated Field, as demonstrated in Figure 5.7.

Figure 5.7
Start the creation of your calculated field by selecting Formulas and then Calculated Field.

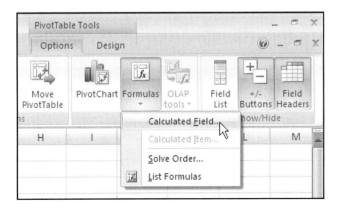

After you select Calculated Field, Excel activates the Insert Calculated Field dialog box, as shown in Figure 5.8.

Figure 5.8
The Insert Calculated Field dialog box assists you in creating a calculated field in your pivot table.

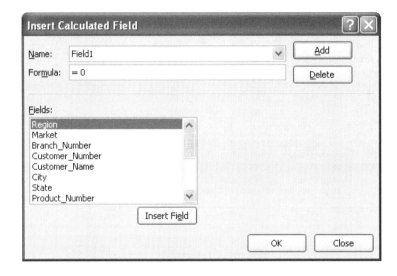

Notice the two input boxes, Name and Formula, at the top of the dialog box. The objective here is to give your calculated field a name and then build the formula by selecting the combination of data fields and mathematical operators that provide the metric you are looking for.

As you can see in Figure 5.9, you first give your calculated field a descriptive name—that is, a name that describes the utility of the mathematical operation. In this case, enter **Average Dollar per Hour** in the Name input box.

Figure 5.9
Give your calculated field a descriptive name.

Next, you go to the Fields list and double-click on the Sales_Amount field. Then enter / to let Excel know you plan to divide the Sales_Amount field by something.

> ___ CAUTION _____
>
> By default, the Formula input box in the Insert Calculated Field dialog box contains = 0. Ensure that you delete the 0 before continuing with your formula.

At this point, your dialog box should look similar to the one shown in Figure 5.10.

Figure 5.10
Start your formula with
= Sales_Amount /.

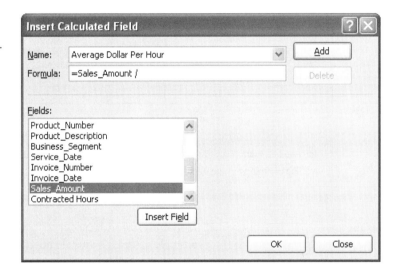

Next, double-click on the Contracted Hours field to finish your formula, as illustrated in Figure 5.11.

Figure 5.11
The full formula, =
Sales_Amount /
'Contracted
Hours', gives you the
calculated field you
need.

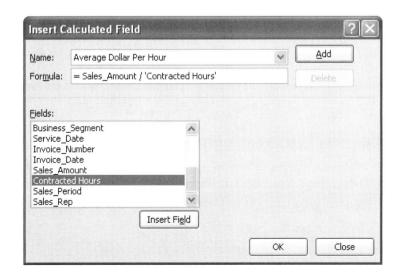

Finally, select Add and then click OK to create your newly created calculated field.

As you can see in Figure 5.12, not only does your pivot table create a new field called Sum of Average Dollar Per Hour, but the PivotTable Field List includes your new calculated field as well.

Figure 5.12
You can change the settings on your new calculated field just as you would any other field (that is, change the field name, change the number format, change the color).

	A	B	C	D	E	F
1						
2					PivotTable Field List	
3		Data				
4	Market	Sales_Amount	Contracted Hours	Sum of Average Dollar Per Hour	Choose fields to add to report:	
5	TULSA	$628,405	9,583	65.57495878	☐ Product_Number	
6	SEATTLE	$179,827	2,889	62.24548633	☐ Product_Description	
7	PHOENIX	$570,255	10,167	56.08882561	☐ Business_Segment	
8	NEWYORK	$873,581	14,213	61.46351298	☐ Service_Date	
9	NEWORLEANS	$333,454	5,057	65.93902511	☐ Invoice_Number	
10	MICHIGAN	$678,705	10,744	63.1706022	☐ Invoice_Date	
11	KANSASCITY	$574,899	8,547	67.26324675	☑ **Sales_Amount**	
12	FLORIDA	$1,450,392	22,640	64.06325088	☑ **Contracted Hours**	
13	DENVER	$645,583	8,641	74.71164101	☐ Sales_Period	
14	DALLAS	$467,089	6,393	73.06264195	☐ Sales_Rep	
15	CHARLOTTE	$890,522	14,535	61.30963787	☑ **Average Dollar Per Hour**	

> **NOTE**
> The resulting values from a calculated field are not formatted. You can easily apply any desired formatting using some of the techniques you learned in Chapter 3, "Customizing a Pivot Table."

Does this mean you have just added a column to your data source? The answer is no. Calculated fields are similar to the pivot table's default subtotal and grand total calculations in that they are all mathematical functions that recalculate when the pivot table changes or is refreshed. Calculated fields merely mimic the hard fields in your data source, allowing you to drag them, change field settings, and use them with other calculated fields.

Take a moment and look at Figure 5.11 closely. Notice the formula you entered is in a format similar to the one used in the standard Excel formula bar. The obvious difference is that instead of using hard numbers or cell references, you are referencing pivot data fields to define the arguments used in this calculation. If you have worked with formulas in Excel before, you will quickly grasp the concept of creating calculated fields.

CASE STUDY

Summarizing Next Year's Forecast

All the branch managers in your company have submitted their initial revenue forecasts for next year. Your task is to take the first-pass numbers they submitted and create a summary report showing the following:

Total revenue forecast by market

Total percent growth over last year

Total contribution margin by market

Because these numbers are first-pass submissions and you know they will change over the course of the next two weeks, you decide to use a pivot table to create the requested forecast summary.

Start by building the initial pivot table, shown here in Figure 5.13, to include Revenue Last Year and Forecast Next Year for each market. After creating the pivot table, you will see that by virtue of adding the Forecast Next Year field in the data area, you have met your first requirement: to show total revenue forecast by market.

Figure 5.13
The initial pivot table is basic, but it provides the data for your first requirement: show total revenue forecast by market.

	A	B	C
1			
2			
3		Data	
4	Market ▼	Revenue Last Year	Forecast Next Year
5	BUFFALO	$450,478.27	$411,245.94
6	CALIFORNIA	$2,254,735.38	$2,423,007.00
7	CANADA	$776,245.27	$746,383.94
8	CHARLOTTE	$890,522.49	$965,360.56
9	DALLAS	$467,089.47	$510,635.34
10	DENVER	$645,583.29	$722,694.95
11	FLORIDA	$1,450,392.00	$1,421,506.58
12	KANSASCITY	$574,898.97	$607,226.32
13	MICHIGAN	$678,704.95	$870,446.73
14	NEWORLEANS	$333,453.65	$366,173.55
15	NEWYORK	$873,580.91	$953,009.86
16	PHOENIX	$570,255.09	$746,721.39
17	SEATTLE	$179,827.21	$214,620.96
18	TULSA	$628,404.83	$661,726.45
19	Grand Total	$10,774,171.78	$11,620,759.57

The next metric you need is percent growth over last year. To get this data, you need to add a calculated field that calculates the following formula:

(Forecast Next Year / Revenue Last Year) – 1

To achieve this, do the following:

1. Activate the Insert Calculated Field dialog box and name your new field **Percent Growth** (see Figure 5.14).
2. Delete the 0 in the Formula input box.
3. Enter **(** (an open parenthesis).
4. Double-click on the Forecast Next Year field.
5. Enter **/** (a division sign).
6. Double-click on the Revenue Last Year field.
7. Enter **)** (a close parenthesis).
8. Enter **-** (a minus sign).
9. Enter the number **1**.

Figure 5.14
Name your new field
Percent Growth.

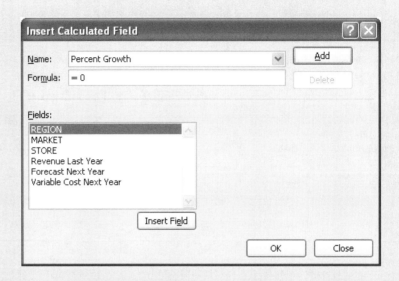

You can use any constant in your pivot table calculations. Constants are static values that do not change. In this example, the number 1 is a constant. Though the value of Revenue Last Year or Forecast Next Year may change based on the available data, the number 1 will always have the same value.

After you have entered the full formula, your dialog box should look similar to the one shown in Figure 5.15.

Figure 5.15
With just a few clicks, you have created a variance formula!

With your formula typed in, you can now click OK to add your new field. After changing the format of the resulting values to percent, you have a nicely formatted Percent Growth calculation in your pivot table. At this point, your pivot table should look like the one shown in Figure 5.16.

Figure 5.16
You have added a Percent Growth calculation to your pivot table.

	A	B	C	D
1				
2				
3		Data		
4	Market ▾	Revenue Last Year	Forecast Next Year	Sum of Percent Growth
5	BUFFALO	$450,478.27	$411,245.94	-9%
6	CALIFORNIA	$2,254,735.38	$2,423,007.00	7%
7	CANADA	$776,245.27	$746,383.94	-4%
8	CHARLOTTE	$890,522.49	$965,360.56	8%
9	DALLAS	$467,089.47	$510,635.34	9%
10	DENVER	$645,583.29	$722,694.95	12%
11	FLORIDA	$1,450,392.00	$1,421,506.58	-2%
12	KANSASCITY	$574,898.97	$607,226.32	6%
13	MICHIGAN	$678,704.95	$870,446.73	28%
14	NEWORLEANS	$333,453.65	$366,173.55	10%
15	NEWYORK	$873,580.91	$953,009.86	9%
16	PHOENIX	$570,255.09	$746,721.39	31%
17	SEATTLE	$179,827.21	$214,620.96	19%
18	TULSA	$628,404.83	$661,726.45	5%
19	Grand Total	$10,774,171.78	$11,620,759.57	8%

With this newly created view into your data, you can easily see that three markets need to resubmit their forecasts to reflect positive growth over last year.

Figure 5.17
You can already discern some information from the calculated field, identifying three problem markets.

	A	B	C	D
1				
2				
3		Data		
4	Market ▾	Revenue Last Year	Forecast Next Year	Sum of Percent Growth
5	BUFFALO	$450,478.27	$411,245.94	-9%
6	CALIFORNIA	$2,254,735.38	$2,423,007.00	7%
7	CANADA	$776,245.27	$746,383.94	-4%
8	CHARLOTTE	$890,522.49	$965,360.56	8%
9	DALLAS	$467,089.47	$510,635.34	9%
10	DENVER	$645,583.29	$722,694.95	12%
11	FLORIDA	$1,450,392.00	$1,421,506.58	-2%
12	KANSASCITY	$574,898.97	$607,226.32	6%
13	MICHIGAN	$678,704.95	$870,446.73	28%
14	NEWORLEANS	$333,453.65	$366,173.55	10%
15	NEWYORK	$873,580.91	$953,009.86	9%
16	PHOENIX	$570,255.09	$746,721.39	31%
17	SEATTLE	$179,827.21	$214,620.96	19%
18	TULSA	$628,404.83	$661,726.45	5%
19	Grand Total	$10,774,171.78	$11,620,759.57	8%

5

Now it's time to focus on your last requirement, which is to find total contribution margin by market. To get this data, you need to add a calculated field that calculates the following formula:

Forecast Next Year + Variable Cost Next Year

> NOTE
>
> A quick look at Figure 5.17 confirms that the Variable Cost Next Year field is not displayed in the pivot table report. Can you build pivot table formulas with fields that are not currently *even in* the pivot table? The answer is yes; you can use any field that is available to you in the PivotTable Field List, regardless of the fact that the field is not shown in the pivot table itself.

To create this field, do the following:

1. Activate the Insert Calculated Field dialog box and name your new field `Contribution Margin`.
2. Delete the 0 in the Formula input box.
3. Double-click on the Forecast Next Year field.
4. Enter + (a plus sign).
5. Double-click on the Variable Cost Next Year field.

After you have entered the full formula, your dialog box should look similar to the one shown in Figure 5.18.

Figure 5.18
With just a few clicks, you have created a formula that calculates contribution margin.

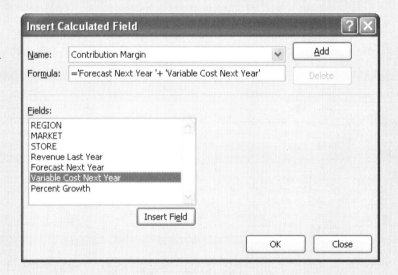

With the creation of the contribution margin, this report is ready to be delivered (see Figure 5.19).

Figure 5.19
Contribution margin is now a data field in your pivot table report thanks to your calculated field.

Market	Revenue Last Year	Forecast Next Year	Sum of Percent Growth	Sum of Contribution Margin
BUFFALO	$450,478.27	$411,245.94	-9%	($169,546)
CALIFORNIA	$2,254,735.38	$2,423,007.00	7%	$1,152,641
CANADA	$776,245.27	$746,383.94	-4%	$118,415
CHARLOTTE	$890,522.49	$965,360.56	8%	$360,343
DALLAS	$467,089.47	$510,635.34	9%	($908,021)
DENVER	$645,583.29	$722,694.95	12%	($697,393)
FLORIDA	$1,450,392.00	$1,421,506.58	-2%	$865,700
KANSASCITY	$574,898.97	$607,226.32	6%	($328,773)
MICHIGAN	$678,704.95	$870,446.73	28%	($92,813)
NEWORLEANS	$333,453.65	$366,173.55	10%	($586,405)
NEWYORK	$873,580.91	$953,009.86	9%	$506,335
PHOENIX	$570,255.09	$746,721.39	31%	$318,496
SEATTLE	$179,827.21	$214,620.96	19%	($163,738)
TULSA	$628,404.83	$661,726.45	5%	($1,193,984)
Grand Total	$10,774,171.78	$11,620,759.57	8%	-$818,743

Now that you've built your pivot table report, you can easily analyze any new forecast submissions by refreshing your report with the new updates.

Creating Your First Calculated Item

As you learned at the beginning of this chapter, a calculated item is a virtual data item you create by executing a calculation against existing items within a data field. Calculated items come in especially handy when you need to group and aggregate a set of data items.

For example, the pivot table in Figure 5.20 gives you sales amount by Sales_Period. Imagine that you need to compare the average performance of the most recent six Sales_Periods to the average of the prior seven periods. That is, you want to take the average of P01–P07 and compare it to the average of P08–P13.

Place your cursor on any data item in the Sales_Period field and then select Formulas from the Tools group. Next, select Calculated Item, as shown in Figure 5.21.

Selecting this option opens the Insert Calculated Item dialog box. A quick glance at Figure 5.22 shows you that the top of the dialog box identifies which field you are working with. In this case, it is the Sales_Period field. In addition, notice the Items list box is automatically filled with all the items in the Sales_Period field.

Your goal is to give your calculated item a name and then build its formula by selecting the combination of data items and operators that provide the metric you are looking for.

5

Figure 5.20
You want to compare the most recent six Sales_Periods to the average of the prior seven periods.

	A	B
1		
2		
3	Sales_Period ▾	Sum of Sales_Amount
4	P01	681,865
5	P02	1,116,916
6	P03	657,611
7	P04	865,498
8	P05	925,802
9	P06	868,930
10	P07	640,587
11	P08	1,170,262
12	P09	604,552
13	P10	891,253
14	P11	949,605
15	P12	887,665
16	P13	513,625
17	Grand Total	10,774,172

Figure 5.21
Start the creation of your calculated item by selecting Formulas and then Calculated Item.

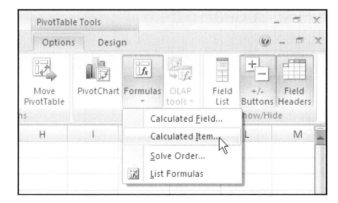

In this example, name your first calculated item **Avg P1-P7 Sales**, as shown in Figure 5.23.

Next, you can build your formula in the Formula input box by selecting the appropriate data items from the Items list. In this scenario, you want to create the following formula:

Average(P01, P02, P03, P04, P05, P06, P07)

Figure 5.22
The Insert Calculated Item dialog box is automatically populated to reflect the field with which you are working.

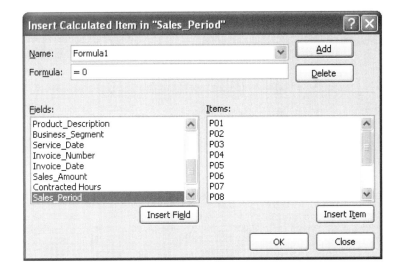

Figure 5.23
Give your calculated item a descriptive name.

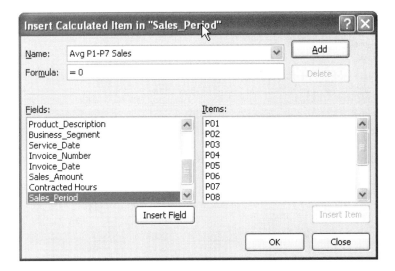

Enter this formula into the Formula input box, as demonstrated in Figure 5.24.

Click OK to activate your new calculated item. As you can see in Figure 5.25, you now have a data item called Avg P1-P7 Sales.

Figure 5.24
Enter a formula that gives you the average of P01–P07.

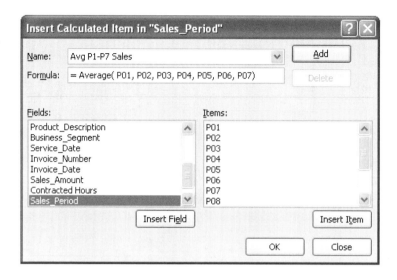

Figure 5.25
You have successfully added a calculated item to your pivot table.

	A	B
1		
2		
3	Sales_Period	Sum of Sales_Amount
4	P01	681,865
5	P02	1,116,916
6	P03	657,611
7	P04	865,498
8	P05	925,802
9	P06	868,930
10	P07	640,587
11	P08	1,170,262
12	P09	604,552
13	P10	891,253
14	P11	949,605
15	P12	887,665
16	P13	513,625
17	Avg P1-P7 Sales	822,458
18	Grand Total	11,596,630

TIP
You can use any worksheet function in both a calculated field and a calculated item. The only restriction is that the function you use cannot reference external cells or named ranges. In effect, this means you can use any worksheet function that does not require cell references or defined names to work (such as COUNT, AVERAGE, IF, OR).

Create a calculated item to represent the average sales for P08–P13, as demonstrated in Figure 5.26.

Figure 5.26
Create a second calculated item.

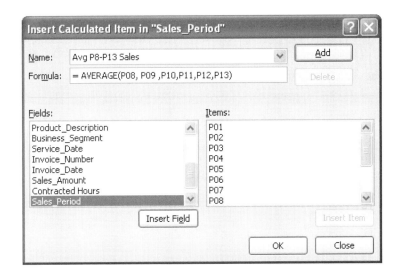

Now you can hide the individual sales periods, leaving only your two calculated items. After a little formatting, your calculated items, shown in Figure 5.27, allow you to compare the average performance of the six most recent Sales_Periods to the average of the prior seven periods.

Figure 5.27
You can now compare the most recent six Sales_Periods to the average of the prior seven periods.

	A	B	C
1			
2			
3	Sales_Period	Average Sales_Amount	
4	Avg P1-P7 Sales	$822,458	
5	Avg P8-P13 Sales	$836,160	
6			

5

CAUTION

If you don't hide the data items you used to create your calculated item, your grand totals and subtotals may show incorrect amounts.

Understanding Rules and Shortcomings of Pivot Table Calculations

Although there is no better way to integrate your calculations into a pivot table than using calculated fields and calculated items, they do come with their own set of drawbacks. It's important you understand what goes on behind the scenes when you use pivot table calculations, and even more important to be aware of the boundaries and limitations of calculated fields and calculated items to avoid potential errors in your data analysis.

The following sections highlight the rules around calculated fields and calculated items that you will most likely encounter when working with pivot table calculations.

Remembering the Order of Operator Precedence

Just as in a spreadsheet, you can use any operator in your calculation formulas, meaning any symbol that represents a calculation to perform (+, −, *, /, %, ^). Moreover, just as in a spreadsheet, calculations in a pivot table follow the order of operator precedence.

In other words, when you perform a calculation that combines several operators, as in (2+3) * 4/50%, Excel evaluates and performs the calculation in a specific order. The order of operations for Excel is as follows:

- Evaluate items in parentheses.
- Evaluate ranges (:).
- Evaluate intersections (spaces).
- Evaluate unions (,).
- Perform negation (−).
- Convert percentages (%).
- Perform exponentiation (^).
- Perform multiplication (*) and division (/), which are of equal precedence.
- Perform addition (+) and subtraction (-), which are of equal precedence.
- Evaluate text operators (&).
- Perform comparisons (=, <>, <=, >=).

> **NOTE**
> Operations that are equal in precedence are performed left to right.

Consider this basic example. The correct answer to (2+3)*4 is 20. However, if you leave off the parentheses, as in 2+3*4, Excel performs the calculation like this: 3*4 = 12 + 2 = 14. The order of operator precedence mandates that Excel perform multiplication before subtraction. Entering 2+3*4 gives you the wrong answer. Because Excel evaluates and performs all calculations in parentheses first, placing 2+3 inside parentheses ensures the correct answer.

Here is another widely demonstrated example. If you enter 10^2, which represents the exponent 10 to the 2nd power as a formula, Excel returns 100 as the answer. If you enter −10^2, you would expect −100 to be the result. Instead, Excel returns 100 yet again. The reason is that Excel performs negation before exponentiation, meaning Excel is converting

10 to –10 before the exponentiation, effectively calculating –10*–10, which indeed equals 100. Using parentheses in the formula, –(10^2), ensures that Excel calculates the exponent before negating the answer, giving you –100.

Understanding the order of operations ensures that you avoid miscalculating your data.

Using Cell References and Named Ranges

When you create calculations in a pivot table, you are essentially working in a vacuum. The only data available to you is the data that exists in the pivot cache. Therefore, you cannot reach outside the confines of the pivot cache to reference cells or named ranges in your formula.

Using Worksheet Functions

You can use any worksheet function that does not require cell references or defined names as an argument. In effect, this means you can use any worksheet function that does not require cell references or defined names to work. Of the many functions that fall into this category, some include COUNT, AVERAGE, IF, AND, NOT, OR.

Using Constants

You can use any constant in your pivot table calculations. Constants are static values that do not change. For example, in the formula [Units Sold]*5, 5 is a constant. Though the value of Units Sold may change based on the available data, 5 will always have the same value.

Referencing Totals

Your calculation formulas cannot reference a pivot table's subtotals or grand total. This means that you cannot use the result of a subtotal or grand total as a variable or argument in your calculated field.

5

Rules Specific to Calculated Fields

Calculated field calculations are always performed against the sum of your data. In basic terms, Excel always calculates data fields, subtotals, and grand totals before evaluating your calculated field. This means that your calculated field is always applied to the sum of the underlying data.

The example shown in Figure 5.28 demonstrates how this can adversely affect your data analysis.

In each quarter, you need to get the total revenue for every product by multiplying the number of units sold by the price. If you look at Q1 first, you can immediately see the problem. Instead of returning the sum of 220+150+220+594, which would give you $1,184, the subtotal is calculating the sum of number of units times the sum of price, which returns the wrong answer.

Figure 5.28
Although the calculated field is correct for the individual data items in your pivot table, the subtotal is mathematically incorrect.

As you can see in Figure 5.29, including the whole year in your analysis compounds the problem.

Figure 5.29
The grand total for the year as a whole is completely wrong.

Unfortunately, there is no solution to this problem, but there is a workaround. In worst-case scenarios, you can configure your settings to eliminate subtotals and grand totals and then calculate your own Totals. Figure 5.30 demonstrates this workaround.

Rules Specific to Calculated Items

You cannot use calculated items in a pivot table that uses averages, standard deviations, or variances. Conversely, you cannot use averages, standard deviations, or variances in a pivot table that contains a calculated item.

You cannot use a page field to create a calculated item, nor can you move any calculated item to the report filter area.

You cannot add a calculated item to a report that has a grouped field, nor can you group any field in a pivot table that contains a calculated item.

When building your calculated item formula, you cannot reference items from a field other than the one you are working with.

Figure 5.30
Calculating your own
Totals can prevent
reporting incorrect data.

	A	B	C	D	E	F	G	H	I	J
1			Data							
2	Qtr	Product	Number of Units	Price	CalcField Unit*Price					
3	Q1	A	10	22	$220					
4		B	5	30	$150					
5		C	5	44	$220					
6		D	11	54	$594					
7	Q2	A	7	19	$133					
8		B	12	25	$300					
9		C	9	39	$351					
10		D	5	52	$260					
11	Q3	A	6	17	$102					
12		B	8	21	$168					
13		C	6	40	$240					
14		D	7	55	$385					
15	Q4	A	8	22	$176					
16		B	7	31	$217					
17		C	6	35	$210					
18		D	10	49	$490					
19										
20										
21				Total	$4,216	<<This is a formula: =SUM(E3:E18)				
22										

As you think about the section you have just read, don't be put off by these shortcomings of pivot tables. Despite the clear limitations highlighted, the capability to create custom calculations directly into your pivot table remains a powerful and practical feature that can enhance your data analysis. Now that you are aware of the inner workings of pivot table calculations and understand the limitations of calculated fields and items, you can avoid the pitfalls and use this feature with confidence.

Managing and Maintaining Your Pivot Table Calculations

In your dealings with pivot tables, you will find that sometimes you won't keep a pivot table for more than the time it takes to say, "Copy, Paste Values." Other times, however, it will be more cost effective to keep your pivot table and all its functionality intact.

When you find yourself maintaining and managing your pivot tables through changing requirements and growing data, you may find the need to maintain and manage your calculated fields and calculated items as well.

Editing and Deleting Your Pivot Table Calculations

When your calculation's parameters change or you no longer need your calculated field or calculated item, you can activate the appropriate dialog box to edit or remove the calculation.

Simply activate the Insert Calculated Field or Insert Calculated Item dialog box and select the Name drop-down, as demonstrated in Figure 5.31.

As you can see in Figure 5.32, after you select a calculated field or item, you have the option of deleting the calculation or modifying the formula.

5

Figure 5.31
Opening the drop-down list under Name reveals all the calculated fields or items in the pivot table.

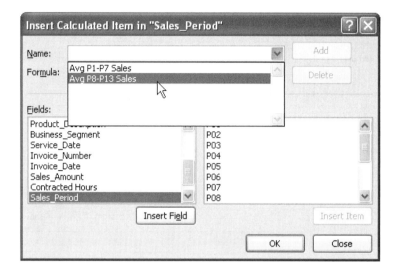

Figure 5.32
After you select the appropriate calculated field or item, you can either delete or modify the calculation.

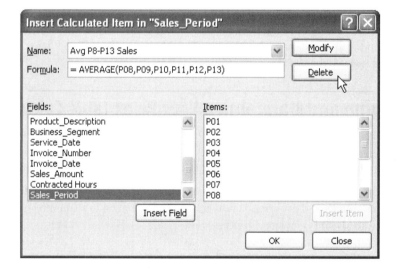

Changing the Solve Order of Your Calculated Items

If the value of a cell in your pivot table is dependent on the results of two or more calculated items, you have the option of changing the solve order of the calculated items. That is, you can specify the order in which the individual calculations are performed.

To get to the Solve Order dialog box, place your cursor anywhere in the pivot table, select Formulas from the Tools group, and then select Solve Order, as shown in Figure 5.33.

Figure 5.33
Activate the Solve Order dialog box by selecting Formulas and then Solve Order.

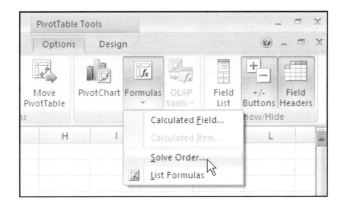

The Solve Order dialog box, shown here in Figure 5.34, lists all the calculated items that currently exist in your pivot table. The idea here is to select any of the calculated items you see listed to enable the Move Up, Move Down, and Delete command buttons. The order you see the formulas in this list is the exact order the pivot table will perform each operation.

Figure 5.34
After you identify the calculated item you are working with, simply move the item up or down to change the solve order. You also have the option of deleting the item in this dialog box.

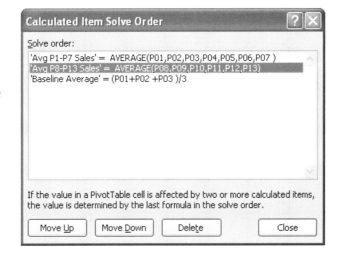

Documenting Your Formulas

Excel provides a nice little function that lists the calculated fields and calculated items used in your pivot table, along with details on the solve order and formulas. This feature comes in especially handy if you need to quickly determine what calculations are being applied in a pivot table and which fields or items those calculations affect.

To list your pivot table calculations, simply place your cursor anywhere in the pivot table and select Formulas and then select List Formulas. Excel creates a new tab in your workbook listing the calculated fields and calculated items in the current pivot table. Figure 5.35 shows a sample output of the List Formulas command.

Figure 5.35
The List Formulas command allows you to document the details of your pivot table calculations quickly and easily.

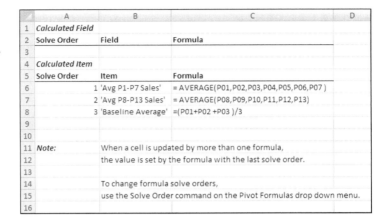

	A	B	C	D
1	*Calculated Field*			
2	Solve Order	Field	Formula	
3				
4	*Calculated Item*			
5	Solve Order	Item	Formula	
6		1 'Avg P1-P7 Sales'	= AVERAGE(P01,P02,P03,P04,P05,P06,P07)	
7		2 'Avg P8-P13 Sales'	= AVERAGE(P08,P09,P10,P11,P12,P13)	
8		3 'Baseline Average'	=(P01+P02 +P03)/3	
9				
10				
11	*Note:*	When a cell is updated by more than one formula,		
12		the value is set by the formula with the last solve order.		
13				
14		To change formula solve orders,		
15		use the Solve Order command on the Pivot Formulas drop down menu.		
16				

Next Steps

In the next chapter, you learn the fundamentals of pivot charts and the basics of representing your pivot data graphically. You also get a firm understanding of the limitations of pivot charts and alternatives to using pivot charts.

5

Using Pivot Charts and Other Visualizations

What Is a Pivot Chart...Really?

When sharing your analyses with others, you will quickly find that there is no getting around the fact that people want charts. Pivot tables are nice, but they leave lots of those pesky numbers that take time to absorb. Charts, on the other hand, enable users to make a split-second determination on what your data is actually revealing. Charts offer instant gratification, allowing users to immediately see relationships, point out differences, and observe trends. The bottom line is that managers today want to absorb data as fast as possible, and nothing delivers that capability faster than a chart. This is where pivot charts come into play. Whereas pivot tables offer the analytical, pivot charts offer the visual.

A common definition of a pivot chart is a graphical representation of the data in your pivot table. Although this definition is technically correct, it somehow misses the mark on what a pivot chart truly does.

When you create a standard chart from data that is not in a pivot table, you feed the chart a range made up of individual cells holding individual pieces of data. Each cell is an individual object with its own piece of data, so your chart treats each cell as an individual data point, charting each one separately.

However, the data in your pivot table is part of a larger object. The pieces of data you see inside your pivot table are not individual pieces of data that occupy individual cells. Rather, they are items inside a larger pivot table object that is occupying space on your worksheet.

When you create a chart from your pivot table, you are not feeding it individual pieces of data inside individual cells; you are feeding it the entire pivot

IN THIS CHAPTER

What Is a Pivot Chart...Really? 141

Creating Your First Pivot Chart 142

Keeping Pivot Chart Rules in Mind 145

Case Study: Creating a Report Showing Invoice Frequency and Revenue Distribution by Product 148

Examining Alternatives to Using Pivot Charts 153

Using Conditional Formatting with Pivot Tables 157

Next Steps 166

table layout. Indeed, a true definition of a pivot chart is a chart that uses a PivotLayout Object to view and control the data in your pivot table.

Using the PivotLayout Object allows your pivot chart to interactively add, remove, filter, and refresh data fields inside the chart just like your pivot table. The result of all this action is a graphical representation of the data you see in your pivot table.

Creating Your First Pivot Chart

With all the complexity behind the make-up of a pivot chart, you may get the impression that creating them is difficult. The reality is that it's quite a simple task.

To demonstrate how simple it is to create a pivot chart, look at the pivot table in Figure 6.1. This pivot table provides for a simple view of revenue by market. The Business Segment field in the report filter area lets you parse out revenue by line of business.

Figure 6.1
This basic pivot table shows revenue by market and allows for filtering by line of business.

	A	B	C
1	Business_Segment (All) ▾		
2			
3	**Row Labels** ▾	**Sum of Sales_Amount**	
4	BUFFALO	$450,478	
5	CALIFORNIA	$2,254,735	
6	CANADA	$776,245	
7	CHARLOTTE	$890,522	
8	DALLAS	$467,089	
9	DENVER	$645,583	
10	FLORIDA	$1,450,392	
11	KANSASCITY	$574,899	
12	MICHIGAN	$678,705	
13	NEWORLEANS	$333,454	
14	NEWYORK	$873,581	
15	PHOENIX	$570,255	
16	SEATTLE	$179,827	
17	TULSA	$628,405	
18	**Grand Total**	**$10,774,172**	
19			

Creating a pivot chart from this data would not only allow for an instant view of the performance of each market, but would also permit you to retain the ability to filter by line of business.

To start the process, place your cursor anywhere inside the pivot table and click the Insert tab on the Application ribbon. On the Insert tab, you can see the Charts group displaying the various types of charts you can create. Here, you can choose the chart type you would like to use for your pivot chart. For this example, click on the Column chart icon and select the first 2-D column chart, as demonstrated in Figure 6.2.

Figure 6.2
Select the chart type you
want to use.

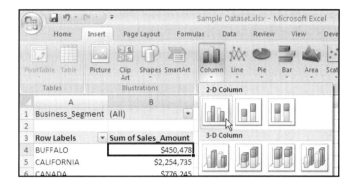

As you can see in Figure 6.3, choosing the chart type causes two objects to appear on your
spreadsheet: a column chart and the PivotChart Filter Pane.

Figure 6.3
Excel creates your pivot
chart on the same sheet
as your pivot table.

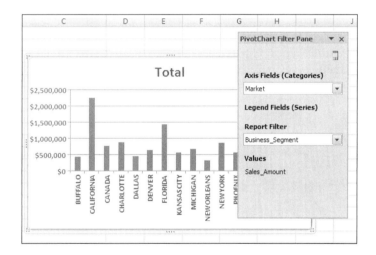

TIP

Notice that pivot charts are now, by default, placed on the same sheet as the source pivot table. If
you long for the days when pivot charts were located on their own chart sheet, you are in luck. All
you have to do is place your cursor inside your pivot table and then press F11 on your keyboard. This
creates a pivot chart on its own sheet.

By the way, you can easily change the location of your pivot charts by simply right-clicking on the
chart itself (outside the plot area) and selecting Move Chart. This activates the Move Chart dialog
box, where you can specify the new location.

6

A Few Words on the PivotChart Filter Pane

In previous versions of Excel, pivot charts displayed the available pivot fields directly on the charts. Using these pivot fields, a user could rearrange a chart and apply filters to the underlying pivot table, thus filtering the chart. In Excel 2007, the pivot fields have been removed from pivot charts. This ensures that pivot charts in Excel 2007 have a clean look and feel consistent with standard charts.

In place of the pivot fields, Excel provides the PivotChart Filter Pane. This task pane allows you to limit the data shown in the pivot chart by applying filters to the underlying pivot table. You can filter your pivot table here using the same techniques highlighted in Chapter 4, "Controlling the Way You View Your Pivot Data." You are also able to call the PivotTable Field List dialog box from here, where you can rearrange the fields in your pivot table.

The PivotChart Filter Pane appears each time you place your cursor inside the pivot chart and disappears when you click outside the pivot chart. You can prevent this task pane from automatically activating by explicitly closing it. After you disable this task pane, you can reactivate it by choosing PivotChart Filter from the Analyze tab on the PivotChart Tools ribbon. Click anywhere inside the pivot chart to activate the PivotChart Tools ribbon.

You now have a chart that is a visual representation of your pivot table. More than that, because the pivot chart is tied to the underlying pivot table, changing the pivot table in any way changes the chart. For example, as Figure 6.4 illustrates, adding the Region field to the pivot table adds a region dimension to your chart.

Figure 6.4
Your pivot chart displays the same fields your underlying pivot table displays.

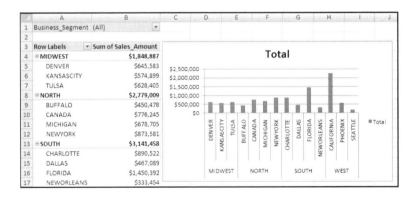

> **NOTE**
> The pivot chart in Figure 6.4 does not display the subtotals shown in the pivot table. When creating a pivot chart, Excel ignores subtotals and grand totals.

In addition, selecting a Business Segment from the page field filters not only the pivot table, but also the pivot chart. All this behavior comes from the fact that pivot charts use the same pivot cache and pivot layout as their corresponding pivot tables. This means that if you add or remove data from your data source and refresh your pivot table, your pivot chart updates to reflect the changes.

Take a moment and think about the possibilities. You can essentially create a fairly robust interactive reporting tool on the power of one pivot table and one pivot chart; no programming necessary.

Creating a Pivot Chart from Scratch

You don't have to build your pivot table before creating a pivot chart. You can go straight from your raw data to a pivot chart. Simply click on any single cell in your data source and select the Insert tab. From there, select PivotTable from the Tables group and choose PivotChart from the drop-down list. This activates the Create PivotChart dialog box. At this point, you go through the same steps you would take if you were building a pivot table.

Keeping Pivot Chart Rules in Mind

As with other aspects of pivot table technology, pivot charts come with their own set of rules and limitations. The following sections give you a better understanding of the boundaries and restrictions of pivot charts.

Changes in the Underlying Pivot Table Affect Your Pivot Chart

The primary rule you should always be cognizant of is that your pivot chart is merely an extension of your pivot table. If you refresh, move a field, add a field, remove a field, hide a data item, show a data item or apply a filter, your pivot chart reflects your changes.

The Placement of Data Fields in Your Pivot Table May Not Be Best Suited for Your Pivot Chart

One common mistake people make when using pivot charts is assuming that Excel will place the values in the column area of the pivot table in the x-axis of the pivot chart.

For instance, the pivot table in Figure 6.5 is in a format that is easy to read and comprehend. The structure chosen shows Sales Periods in the column area and the Region in the row area. This structure works fine in the pivot table view.

Figure 6.5
The placement of your data fields works for a pivot table view.

	A	B	C	D	E	F
1						
2						
3	Sales_Amount	Sales_Period ▾				
4	Region ▾	P01	P02	P03	P04	P05
5	MIDWEST	$109,498	$207,329	$101,861	$155,431	$159,298
6	NORTH	$180,772	$260,507	$183,151	$214,665	$235,369
7	SOUTH	$198,415	$334,189	$189,493	$255,558	$283,012
8	WEST	$193,180	$314,891	$183,106	$239,843	$248,124
9	Grand Total	$681,865	$1,116,916	$657,611	$865,498	$925,802
10						

6

Suppose you decide to create a pivot chart from this pivot table. You would instinctively expect to see fiscal periods across the x-axis and lines of business along the y-axis. However, as you can see in Figure 6.6, your pivot chart comes out with Region in the x-axis and Sales Period in the y-axis.

Figure 6.6
Creating a pivot chart from your nicely structured pivot table does not yield the results you were expecting.

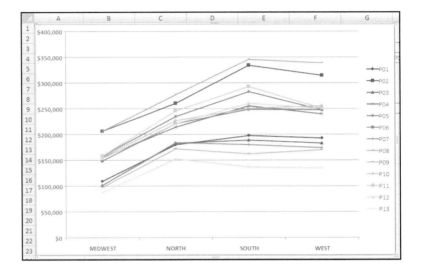

So why does the structure in your pivot table not translate to a clean pivot chart? The answer has to do with the way pivot charts handle the different areas of your pivot table.

In a pivot chart, both the x-axis and y-axis correspond to a specific area in your pivot table:

- **Y-axis**—Corresponds to the column area in your pivot table and makes up the y-axis of your pivot chart
- **X-axis**—Corresponds to the row area in your pivot table and makes up the x-axis of your pivot chart

Given this new information, look at the pivot table in Figure 6.5 again. This structure says that the Sales_Period field will be treated as the y-axis because it is in the column area. Meanwhile, the Region field will be treated as the x-axis because it is in the row area.

Now suppose you were to rearrange the pivot table to show fiscal periods in the row area and lines of business in the column area, as shown in Figure 6.7.

This arrangement generates the pivot table shown in Figure 6.8.

A Few Formatting Limitations Still Exist in Excel 2007

With previous versions of Excel, many users avoided using pivot charts because of the many formatting limitations that came with them. These limitations included the inability to resize or move key components of the pivot chart, the loss of formatting when underlying pivot tables were changed, and the inability to use certain chart types. All these limitations led to pivot charts being viewed by most users as too clunky and impractical to use.

Figure 6.7
This format makes for slightly more difficult reading in a pivot table view but allows your pivot chart to give you the effect you are looking for.

	A	B	C	D	E	F
1						
2						
3	Sales_Amount	Region				
4	Sales_Period	MIDWEST	NORTH	SOUTH	WEST	Grand Total
5	P01	$109,498	$180,772	$198,415	$193,180	$681,865
6	P02	$207,329	$260,507	$334,189	$314,891	$1,116,916
7	P03	$101,861	$183,151	$189,493	$183,106	$657,611
8	P04	$155,431	$214,665	$255,558	$239,843	$865,498
9	P05	$159,298	$235,369	$283,012	$248,124	$925,802
10	P06	$149,426	$221,791	$249,258	$248,456	$868,930
11	P07	$101,809	$184,350	$180,146	$174,282	$640,587
12	P08	$207,278	$277,905	$345,842	$339,236	$1,170,262
13	P09	$98,129	$172,271	$163,153	$171,000	$604,552
14	P10	$156,974	$227,469	$251,042	$255,769	$891,253
15	P11	$159,130	$246,435	$293,184	$250,855	$949,605
16	P12	$154,276	$221,242	$261,113	$251,034	$887,665
17	P13	$88,448	$153,083	$137,053	$135,041	$513,625
18	Grand Total	$1,848,887	$2,779,009	$3,141,458	$3,004,818	$10,774,172

Figure 6.8
With the new arrangement in your pivot table, you get a pivot chart that makes sense.

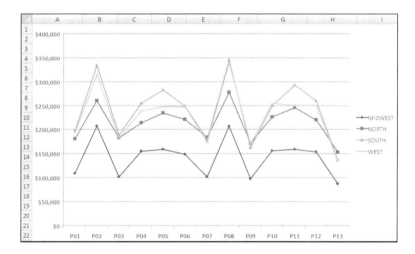

Excel 2007 brings vast improvements to pivot charts. Users can now format almost every property and component of a pivot chart. In addition, pivot charts in Excel 2007 no longer lose their formatting when the underlying pivot table changes. And as you've seen, pivot charts are now (by default) placed on the same worksheet as the source pivot table. Overall, the look and feel of pivot charts in Excel 2007 are very much that of standard charts, making them much more of a viable reporting option.

However, a few limitations persist in this version of Excel that you should keep in mind:

- You still cannot use XY (scatter) charts, bubble charts, or stock charts when creating a pivot chart.
- Applied trend lines are often lost when adding or removing fields in the underlying pivot table.

6

- You cannot switch the data source feed from rows to columns (or vice versa) as with a standard chart.
- The data labels in the pivot chart cannot be resized.

> **TIP**
> Although you cannot resize the data labels in a pivot chart, you can change the font of a data label. Making the font bigger or smaller indirectly resizes the data label.

CASE STUDY

Creating a Report Showing Invoice Frequency and Revenue Distribution by Product

You have been asked to provide both region and market managers with an interactive reporting tool that will allow them to easily see the frequency and distribution of revenues across products. Your solution needs to give managers the flexibility to filter out a region or market if needed.

Given the amount of data in your source table and possibility that this will be a recurring exercise, you decide to use a pivot chart. Start by building the pivot chart you see in Figure 6.9.

Figure 6.9
The initial pivot table meets all the data requirements.

	A	B	C
1	Region	(All)	
2	Market	(All)	
3			
4		Values	
5	Product_Description	Count of Invoice_Number	Sum of Sales_Amount
6	Cleaning & Housekeeping Services	2,534	$1,138,593
7	Facility Maintenance and Repair	21,351	$2,361,158
8	Fleet Maintenance	18,623	$2,627,798
9	Green Plants and Foliage Care	8,357	$1,276,783
10	Landscaping/Grounds Care	6,077	$1,190,915
11	Predictive Maintenance/Preventative Maintenance	11,672	$2,178,925
12	Grand Total	68,614	$10,774,172

Next, place your cursor anywhere inside the pivot table and click on Insert. On the Insert tab, you can see the Charts menu displaying the various types of charts you can create. Choose the Column chart icon and select the first 2-D column chart. You immediately see the chart in Figure 6.10.

> **TIP**
> The next few steps in this case study expose you to some basic chart formatting techniques. To keep the focus of this book on pivot tables, any explanation on the techniques shown here is in the context of this case study. For a detailed look at creating, formatting, and managing charts in Excel 2007, check out Charts and Graphs for Microsoft Office Excel 2007 (ISBN: 0789736101).

Figure 6.10
Your raw pivot chart needs some formatting to meet requirements.

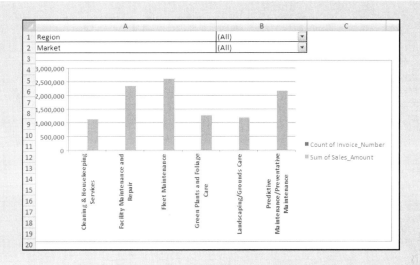

The first thing you will notice is that only one of the two data series is visible (the series that represents Sales_Amount). The reason is that the two series are on such different scale ranges that the scale on the bigger series actually represses the other. To fix this problem, you have to place one of the series on a secondary axis.

Right-click on the Sales_Amount data series and select Format Data Series. After the Format Data Series dialog box activates, click the Secondary Axis radio button, as demonstrated in Figure 6.11.

Figure 6.11
Place the Sales_Amount series on a secondary axis.

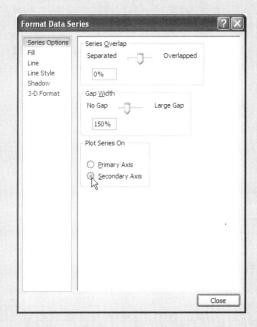

6

Next, right-click on the Sales_Amount series again and select Change Series Chart Type. Here, you select the Line with Markers chart type, as illustrated in Figure 6.12.

Figure 6.12
Change the chart type for the Sales_Amount data series to a line chart.

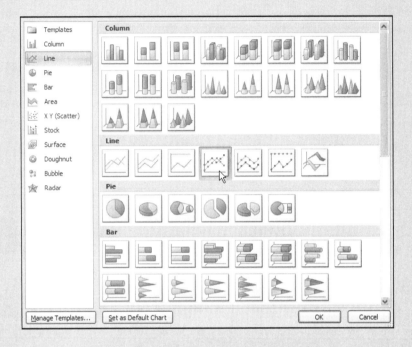

At this point, your pivot chart should look similar to the one in Figure 6.13. As you can see, the bars represent the number of invoices generated for each product, and the line represents the revenue for each product.

Figure 6.13
All that is required now is some final formatting.

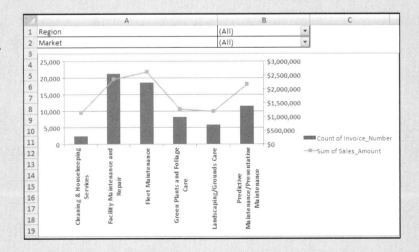

Now change the data series names to be a bit more user-friendly. Activate the PivotTable Field List and change the names of the data fields in the pivot table from Count of Invoice_Number and Sum of Sales_Amount to something more appropriate. As you can see in Figure 6.14, Invoice Count and Revenue work well in this scenario.

Figure 6.14
The names on the data series are now a bit more user-friendly.

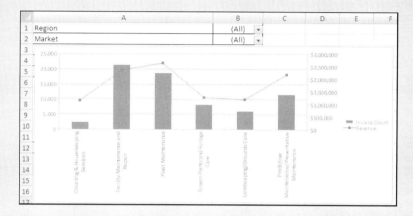

On an aesthetic note, try applying one of Excel's Quick Style designs to your chart. To get to the Quick Style menu, click on the chart and select Design on the Chart Tools ribbon. The idea is to select the style that best suits your taste. As you can see in Figure 6.15, after your style is applied, you have quite the professional-looking chart.

Figure 6.15
Applying one of Excel's Quick Styles gives your pivot chart a professional look and feel.

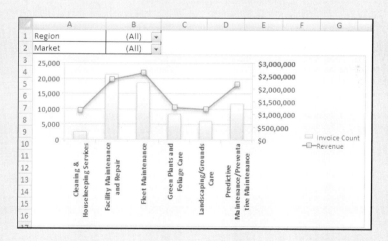

The final step is to remove the line from the Revenue data series. Because this data series does not represent a trend over time, the line between the data points is not necessary and may cause confusion. To remove the line, right-click on the Revenue data series and select Format Data Series. This activates a dialog box where you can specify that no line should be shown for this data series. Figure 6.16 demonstrates how this is done.

6

Figure 6.16
Remove the line from the Revenue data series to avoid implying that this data point is a trend.

Your final pivot chart should look similar to the one in Figure 6.17.

Figure 6.17
Your final report meets all the requirements of content and interactivity.

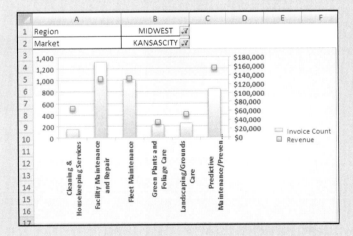

You now have a pivot chart that allows a manager to see the frequency a product is invoiced and the revenue it generates. This pivot chart also gives anyone using this report the ability to filter by region and market.

Examining Alternatives to Using Pivot Charts

There are generally two reasons why you would need an alternative to using pivot charts. First, you do not want the overhead that comes with a pivot chart. Second, you want to avoid some of the formatting limitations of pivot charts.

In fact, sometimes you might create a pivot table simply to summarize and shape your data in preparation for charting. In these situations, you don't plan on keeping your source data, and you definitely don't want a pivot cache taking up memory and file space.

In the example in Figure 6.18, you can see a pivot table that summarizes revenue by quarter for each product.

Figure 6.18
This pivot table was created to summarize and chart revenue by quarter for each product.

	A	B	C	D	E
1					
2	Sum of Sales_Amount	Filter column			
3	Filter rows	Qtr1	Qtr2	Qtr3	Qtr4
4	Cleaning & Housekeeping Services	$257,218	$290,074	$297,251	$294,049
5	Facility Maintenance and Repair	$563,799	$621,715	$600,810	$574,834
6	Fleet Maintenance	$612,496	$691,440	$674,592	$649,269
7	Green Plants and Foliage Care	$293,194	$325,276	$329,787	$328,527
8	Landscaping/Grounds Care	$288,797	$310,670	$303,086	$288,363
9	Predictive Maintenance/Preventativ	$533,127	$567,391	$552,380	$526,027

The idea here is that you created this pivot table only to summarize and shape your data for charting. You don't want to keep the source data, nor do you want to keep the pivot table with all its overhead. The problem is if you try to create a chart using the data in the pivot table, you inevitably create a pivot chart. This effectively means you have all the overhead of the pivot table looming in the background. Of course, this could be problematic if you do not want to share your source data with end users or you don't want to inundate them with unnecessarily large files.

The good news is there are a few simple techniques that allow you to create a chart from a pivot table, but not end up with a pivot chart. Any one of the following methods does the trick.

Method 1: Turn Your Pivot Table into Hard Values

After you have created and structured your pivot table appropriately, select the entire pivot table and copy it. Then select Paste Values from the Insert tab, as demonstrated in Figure 6.19.

This action essentially deletes your pivot table, leaving you with the last values that were displayed in the pivot table. These values can subsequently be used to create a standard chart.

> **NOTE**
> This technique effectively disables the dynamic functionality of your pivot chart. That is, your pivot chart becomes a standard chart that cannot be interactively filtered or refreshed. This is also true for method 2 and method 3 outlined next.

6

Figure 6.19
The Paste Values func-
tionality is useful when
you want to create hard-
coded values from pivot
tables.

Method 2: Delete the Underlying Pivot Table

If you have already created your pivot chart, you can turn it into a standard chart by simply deleting the underlying pivot table. To do this, select the entire pivot table and press the Delete key on the keyboard. Keep in mind that with this method, unlike method 1, you are not left with any of the values that made up the source data for the chart. In other words, if anyone asks for the data that feeds the chart, you don't have it.

> **TIP**   Here is a handy tip to keep in the back of your mind. If you ever find yourself in a situation in which you have a chart but the data source is not available, activate the chart's data table. The data table lets you see the data values that feed each series in the chart.

Method 3: Distribute a Picture of the Pivot Chart

Now, it may seem strange to distribute pictures of pivot chart, but this is an entirely viable method of distributing your analysis without a lot of overhead. In addition to very small file sizes, you also get the added benefit of controlling what your clients get to see.

To use this method, simply copy the pivot chart by right-clicking on the chart itself (outside the plot area) and selecting Copy. Then open a new workbook. Right-click anywhere in the new workbook and select Paste Special; then select the picture format you prefer. A picture of your pivot chart is then placed in the new workbook.

Method 4: Use Cells Linked Back to the Pivot Table as the Source Data for Your Chart

Many Excel users shy away from using pivot charts solely based on the formatting restrictions and issues they encounter when working with them. Often these users give up the functionality of a pivot table to avoid the limitations of pivot charts.

However, if you want to retain key functionality in your pivot table such as report filters and top 10 ranking, there is a way to link a standard chart to your pivot table without creating a pivot chart.

In the example in Figure 6.20, a pivot table shows the top 10 markets by contracted hours along with their total revenue. Notice that the report filter area allows you to filter by business segment so you can see the top 10 markets segment.

Figure 6.20
This pivot table allows you to filter by business segment to see the top 10 markets by total contracted hours and revenue.

	A	B	C
1			
2	Business_Segment	(All)	
3			
4		Values	
5	Market	Contracted Hours	Sales_Amount
6	CALIFORNIA	33,014	$2,254,735
7	CANADA	12,103	$776,245
8	CHARLOTTE	14,525	$890,522
9	DENVER	8,641	$645,583
10	FLORIDA	22,640	$1,450,392
11	KANSASCITY	8,547	$574,899
12	MICHIGAN	10,744	$678,705
13	NEWYORK	14,213	$873,581
14	PHOENIX	10,167	$570,255
15	TULSA	9,583	$628,405
16	Grand Total	144,177	$9,343,323

Suppose you want to turn this view into an XY scatter chart to be able to point out the relationship between the contracted hours and revenues. You need to keep the functionality of being able to filter out 10 records by model number; however, you want to avoid the inability to create XY.

Well, a pivot chart is definitely out because you can't build pivot charts with certain chart types (such as XY scatter charts). The techniques outlined in methods 1, 2, and 3 are also out because those methods disable the interactivity you need. So what's the solution? Use the cells around the pivot table to link back to the data you need and then chart those cells. In other words, you can build a mini dataset that feeds your standard chart. This dataset links back to the data items in your pivot table, so when your pivot table changes, so does your dataset.

Click your cursor in a cell next to your pivot table, as demonstrated in Figure 6.21, and reference the first data item that you need to create the range you will feed your standard chart.

Now copy the formula you just entered and paste that formula down and across to create your complete dataset. At this point, you should have a dataset that looks similar to Figure 6.22.

After your linked dataset is complete, you can use it to create a standard chart. In this example, shown in Figure 6.23, you are creating an XY scatter chart with this data. You could never do this with a pivot chart.

6

Figure 6.21
Start your linked dataset by referencing the first data item you need to capture.

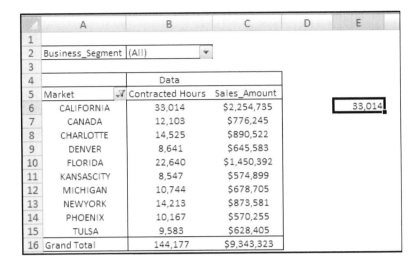

Figure 6.22
Copy the formula and paste it down and across to create your complete dataset.

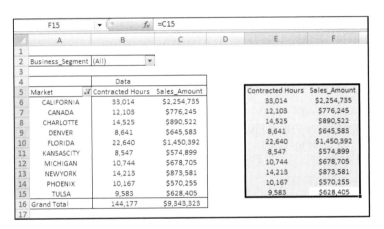

Figure 6.24 demonstrates how this solution offers the best of both worlds. You have kept the ability to filter out a particular business segment using the page field, and you have all the formatting freedom of a standard chart without any of the issues related to using a pivot chart.

Figure 6.23
Use your completed linked dataset to create a standard chart.

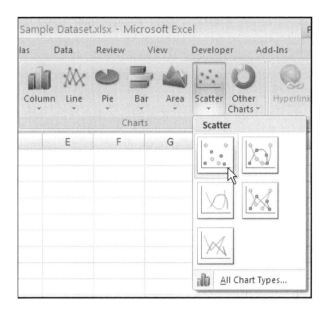

Figure 6.24
This solution allows you to continue using the functionality of your pivot table without any of the formatting limitations you would have with a pivot chart.

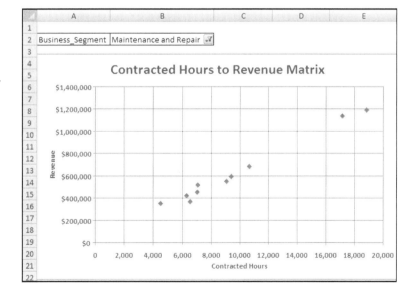

Using Conditional Formatting with Pivot Tables

One of the most impressive new features of Excel 2007 is the improved conditional formatting functionality. In previous versions of Excel, conditional formatting simply allowed you to dynamically change the color or formatting of a value or a range of cells based on a set of conditions you defined.

In Excel 2007, conditional formatting includes a more robust set of visualizations including data bars, color scales, and icon sets. These new visualizations allow users to build dashboard-style reporting that goes far beyond the traditional red, yellow, and green designations. What's more, conditional formatting has been extended to integrate with pivot tables. This means that conditional formatting is now applied to a pivot table's structure, not just the cells it occupies.

In this section, you learn how to leverage the magic combination of pivot tables and conditional formatting to create interactive visualizations that serve as an alternative to pivot charts.

To start the first example, create the pivot table shown in Figure 6.25.

Figure 6.25
Create this pivot table.

	A	B
1	Market	(All) ▼
2		
3	Sales_Period ▼	Sales_Amount
4	P01	$681,865
5	P02	$1,116,916
6	P03	$657,611
7	P04	$865,498
8	P05	$925,802
9	P06	$868,930
10	P07	$640,587
11	P08	$1,170,262
12	P09	$604,552
13	P10	$891,253
14	P11	$949,605
15	P12	$887,665
16	P13	$513,625
17	Grand Total	$10,774,172

6

Suppose you want to create a report that allows your managers to see the performance of each sales period graphically. You could build a pivot chart, but you decide to use conditional formatting. In this example, let's go the easy route and quickly apply some data bars.

First, select all the Sales_Amount values in the values area. After you have highlighted the revenue for each Sales_Period, click on the Home tab and select Conditional Formatting in the Styles group to data bars, as demonstrated in Figure 6.26.

As you can see in Figure 6.27, you now have a set of bars that correspond to the values in your pivot table. This visualization looks like a sideway chart, doesn't it? What's more impressive is that as you filter the markets in the report filter area, the data bars dynamically update to correspond with the data for the selected market.

How can it be that you did not have to trudge through a dialog box to define the condition levels?

Figure 6.26
Apply data bars to the values in your pivot table.

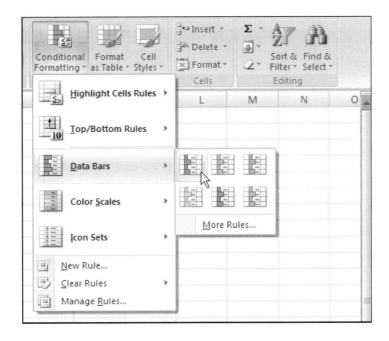

Figure 6.27
You have applied conditional data bars with just three easy clicks!

	A	B
1	Market	DALLAS
2		
3	Sales_Period ▼	Sales_Amount
4	P01	$26,215
5	P02	$52,257
6	P03	$23,058
7	P04	$40,857
8	P05	$35,791
9	P06	$39,518
10	P07	$26,000
11	P08	$55,795
12	P09	$23,367
13	P10	$41,911
14	P11	$38,613
15	P12	$41,747
16	P13	$21,962
17	Grand Total	$467,089

Excel 2007 has a handful of preprogrammed scenarios that can be leveraged when you want to spend less time configuring your conditional formatting and more time analyzing your data. For example, to create the data bars you've just employed, Excel uses a predefined algorithm that takes the largest and smallest values in the selected range and calculates the condition levels for each bar.

Other examples of preprogrammed scenarios include

- Top *N*th Items
- Top *N*th %
- Bottom *N*th Items
- Bottom *N*th %
- Above Average
- Below Average

As you can see, Excel 2007 makes an effort to offer the conditions that are most commonly used in data analysis.

> **NOTE**
> To remove the applied conditional formatting, place your cursor inside the pivot table, click on the Home tab, and select Conditional Formatting in the Styles group. From there, select Clear Rules and then select This PivotTable.

It's important to note that you are by no means limited to these preprogrammed scenarios. You can still create your own custom conditions. To help illustrate this, create the pivot table shown in Figure 6.28.

Figure 6.28
This pivot shows
Sales_Amount,
Contracted_Hours, and a
calculated field that cal-
culates Dollars per Hour.

	A	B	C	D
1	Product_Description	(All)		
2				
3		Values		
4	Market	Sales_Amount	Contracted Hours	Dollars per Hour
5	BUFFALO	$450,478	6,864	$65.63
6	CALIFORNIA	$2,254,735	33,014	$68.30
7	CANADA	$776,245	12,103	$64.14
8	CHARLOTTE	$890,522	14,525	$61.31
9	DALLAS	$467,089	6,393	$73.06
10	DENVER	$645,583	8,641	$74.71
11	FLORIDA	$1,450,392	22,640	$64.06
12	KANSASCITY	$574,899	8,547	$67.26
13	MICHIGAN	$678,705	10,744	$63.17
14	NEWORLEANS	$333,454	5,057	$65.94
15	NEWYORK	$873,581	14,213	$61.46
16	PHOENIX	$570,255	10,167	$56.09
17	SEATTLE	$179,827	2,889	$62.25
18	TULSA	$628,405	9,583	$65.57
19	Grand Total	$10,774,172	165,380	$65.15

In this scenario, you want to evaluate the relationship between total revenue and dollars per hour. The idea is that some strategically applied conditional formatting helps identify opportunities for improvement.

Start by placing your cursor in the Sales_Amount column. Click the Home tab and select Conditional Formatting. Then select New Rule. This activates the New Formatting Rule dialog box, shown in Figure 6.29.

Figure 6.29
The New Formatting
Rule dialog box.

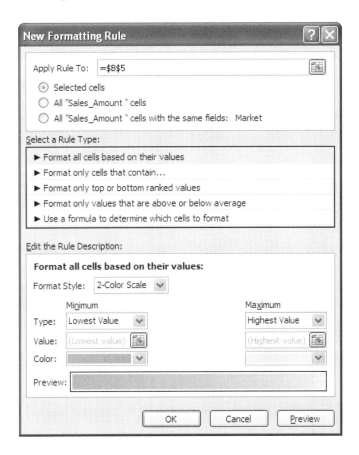

The objective in this dialog box is to identify the cells where the conditional formatting will be applied, specify the rule type to use, and define the details of the conditional formatting.

First, you must identify the cells where your conditional formatting will be applied. You have three choices:

- **Selected Cells**—This selection applies conditional formatting to only the selected cells.
- **All "Sales_Amount" Cells**—This selection applies conditional formatting to all values in the Sales_Amount column, including all subtotals and grand totals. This selection is ideal for use in analyses in which you are using averages, percentages, or other calculations where a single conditional formatting rule makes sense for all levels of analysis.

■ **All "Sales_Amount" Cells with the Same Fields: Market:** This selection applies conditional formatting to all values in the Sales_Amount column at the Market level only (excludes subtotals and grand totals). This selection is ideal for use in analyses where you are using calculations that make sense only within the context of the level being measured.

> **NOTE** The words *Sales_Amount* and *Market* are not permanent fixtures of the New Formatting Rule dialog box. These words change to reflect the fields in your pivot table. Sales_Amount is used because your cursor is in that column. Market is used because the active data items in the pivot table are in the Market field.

In this example, the third selection (All "Sales_Amount" Cells with the Same Fields: Market) makes the most sense, so click that radio button, as demonstrated in Figure 6.30.

Figure 6.30
Click the radio button next to All "Sales_Amount" Cells with the Same Fields: Market.

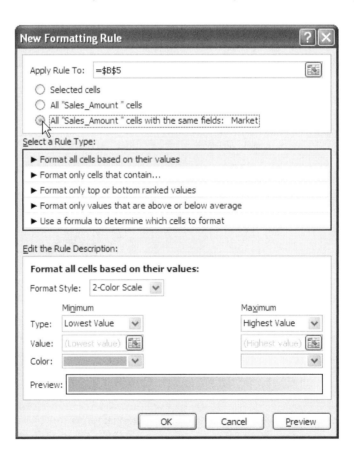

Next, in the Select a Rule Type section, you need to specify the rule type you want to use for the conditional format. You can select one of five rule types:

- **Format All Cells Based on Their Values**—This selection allows you to apply conditional formatting based on some comparison of the actual values of the selected range. That is, the values in the select range are measured against each other. This selection is ideal when you want to identify general anomalies in your dataset.

- **Format Only Cells That Contain**—This selection allows you to apply conditional formatting to those cells that meet specific criteria you define. Keep in mind that the values in your range are not measured against each other when you use this rule type. This selection is useful when you are comparing your values against a predefined benchmark.

- **Format Only Top or Bottom Ranked Values**—This selection allows you to apply conditional formatting to those cells that are ranked in the top or bottom Nth number or percent of all the values in the range.

- **Format Only Values That Are Above or Below the Average**—This selection allows you to apply conditional formatting to those values that are mathematically above or below the average of all values in the selected range.

- **Use a Formula to Determine Which Cells to Format**—This selection allows you to specify your own formula and evaluate each value in the selected range against that formula. If the values evaluate as true, then the conditional formatting is applied. This selection comes in handy when you are applying conditions based on the results of an advanced formula or mathematical operation.

> **NOTE**
> Data bars, color scales, and icon sets can be used only when the selected cells are formatted based on their values. This means that if you want to use data bars, color scales, and icon sets, you must select the Format All Cells Based on Their Values rule type.

In this scenario, you want to identify problem areas using icon sets; therefore, you want to format the cells based on their values.

Finally, you need to define the details of the conditional formatting in the Edit the Rule Description section. Again, you want to identify problem areas using the slick new icon sets that are offered by Excel 2007. In that light, select Icon Sets from the Format Style drop-down box.

After selecting Icon Sets, select 3 Signs from the Icon Style drop-down. This style of icon is ideal in situations in which your pivot tables cannot always be viewed in color.

At this point, your New Formatting Rule dialog box should look similar to Figure 6.31.

With this configuration, Excel applies the sign icons based on the percentile bands >=67, >=33, and <33. Keep in mind that the actual percentile bands could be changed based on your needs. In this scenario, the default percentile bands are sufficient.

6

Figure 6.31
Select Icon Sets from the
Format Style drop-down
box.

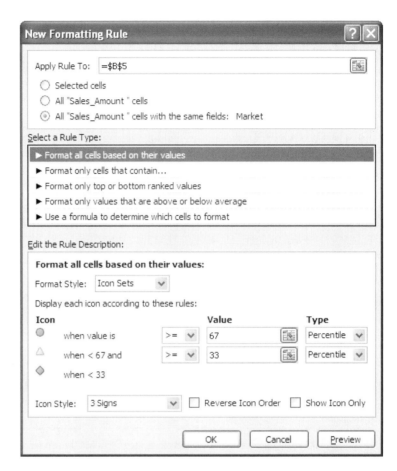

Click the OK button to apply the conditional formatting. As you can see in Figure 6.32, you now have icons that allow you to quickly determine where each market falls in relation to other markets as it pertains to revenue.

Now apply the same conditional formatting to the Dollars per Hour field. When you are done, your pivot table should look similar to one shown in Figure 6.33.

Take a moment to analyze what you have here. With this view, a manager can analyze the relationship between total revenue and dollars per hour. So, for example, the Dallas market manager can see that he is in the bottom percentile for revenue but in the top percentile for dollars per hour. With this information, he immediately sees that his dollars per hour rates may be too high for his market. Conversely, the New York market manager can see that she is in the top percentile for revenue but in the bottom percentile for dollars per hour. This tells her that her dollars per hour rates may be too low for her market.

Figure 6.32
You have applied your
first custom conditional
formatting!

	A	B	C	D
1	Product_Description	(All) ▾		
2				
3		Values		
4	Market ▾	Sales_Amount	Contracted Hours	Dollars per Hour
5	BUFFALO	◇ $450,478	6,864	$65.63
6	CALIFORNIA	◯ $2,254,735	33,014	$68.30
7	CANADA	△ $776,245	12,103	$64.14
8	CHARLOTTE	◯ $890,522	14,525	$61.31
9	DALLAS	◇ $467,089	6,393	$73.06
10	DENVER	△ $645,583	8,641	$74.71
11	FLORIDA	◯ $1,450,392	22,640	$64.06
12	KANSASCITY	△ $574,899	8,547	$67.26
13	MICHIGAN	△ $678,705	10,744	$63.17
14	NEWORLEANS	◇ $333,454	5,057	$65.94
15	NEWYORK	◯ $873,581	14,213	$61.46
16	PHOENIX	◇ $570,255	10,167	$56.09
17	SEATTLE	◇ $179,827	2,889	$62.25
18	TULSA	△ $628,405	9,583	$65.57
19	Grand Total	$10,774,172	165,380	$65.15

Figure 6.33
You have successfully
created an interactive
visualization.

	A	B	C	D
1	Product_Description	(All) ▾		
2				
3		Values		
4	Market ▾	Sales_Amount	Contracted Hours	Dollars per Hour
5	BUFFALO	◇ $450,478	6,864	△ $65.63
6	CALIFORNIA	◯ $2,254,735	33,014	◯ $68.30
7	CANADA	△ $776,245	12,103	△ $64.14
8	CHARLOTTE	◯ $890,522	14,525	◇ $61.31
9	DALLAS	◇ $467,089	6,393	◯ $73.06
10	DENVER	△ $645,583	8,641	◯ $74.71
11	FLORIDA	◯ $1,450,392	22,640	△ $64.06
12	KANSASCITY	△ $574,899	8,547	◯ $67.26
13	MICHIGAN	△ $678,705	10,744	◇ $63.17
14	NEWORLEANS	◇ $333,454	5,057	△ $65.94
15	NEWYORK	◯ $873,581	14,213	◇ $61.46
16	PHOENIX	◇ $570,255	10,167	◇ $56.09
17	SEATTLE	◇ $179,827	2,889	◇ $62.25
18	TULSA	△ $628,405	9,583	△ $65.57
19	Grand Total	$10,774,172	165,380	$65.15

6

Remember that this in an interactive report. Each manager can view the same analysis by product by simply filtering the report filter area!

Next Steps

In the next chapter, you learn how to bring together disparate data sources into one pivot table. You create a pivot table from multiple data sets, and you learn the basics of creating pivot tables from other pivot tables.

Analyzing Disparate Data Sources with Pivot Tables

7

Until this point, you have been working with one local table located in the worksheet within which you are operating. Indeed, it would be wonderful if every dataset you came across were neatly packed in one easy-to-use Excel table. Unfortunately, the business of data analysis does not always work out that way.

The reality is that some of the data you encounter will come from disparate data sources—meaning sets of data that are from separate systems, stored in different locations, or saved in a variety of formats. In an Excel environment, disparate data sources generally fall into one of two categories: external data and multiple ranges.

External data is exactly what it sounds like—data that is not located in the Excel workbook in which you are operating. Some examples of external data sources are text files, Access tables, SQL Server tables, and other Excel workbooks.

Multiple ranges are separate datasets located in the same workbook but separated either by blank cells or by different worksheets. For example, if your workbook has three tables on three different worksheets, each of your datasets covers a range of cells. You are therefore working with multiple ranges.

A pivot table can be an effective tool when you need to summarize data that is not neatly packed into one table. With a pivot table, you can quickly bring together either data found in an external source or data found in multiple tables within your workbook. In this chapter, you discover how to work with external data sources and datasets located in multiple ranges within your workbook.

IN THIS CHAPTER

Using Multiple Consolidation Ranges 168

Analyzing the Anatomy of a Multiple Consolidation Range Pivot Table 174

Case Study: Consolidating and Analyzing Datasets 176

Building a Pivot Table Using External Data Sources 179

Next Steps............................187

Using Multiple Consolidation Ranges

If you need to analyze data dispersed in multiple ranges, your options are somewhat limited. For example, the data in Figure 7.1 shows you three ranges that you need to bring together to analyze as a group.

Figure 7.1
Someone passed you a file that has three ranges of data. You need to bring the three ranges together so you can analyze them as a group.

	A	B	C	D	E	F
1	NORTH					
2	Line of Business	Lob Manager	Jan	Feb	Mar	Apr
3	Copier Sale	Jim Graham	$1,670,642	$1,908,785	$2,185,037	$2,239,371
4	Parts	Mike Alexander	$2,378,240	$2,372,974	$2,537,793	$2,429,561
5	Printer Sale	Allan Howe	$1,443,106	$1,628,517	$1,745,271	$1,545,072
6	Service Plan	Kelly Richardson	$17,098,331	$17,045,471	$17,497,027	$16,903,477
7						
8	SOUTH					
9	Line of Business	Lob Manager	Jan	Feb	Mar	Apr
10	Copier Sale	Jim Graham	$2,703,264	$2,923,311	$2,869,761	$2,892,764
11	Parts	Mike Alexander	$2,457,824	$2,658,591	$2,736,089	$2,493,456
12	Printer Sale	Allan Howe	$2,016,462	$2,378,109	$2,467,409	$2,089,987
13	Service Plan	Kelly Richardson	$18,922,385	$19,240,187	$19,100,783	$19,072,738
14						
15	WEST					
16	Line of Business	Lob Manager	Jan	Feb	Mar	Apr
17	Copier Sale	Jim Graham	$1,672,342	$1,913,201	$2,000,897	$2,073,048
18	Parts	Mike Alexander	$1,840,374	$2,041,408	$1,899,784	$2,028,641
19	Printer Sale	Allan Howe	$1,383,284	$1,630,537	$1,676,003	$1,495,751
20	Service Plan	Kelly Richardson	$12,840,822	$12,878,362	$12,728,642	$12,405,450
21						

You essentially have three paths you can take to get to the point where you can analyze all three ranges together:

1. You can obtain the original data used to create this summary. This seems like a good choice, but in most cases, you could find another solution by the time it took you to obtain the original data—if you have access to it at all.
2. You can manually shape the data into a proper tabular dataset and then do your analysis. In reality, this option would be the best one if you had the time to spare or you were planning to use this data on an ongoing basis. However, if this is a one-time analysis or if you're in a crunch, you would not want to spend the time to manually format this data.
3. You can create a pivot table using multiple consolidation ranges. With this pivot table option, you can quickly and easily consolidate all the data from your selected ranges into a single pivot table. This is the best option if you need to perform only a one-time analysis on multiple ranges or if you need to analyze multiple ranges in a hurry.

To start the process of bringing this data together with a pivot table, you have to activate the classic PivotTable and PivotChart Wizard.

Activating the Classic PivotTable and PivotChart Wizard

As you learned in Chapter 2, "Creating a Basic Pivot Table," Microsoft has abandoned the classic PivotTable and PivotChart Wizard for a streamlined dialog box. Unfortunately, some of the functionality exposed in the classic wizard was not brought over with the new pivot table interfaces. The capability to create multiple consolidation range pivot tables is one example of functionality that did not make its way to Excel 2007's new UI.

The good news is that Excel does allow you to activate the classic wizard (complete with all the old functionality) through a custom toolbar command. The idea is to add the PivotTable and PivotChart Wizard custom toolbar command to the Quick Access toolbar. After it's on the Quick Access toolbar, you can call up the classic wizard simply by clicking on the icon.

Follow these steps to add the PivotTable and PivotChart Wizard custom toolbar command to the Quick Access toolbar:

1. Click the Office icon in the upper-left corner of your screen.

2. Select Excel Options to open the Options dialog box.

3. Select Customize to bring up all the available commands that can be added to the Quick Access toolbar.

4. In the Choose Commands From drop-down box, select Commands Not in the Ribbon.

5. Select the PivotTable and PivotChart Wizard from the list of commands and click the Add button.

6. Click OK.

As you can see in Figure 7.2, your reward is an easily accessible icon that calls the classic PivotTable and PivotChart Wizard.

TIP

You can also activate the classic PivotTable and PivotChart Wizard by pressing Alt+D+P on your keyboard. Keep in mind this approach does not add an icon to the Quick Access toolbar.

Figure 7.2
Add the PivotTable and PivotChart Wizard command to the Quick Access toolbar.

After you have access to the PivotTable and PivotChart Wizard, activate it and then select Multiple Consolidation Ranges, as demonstrated in Figure 7.3. Then select Next.

In the next step, you specify whether you want Excel to create one page field for you, or whether you would like to create your own. In most cases, the page fields that Excel creates are ambiguous and of no value. Therefore, in almost all cases, you should select the option of creating your own page fields, as illustrated in Figure 7.4. Then select Next.

Next, you need to point Excel to each of your individual datasets one by one. Simply select the entire range of your first data set and select Add, as shown in Figure 7.5.

> **CAUTION**
>
> For your pivot table to generate properly, the first line of each range must include column labels.

Figure 7.3
Start the PivotTable and PivotChart Wizard and select Multiple Consolidation Ranges. Select Next to move to the next step.

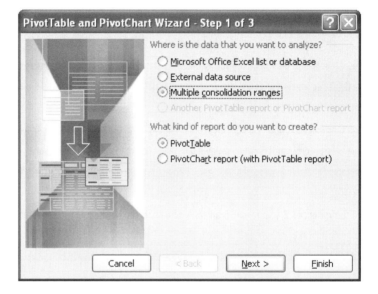

Figure 7.4
Specify that you want to create your own page fields and then select Next.

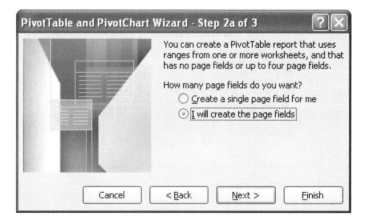

Figure 7.5
Select the entire range of
your first data set and
select Add.

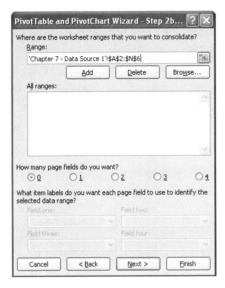

Select the rest of your ranges and add them to your list of ranges. At this point, your dialog box should look similar to the one in Figure 7.6.

Notice that each of your datasets belongs to a Region (North, South, or West). When your pivot table brings your three datasets together, you need a way to parse out each Region again.

Figure 7.6
Add the other two
dataset ranges to your
range list.

7

To ensure you have that capability, you need to tag each range in your list of ranges with a name identifying which dataset that range came from. The result is the creation of a Page field that allows you to filter each region as needed.

The first thing you have to do to create your Region page field is specify how many page fields you want to create. In your case, you want to create only one page field for your region identifier, so simply click on the radio button next to the number 1, as demonstrated in Figure 7.7. This action enables the Field One input box. As you can see, you can create up to four page fields.

Figure 7.7
To be able to filter by Region when your pivot table is complete, you have to create a page field. Click on the radio button next to the number 1 to create one page field. This action enables the Field One input box.

You have to tag each range one by one, so click on the first range in your range list to highlight it. Enter the region name into the Field One input box. As you can see in Figure 7.8, the first range is made up of data from the North region, so you enter **North** in the input box.

Figure 7.8
Select the first range that represents the dataset for the North region and enter the word **North** in the input box.

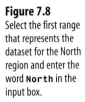

Repeat the process for the other regions, as illustrated in Figure 7.9. When you're done, select Next and then select Finish.

Figure 7.9
Repeat the process until you have tagged all your datasets. When you're done, select Next and then select Finish.

You have successfully brought three data sources together into one pivot table, as shown in Figure 7.10.

Figure 7.10
You now have a pivot table that contains data from three data sources.

	A	B	C	D	E	F	G	H	I	J	K	L	M	N	O
1	Page1	(All)													
2															
3	Count of Value	Column Labels													
4	Row Labels	Jan	Feb	Mar	Apr	May	Jun	Jul	Aug	Sep	Oct	Nov	Dec	Lob Manager	Grand Total
5	Copier Sale	3	3	3	3	3	3	3	3	3	3	3	3	3	39
6	Parts	3	3	3	3	3	3	3	3	3	3	3	3	3	39
7	Printer Sale	3	3	3	3	3	3	3	3	3	3	3	3	3	39
8	Service Plan	3	3	3	3	3	3	3	3	3	3	3	3	3	39
9	Grand Total	12	12	12	12	12	12	12	12	12	12	12	12	12	156
10															

Analyzing the Anatomy of a Multiple Consolidation Range Pivot Table

Take a moment to analyze your new pivot table. You may notice a few interesting things here. First, your field list includes a field call Row, a field called Column, a field called Value, and a field called Page1.

It is important to keep in mind that pivot tables using multiple consolidation ranges as their data source can have only three base fields: Row, Column, and Value. In addition to these base fields, you can create up to four page fields.

> **TIP**
>
> Notice that the fields generated with your pivot table have fairly generic names (Row, Column, Value, Page). You can customize the field settings for these fields to rename and format them to better suit your needs. See Chapter 3, "Customizing a Pivot Table," for a more detailed look at customizing field settings.

The Row Field

The Row field is always made up of the first column in your data source. Note that in Figure 7.1, the first column in your data source is Line of Business. Therefore, the Row field in your newly created pivot table contains Line of Business.

The Column Field

The Column field contains the remaining columns in your data source. Pivot tables that use multiple consolidation ranges combine all the fields in your original datasets (minus the first column, which is used for the Row field) into a kind of super field called the Column field. The fields in your original datasets become data items under the Column field.

Notice that your pivot table initially applies Count to your Column field. If you change the field setting of the Column field to Sum, all the data items under the Column field are affected. Figure 7.11 shows the same data as Figure 7.10, except the summarize type is set to Sum instead of the default (Count).

Figure 7.11

The data items under the Column field are treated as one entity. When you change the calculation of the Column field from Count to Sum, the change applies to all items under the Column field.

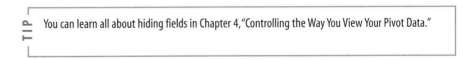

	A	B	C	D	E	F	G	N	O
1	Page1	(All)							
2									
3	Sum of Value	Column Label							
4	Row Labels	Jan	Feb	Mar	Apr	May	Jun	Lob Manager	Grand Total
5	Copier Sale	$6,046,248	$6,745,297	$7,055,695	$7,205,183	$7,314,876	$7,307,057	$0	$86,581,689
6	Parts	$6,676,438	$7,072,973	$7,173,666	$6,951,658	$7,034,322	$6,787,727	$0	$83,938,493
7	Printer Sale	$4,842,852	$5,637,163	$5,888,683	$5,130,810	$5,859,476	$5,985,190	$0	$68,368,778
8	Service Plan	$48,861,538	$49,164,020	$49,326,452	$48,381,665	$49,363,401	$47,116,246	$0	$574,506,079
9	Grand Total	$66,427,076	$68,619,453	$69,444,496	$67,669,316	$69,572,075	$67,196,220	$0	$813,395,039

The Value Field

The Value field contains the value for all data items under the Column field. Notice that even fields that were originally text fields in your dataset are treated as numerical values. An example is Lob Manager, shown in Figure 7.11. Although this field contained manager names in the original dataset, it is now treated as a number in your pivot table.

As mentioned before, pivot tables that use multiple consolidation ranges merge the fields in your original datasets (minus the first field), making them data items in the Column field. Therefore, although you may recognize fields like Lob Manager as text fields that contain their own individual data items, they no longer hold data of their own. They have been transformed into data items themselves—data items with a value.

The net effect of this behavior is that fields originally holding text or dates show up in your pivot table as a meaningless numerical value. It's usually a good idea to simply hide these fields to avoid confusion.

> **TIP**
>
> You can learn all about hiding fields in Chapter 4, "Controlling the Way You View Your Pivot Data."

The Page Fields

Page fields are the only fields in multiple consolidation range pivot tables that you have direct control over. You can create and define up to four page fields. The useful feature of these fields is that you can drag them to the row area or column area to add layers to your pivot table.

The Page1 field shown in the pivot table in Figure 7.11 was created to be able to filter by region. However, if you move the Page1 field to the row area of your pivot table, you can create a one-shot view of all your data by region. Figure 7.12 demonstrates this view.

7

Figure 7.12
Dragging the Page1 field to the row area adds a layer to your pivot table report, giving you a one-shot view of all your data by region.

	A	B	C	D	E	F	G	H	O	P
1										
2										
3	Sum of Value		Column							
4	Page1	Row	Jan	Feb	Mar	Apr	May	Jun	Lob Manager	Grand Total
5	⊟North	Copier Sale	$1,670,642	$1,908,785	$2,185,037	$2,239,371	$2,121,648	$2,133,291	$0	$25,893,618
6		Parts	$2,378,240	$2,372,974	$2,537,793	$2,429,561	$2,419,169	$2,271,298	$0	$29,063,171
7		Printer Sale	$1,443,106	$1,628,517	$1,745,271	$1,545,072	$1,808,141	$1,785,903	$0	$20,621,317
8		Service Plan	$17,098,331	$17,045,471	$17,497,027	$16,903,477	$17,157,864	$16,422,091	$0	$201,414,511
9	North Total		$22,590,319	$22,955,747	$23,965,128	$23,117,481	$23,506,822	$22,612,583	$0	$276,992,617
10	⊟South	Copier Sale	$2,703,264	$2,923,311	$2,869,761	$2,892,764	$3,203,760	$3,192,643	$0	$36,711,470
11		Parts	$2,457,824	$2,658,591	$2,736,089	$2,493,456	$2,583,428	$2,572,431	$0	$31,205,269
12		Printer Sale	$2,016,462	$2,378,109	$2,467,409	$2,089,987	$2,351,109	$2,480,684	$0	$28,153,264
13		Service Plan	$18,922,385	$19,240,187	$19,100,783	$19,072,738	$19,193,191	$18,400,440	$0	$223,750,307
14	South Total		$26,099,935	$27,200,198	$27,174,042	$26,548,945	$27,331,488	$26,646,198	$0	$319,820,310
15	⊟West	Copier Sale	$1,672,342	$1,913,201	$2,000,897	$2,073,048	$1,989,468	$1,981,123	$0	$23,976,601
16		Parts	$1,840,374	$2,041,408	$1,899,784	$2,028,641	$2,031,725	$1,943,998	$0	$23,670,053
17		Printer Sale	$1,383,284	$1,630,537	$1,676,003	$1,495,751	$1,700,226	$1,718,603	$0	$19,594,197
18		Service Plan	$12,840,822	$12,878,362	$12,728,642	$12,405,450	$13,012,346	$12,293,715	$0	$149,341,261
19	West Total		$17,736,822	$18,463,508	$18,305,326	$18,002,890	$18,733,765	$17,937,439	$0	$216,582,112
20	Grand Total		$66,427,076	$68,619,453	$69,444,496	$67,669,316	$69,572,075	$67,196,220	$0	$813,395,039

TIP

Your pivot table may have a different layout than Figure 7.12. You can achieve the same layout by selecting Design from the PivotTable Tools tab and then selecting Report Layout in the Layout group. Here, you can select Show in Tabular Form to get the same layout.

Redefining Your Pivot Table

You may run into a situation in which you need to redefine your pivot table. That is, you need to add a data range, remove a data range, or redefine your page fields. To redefine your pivot table, simply activate the classic PivotTable and PivotChart Wizard and then select the Back button until you get to the dialog box you need.

CASE STUDY

Consolidating and Analyzing Datasets

Your manager forwarded you the spreadsheet shown in Figure 7.13 and asked you to extract a two-year average revenue by quarter for each model number. Your manager requires these figures for a meeting that starts in 15 minutes, so you have little time to organize and summarize this data.

Given that this is a one-time analysis that needs to be completed quickly, you decide to use a pivot table. To create it, follow these steps:

1. Start the classic PivotTable and PivotChart Wizard and select Multiple Consolidation Ranges as your data source. Select Next.
2. Select I Will Create the Page Fields and then select Next.
3. Add your first data range and then select the radio button next to the number 1 to activate the Field One input box. Enter **2006** into the input box.

   At this point, your dialog box should look like the one shown in Figure 7.14.

Figure 7.13
You need to analyze the data in this spreadsheet and quickly extract the two-year average revenue by quarter for each model number.

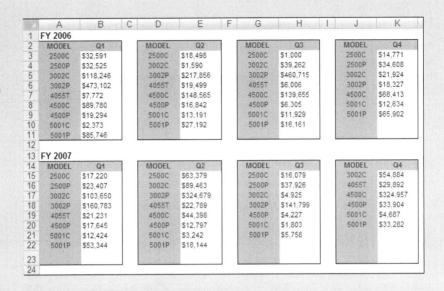

Figure 7.14
After you add your first data range, your dialog box should look like this one.

4. Repeat step 3 for each of your datasets until you have added all your data ranges. Be sure to enter **2007** for all the datasets under FY 2007 and enter **2006** for all the datasets under FY 2006.

At this point, your dialog box should look like the one shown in Figure 7.15.

Figure 7.15
After adding all your data ranges, select Finish to finalize your pivot table.

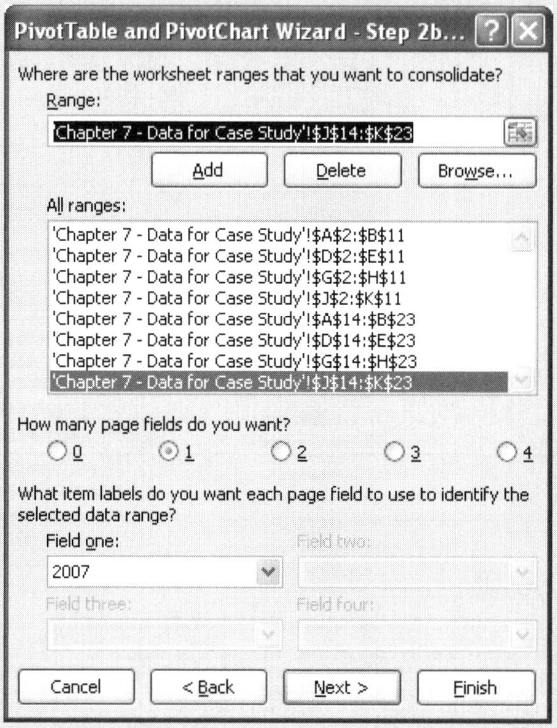

5. Select Finish.

You have successfully consolidated your data into one pivot table! As you can see in Figure 7.16, you have to change the field settings on your Value fields to calculate the Average instead of Count.

Figure 7.16
After generating your pivot table, you need to change the field settings on your value fields to calculate Average instead of Count.

	A	B	C	D	E	F
1	Page1	(All)				
2						
3	Count of Value	Column				
4	Row	Q1	Q2	Q3	Q4	Grand Total
5	2500C	2	2	2	1	7
6	2500P	2		1	1	4
7	3002C	2	2	2	2	8
8	3002P	2	2	2	1	7
9	4055T	2	2	1	1	6
10	4500C	1	2	1	2	6
11	4500P	2	2	2	1	7
12	5001C	2	2	2	2	8
13	5001P	2	2	2	2	8
14	(blank)					
15	Grand Total	17	16	15	13	61

After a little formatting and renaming of fields, you have completed your task, as shown in Figure 7.17. Now, to enhance your analysis, you can reorganize your pivot table's fields.

Figure 7.17
You've enhanced your pivot table report by formatting and renaming your fields, but you want to go a step further and reorganize your fields to provide a better view of the data.

	A	B	C	D	E	F
1	Year	(All) ▼				
2						
3	Average of Value	Quarte ▼				
4	Model ▼	Q1	Q2	Q3	Q4	Grand Total
5	2500C	24,906	40,939	8,540	14,771	23,363
6	2500P	27,966		37,926	34,608	32,117
7	3002C	110,948	45,527	22,094	38,404	54,243
8	3002P	316,943	271,268	301,257	18,327	256,752
9	4055T	14,502	21,144	6,006	29,892	17,865
10	4500C	89,780	96,482	139,655	196,685	135,961
11	4500P	18,470	14,820	5,266	33,904	15,859
12	5001C	7,399	8,217	6,866	8,661	7,785
13	5001P	69,545	22,668	10,960	49,592	38,191
14	(blank)					
15	Grand Total	74,773	65,133	59,570	55,245	64,344

With the streamlined structure you see in Figure 7.18, you are showing the optimal amount of data in an easy-to-read format.

Figure 7.18
With your reorganized pivot table report, you have provided your manager with a report that shows the average revenue for each model number by quarter, by year, and as a two-year average.

	A	B	C	D	E	F	G
1							
2	Average of		Quarter ▼				
3	Model ▼	Year ▼	Q1	Q2	Q3	Q4	Grand Total
4	⊟2500C	2006	32,591	18,498	1,000	14,771	16,715
5		2007	17,220	63,379	16,079	0	32,226
6	2500C Total		24,906	40,939	8,540	14,771	23,363
7	⊟2500P	2006	32,525	0	0	34,608	33,567
8		2007	23,407	0	37,926	0	30,667
9	2500P Total		27,966	0	37,926	34,608	32,117
10	⊟3002C	2006	118,246	1,590	39,262	21,924	45,256
11		2007	103,650	89,463	4,925	54,884	63,231
12	3002C Total		110,948	45,527	22,094	38,404	54,243
13	⊟3002P	2006	473,102	217,856	460,715	18,327	292,500
14		2007	160,783	324,679	141,799	0	209,087
15	3002P Total		316,943	271,268	301,257	18,327	256,752
16	⊟4055T	2006	7,772	19,499	6,006	0	11,092

7

Building a Pivot Table Using External Data Sources

There is no argument that Excel is good at processing and analyzing data. In fact, pivot tables themselves are a testament to the analytical power of Excel. However, despite all its strengths, Excel makes for a poor data management platform, primarily for three reasons:

- A dataset's size has a significant impact on performance, making for less efficient data crunching. The reason for this is the fundamental way Excel handles memory. When you open an Excel file, the entire file is loaded into RAM to ensure quick data processing and access. The drawback to this behavior is that Excel requires a great deal of RAM to process even the smallest change in your spreadsheet (typically giving you a "Calculating" indicator in the status bar). So although Excel 2007 offers over 1 million rows and over 16,000 columns, creating and managing large datasets causes Excel to slow down considerably, making data analysis a painful endeavor.

- The lack of a relational data structure forces the use of flat tables that promote redundant data. It also increases the chance for errors.

- There is no way to index data fields in Excel to optimize performance when you're attempting to retrieve large amounts of data.

In smart organizations, the task of data management is not performed by Excel; rather, it is primarily performed by relational database systems such as Microsoft Access and SQL Server. These databases are used to store millions of records that can be rapidly searched and retrieved.

The effect of this separation in tasks is that you have a data management layer (your database) and a presentation layer (Excel). The trick is to find the best way to get information from your data management layer to your presentation layer for use by your pivot table.

Managing your data is the general idea behind building your pivot table using an external data source. Building your pivot tables from external systems allow you to leverage environments that are better suited to data management. This means you can let Excel do what it does best: analyze and create a presentation layer for your data. The following sections walk you through several techniques that enable you to build pivot tables using external data.

Building a Pivot Table with Microsoft Access Data

Often Access is used to manage a series of tables that interact with each other, such as a Customers table, an Orders table, and an Invoices table. Managing data in Access provides the benefit of a relational database where you can ensure data integrity, prevent redundancy, and easily generate datasets via queries.

The modus operandi of most Excel users is to use an Access query to create a subset of data and then import that data into Excel. From there, the data can be analyzed with pivot tables. The problem with this method is that it forces the Excel workbook to hold two copies of the imported datasets: one on the spreadsheet and one in the pivot cache. Holding two copies obviously causes the workbook to be twice as big as it needs to be, and it introduces the possibility of performance issues.

Excel 2007 offers a surprisingly easy way to use your Access data without creating two copies of your data. To see how easy it is, open Excel and start a new workbook. Then click on the Data tab and look for the group called Get External Data. Here, you find the From Access selection, as shown in Figure 7.19.

Figure 7.19
Click the From Access
button to get data from
your Access database.

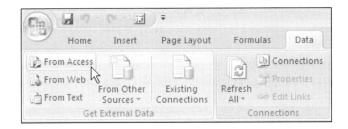

Selecting the From Access button activates a dialog box asking you to select the database
you want to work with. Select your database.

> **TIP**
>
> The sample database used in this chapter is available for download from www.MrExcel.com/pivot-
> bookdata2007.html.

After your database has been selected, the dialog box shown in Figure 7.20 activates. This
dialog box lists all the tables and queries available. In this example, select the query called
Sales_By_Employee and click the OK button.

Figure 7.20
Select the table or query
you want to analyze.

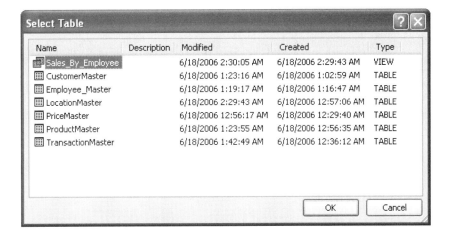

> **NOTE**
>
> In Figure 7.20, notice that the Select Table dialog box contains a column called Type. There are two
> types of Access objects you can work with: Views and Tables. View indicates that the dataset listed is
> an Access query, and Table indicates that the dataset is an Access table.
>
> In this example, notice that Sales_By_Employee is actually an Access query. This means that you
> import the results of the query. This is true interaction at work; Access does all the back-end data
> management and aggregation, and Excel handles the analysis and presentation!

Next, you see the Import Data dialog box, where you select the format in which you want to import the data. As you can see in Figure 7.21, you have the option of importing the data as a table, as a pivot table, or as a pivot table with an accompanying pivot chart. You also have the option to tell Excel where to place the data.

Select the radio button next to PivotTable Report and click the OK button.

Figure 7.21
Select the radio button next to PivotTable Report.

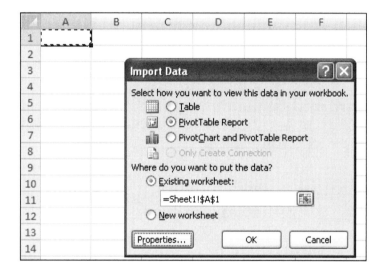

At this point, you should see the PivotTable Field List shown in Figure 7.22. From here, you can use this pivot table just as you normally would.

Figure 7.22
Your pivot table is ready to use.

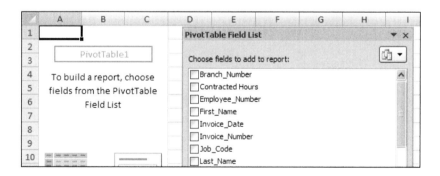

The wonderful thing about this technique is that the only copy of the data resides inside the pivot cache. You won't find the data in any of the other tabs. Does this present a problem when you need to get to the raw data in the pivot cache? The answer is no.

You can tell the pivot cache to output a raw dataset for any dimension in the pivot table simply by double-clicking on the data for that dimension. For example, Figure 7.23 illustrates how double-clicking the Grand Total for Mr. Gall outputs all the raw records that make up his Grand Total. The output is automatically placed into a separate tab.

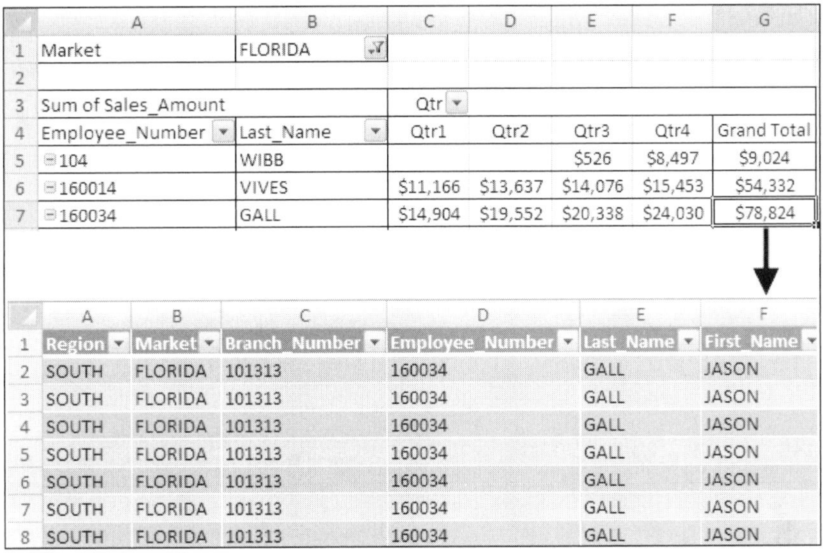

	A	B	C	D	E	F	G
1	Market	FLORIDA					
2							
3	Sum of Sales_Amount		Qtr				
4	Employee_Number	Last_Name	Qtr1	Qtr2	Qtr3	Qtr4	Grand Total
5	104	WIBB			$526	$8,497	$9,024
6	160014	VIVES	$11,166	$13,637	$14,076	$15,453	$54,332
7	160034	GALL	$14,904	$19,552	$20,338	$24,030	$78,824

	A	B	C	D	E	F
1	Region	Market	Branch_Number	Employee_Number	Last_Name	First_Name
2	SOUTH	FLORIDA	101313	160034	GALL	JASON
3	SOUTH	FLORIDA	101313	160034	GALL	JASON
4	SOUTH	FLORIDA	101313	160034	GALL	JASON
5	SOUTH	FLORIDA	101313	160034	GALL	JASON
6	SOUTH	FLORIDA	101313	160034	GALL	JASON
7	SOUTH	FLORIDA	101313	160034	GALL	JASON
8	SOUTH	FLORIDA	101313	160034	GALL	JASON

Figure 7.23
Double-clicking on the totals in the data area of a pivot table outputs the raw records that make up that total into a separate tab.

CAUTION

If you create a pivot table that uses an Access database as its source, you can refresh that pivot table only if the table or view is available. That is, deleting, moving, or renaming the database used to create the pivot table destroys the link to the external dataset, thus destroying your ability to refresh the data. Deleting or renaming the source table or query has the same effect.

Following that reasoning, any clients using your linked pivot table cannot refresh the pivot table unless the source is available to them. If you need your clients to be able to refresh, you may want to make the data source available via a shared network directory.

Building a Pivot Table with SQL Server Data

In the spirit of collaboration, Excel 2007 vastly improves your ability to connect to transactional databases such as SQL Server. With its new connection functionality found in Excel, creating a pivot table from SQL Server data is as easy as ever.

Start on the Data tab and select From Other Sources to see the drop-down menu shown Figure 7.24. Then select From SQL Server.

Selecting this option activates the Data Connection Wizard, as shown in Figure 7.25. The idea here is that you configure your connection settings so Excel can establish a link to the server.

NOTE

There is no sample file for this case study. The essence of this demonstration is the interaction between Excel and a SQL server data source. The actions you take to connect to your particular database are the same as demonstrated here.

Figure 7.24
Select From SQL Server from the drop-down menu.

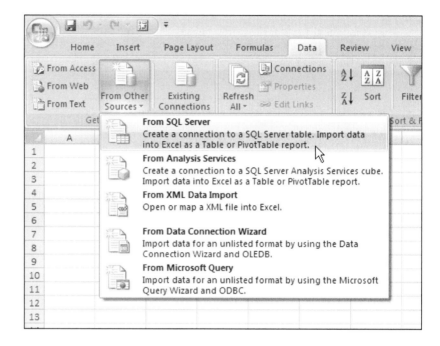

The first step in this endeavor is to provide Excel with some authentication information. As you can see in Figure 7.25, you enter the name of your server as well as your username and password.

Figure 7.25
Enter your authentication information and click the Next button.

N O T E If you are typically authenticated via Windows authentication, you simply select the Use Windows Authentication option.

Next, you select the database with which you are working from a drop-down menu containing all available databases on the specified server. As you can see in Figure 7.26, a database called Facility_Svcs_Database has been selected in the drop-down box. Selecting this database causes all the tables and views in it be exposed in the list of objects below the drop-down menu. All there is left to do in this screen is to choose the table or view you want to analyze and then click the Next button.

Figure 7.26
Specify your database and then choose the table or view you want to analyze.

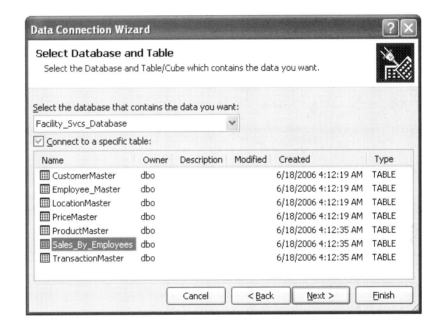

In Figure 7.26, notice the check box titled Connect to a Specific Table. In most cases, you connect to one table or view that has been created to give you an aggregation or a smaller subset of data for analysis. For this reason, the Connect to Specific Table check box is checked by default, allowing you to make only one selection.

If you were to uncheck the check box, all the objects in the specified database would be selected, giving you access to all the tables and views available. Enabling the selection of all objects in the database allows you to create your own aggregations and queries using MS Query.

7

The next screen in the wizard, shown in Figure 7.27, allows you to enter some descriptive information about the connection you've just created.

Figure 7.27
Edit descriptive information for your connection.

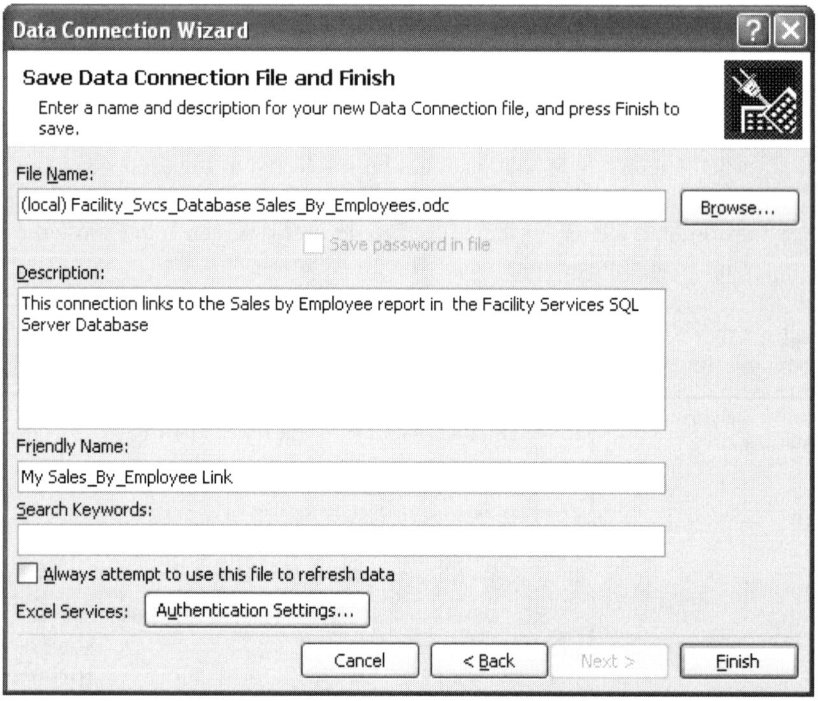

> **NOTE**
> All the fields in the screen shown in Figure 7.27 are optional edits only. That is, if you bypass this screen without editing anything, your connection will work fine.

The fields that you use most often are

- **File Name**—In the File Name input box, you can change the filename of the `.odc` (Office Data Connection) file generated to store the configuration information for the link you just created.
- **Save Password in File**—Under the File Name input box, you have the option of saving the password for your external data in the file itself (via the Save Password in File check box). Placing a check in this check box actually enters your password in the file. Keep in mind that this password is not encrypted, so anyone interested enough could potentially get the password for your data source simply by viewing your file with a text editor.
- **Description**—In the Description field, you can enter a plain description of what this particular data connection does.

7

■ **Friendly Name**—The Friendly Name field allows you to specify your own name for the external source. You typically enter a name that is descriptive and easy to read.

When you are satisfied with your descriptive edits, click the Finish button to finalize your connection settings. You immediately see the Import Data dialog box, shown in Figure 7.28. From here, you select a pivot table and then click the OK button to start building your pivot table.

Figure 7.28
When your connection is finalized, you can start building your pivot table.

Next Steps

Chapter 8 introduces you to the world of OLAP reporting where OLAP cubes enhance your interaction with pivot tables. You learn how OLAP functionality can give your pivot tables access to millions of records in databases far larger than the ones you can create with Microsoft Access.

7

Sharing Pivot Tables with Others

In the area of sharing your pivot tables with others, Excel 2007 took a giant step backward for all customers and a giant leap forward for select corporate customers.

All customers have the annoyance that pivot tables created in Excel 2007 cannot be used by customers using Excel 97 through Excel 2003. This chapter demonstrates the hoops that you must jump through to be able to share your pivot tables.

All customers have lost the ability to publish interactive pivot tables to a web page. If you were a fan of this technology, you might want to keep Office 2003 installed on your computer to continue to access the feature. If you attempt to save your pivot tables to a web page, you are given a boring static view of the pivot table.

If you happen to work for a large corporation that has invested in Windows Server, the Enterprise Edition of SharePoint Server, and the Enterprise Edition of Excel 2007, then you are able to publish an interactive version of your Excel 2007 pivot tables to your company's SharePoint server. This chapter briefly touches on setting up the parameter cells necessary for successful use of this feature.

Overall, 99% of Excel customers will be disappointed with the annoyances in this chapter.

Sharing a Pivot Table with Other Versions of Office

A version property is attached to every pivot table. This property controls certain behaviors for compatibility with previous versions of Excel.

New Excel pivot tables created in Excel 2007 have a version number of 12. Pivot tables that were originally created in Excel 2002 or 2003 have a version number of 10.

IN THIS CHAPTER

Sharing a Pivot Table with Other Versions of Office 189

Saving Pivot Tables to the Web 191

Publishing Pivot Tables to Excel Services ...193

Next Steps 199

Features Unavailable in Excel 2003 Pivot Tables

If you open a version 10 pivot table in Excel 2007, several features are not available:

- Label filtering is grayed out. For example, this is the menu item where you could choose all customers whose names start with *A*.
- Most Value filtering is unavailable. The only exception is the Top 10 filter.
- Manual Inclusive filtering is unavailable.
- Formatting of hidden items is unavailable. In Excel 2007, if you format a field, remove the field from the table, and then later add it back to the table, the format is remembered. This functionality is not present in version 10 pivot tables.
- The capability to hide intermediate levels of hierarchies in OLAP data sources is not available.
- The use of key performance indicators from a SQL Server Analysis Services 2005 dataset is disabled.
- The number of rows is limited to 64,000 instead of 1 million.
- The number of columns is limited to 255 instead of 16,000.
- The maximum number of unique items in a pivot table is limited to 32,000 instead of 1 million.
- Field labels are truncated after 255 characters instead of 32,000 characters.
- The number of fields in the field list is limited to 255 instead of 16,000.

Excel 2007 Compatibility Mode

To a certain extent, version number is controlled in Excel 2007 by compatibility mode. If you create a new pivot table in a workbook that is still in compatibility mode, the pivot table is created as a version 10 pivot table.

When you save the workbook from compatibility mode to one of the new file formats, all the pivot tables are marked for upgrade. You must go through and refresh each pivot table to convert the pivot table to a version 12 pivot table.

No Downgrade Path Available from Version 12 Pivot Tables

After a pivot table has been upgraded to version 12, it no longer functions in previous versions of Excel. Even if you save the file in compatibility mode, the pivot table is no longer refreshable.

Strategies for Sharing Pivot Tables

Version 12 pivot tables cannot be refreshed by anyone using Excel 2003 or earlier.

If you want to share a pivot table with someone using Excel 2003, you must take extra care to make sure that the pivot table never existed as a version 12 pivot table.

You can follow these steps to create a version 10 pivot table:

1. Open a new Excel workbook.

2. Save the workbook as Excel 97–2003 format.

3. Copy and paste your dataset from the Excel 2007 workbook to the Excel 2003 workbook.

4. Create the pivot table in the Excel 2003 workbook while in compatibility mode.

Saving Pivot Tables to the Web

If you saved your pivot tables to the web in prior versions of Excel, you will be disappointed with Excel 2007.

In Excel 2003, you could use Office Web Components to create an interactive web page. From Excel 2003, you would choose File, Save as Web Page, Publish. You could then specify that the web page should have pivot table functionality, as shown in Figure 8.1.

Figure 8.1
In Excel 2003, you could save the pivot table with pivot table interactivity.

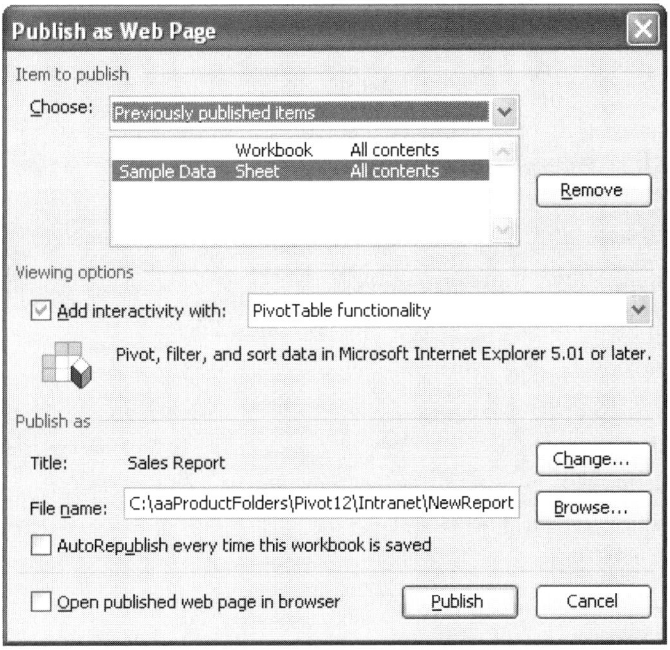

When you opened the resulting web page in a browser, you could drag fields around to create a pivot table in a browser, as shown in Figure 8.2.

Microsoft has decided to no longer invest in Office Web Components. It is instead investing in Office Services for SharePoint. While this might be a better technology, it is not available to most of the 400 million people using Excel.

Figure 8.2
When opened in Internet Explorer, the web page offered pivot table functionality.

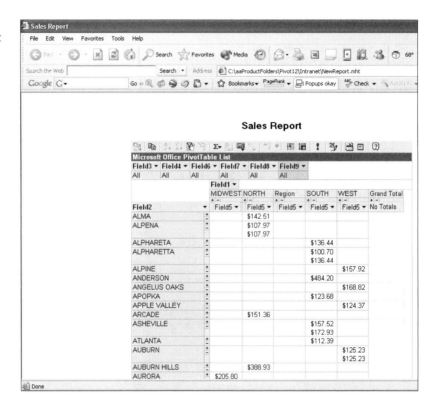

Your ability to save from Excel 2007 to a web page is severely limited. Follow these steps to create a static image of the pivot table:

1. From the Office icon, choose Save As, Other Formats.

2. In the Save as Type drop-down, choose Web Page.

3. Click the Publish button to display the Publish as Web Page dialog box, as shown in Figure 8.3.

4. Click the Title button to specify a title for the web page.

5. If you want the web page updated every time the file is saved, click the AutoRepublish check box.

6. Specify a filename for the resulting web page.

7. Click Publish. Excel writes out a static view of the web page, as shown in Figure 8.4.

Figure 8.3
In the Publish as Web Page dialog box, you can specify a few options for the web page.

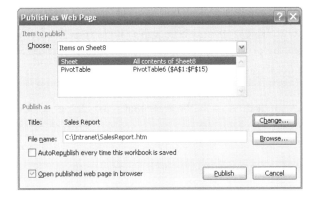

Figure 8.4
The resulting web page is a static view of the data.

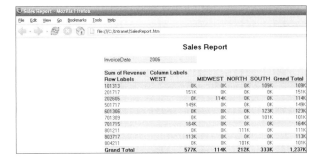

Publishing Pivot Tables to Excel Services

Excel Services represents a dramatic investment for Microsoft. This is still the "version 1.0" release of Excel Services, and it promises to get even better in future versions of Office.

Excel Services is a new technology for Excel 2007. It supports loading, calculating, and rendering Excel spreadsheets on servers. The person reading the Excel spreadsheet accesses the file through his browser.

As the author of the file, you can specify certain cells that the end user can change in the browser. These fields can even be filter fields in your pivot table. Imagine the possibilities for creating fantastic ad hoc reporting tools that people can use to query your data.

Even better, if your Excel spreadsheet is querying a SQL Server database, every time the browser is refreshed, the Excel file pulls new data from SQL Server, providing real-time business intelligence.

There are three likely scenarios when you want to use Office Services:

- Allow everyone to have read-only access to a single version of an important spreadsheet. This eliminates the problem of multiple versions of the spreadsheet floating around.
- Encapsulate several ranges of various spreadsheets into an executive dashboard running in a browser.
- Build a custom application in the browser that reuses logic already designed in the Excel spreadsheet.

Requirements to Render Spreadsheets with Excel Services

The requirements for Excel Services are fairly high-end. Your organization needs to provide a server running Windows Server 2003 or Vista Server. You need the Enterprise Editions of SharePoint Server and Excel Services for SharePoint.

As the author of the spreadsheet, you need read-write access to the server.

Preparing Your Spreadsheet for Excel Services

You need to carefully decide which cells in your spreadsheet can be edited by the end user.

In a pivot table spreadsheet, these fields are likely the value fields in the Report Filter section of the report.

You need to assign each of these cells a name. To assign a name, follow these steps:

1. Select the desired cell.
2. To the left of the formula bar is the Name box. Typically, this box shows the cell address, such as A1. Click in this box and type a name for the cell. Do not use spaces in the name. "WhichYear" or "Which_Year" are valid. "Which Year" is not valid.
3. Press the Enter key to accept the name.

If you need to later change or delete a name, use the Name Manager icon on the Formulas ribbon.

Publishing Your Spreadsheet to Excel Services

The first time you publish your spreadsheet, you have to go through a few extra steps to specify the parameter cells. Make sure that you have assigned range names to the parameter cells before starting this process. Then do the following:

1. From the Office icon, choose Publish, Excel Services, as shown in Figure 8.5.

Figure 8.5
Access Excel Services through the Office icon.

2. Specify a path and filename in the Save As dialog box.

3. If this is the first time you are publishing the workbook, click the Excel Services Options button, shown in Figure 8.6. Excel displays the Excel Services Options dialog box.

Figure 8.6
Click the Excel Services Options button to access the parameter selection.

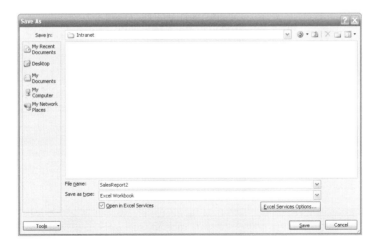

8

4. There are two tabs in the Excel Services Options dialog box. On the Show tab, choose which spreadsheet(s) you would like to include in the browser. In Figure 8.7, the Sheet8 spreadsheet is the target spreadsheet.

Figure 8.7
On the Show tab, define the worksheets to be rendered in the browser.

5. Click the Parameters tab. Click the Add button to display the Add Parameters dialog box.

6. On the Add Parameters dialog box, you see a list of all named ranges in the worksheet. Click the ranges that you would like to specify as parameters (see Figure 8.8).

7. Click OK to close the Add Parameters dialog box.

8. Click OK to close the Excel Services Options dialog box.

9. Click Save to save the worksheet for Excel Services.

What the End User Sees in Excel Services

The goals of Excel Services are to allow the end user to view data in the spreadsheet, navigate around the spreadsheet, perform further exploration of the data in the spreadsheet, and change parameters to facilitate what-if analysis.

Microsoft has enabled a limited subset of features that allow the end user to achieve these four goals. Excel Services is not designed to allow someone to completely author a new spreadsheet; she would need to own Excel 2007 to do this. Instead, Excel Services allows

- Support for basic Excel formatting (row height, column width, font, color, gridlines, text rotation). Surprisingly, Excel Services supports data bars, color scales, and table style formatting as well.
- Switching between sheets in the workbook.

Figure 8.8
On the Add Parameters dialog box, choose which named ranges to use as parameters.

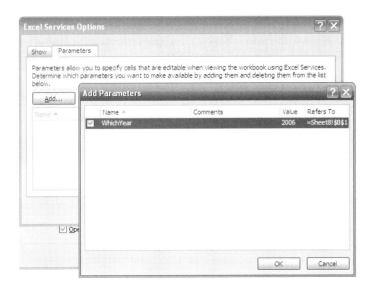

- Support for the use of expand and collapse buttons, either in pivot tables or using the group and outline buttons.
- Support for querying external data and refreshing that data.
- Support for the Find utility.
- Support for displaying charts.
- Support for autofiltering and sorting within a defined table.
- Support for filtering and sorting within a pivot table.

As the author of the worksheet, you have a certain amount of control in this support. You can specify, for example, that you don't want interactivity to be enabled for the spreadsheet.

One difference between Excel and Excel Services is that Excel Services creates sections of the worksheet and serves up only one section at a time. A typical section contains 75 rows and 20 columns. This is primarily a performance consideration; you don't want the browser attempting to render 20 million cells at once.

What You Cannot Do with Excel Services

Although Excel Services handles many aspects of Excel files, it does not support several features. Any of the items below cause the Excel workbook not to load in Excel Services.

Features Disallowed in Excel Services

- Spreadsheets with code. This includes spreadsheets with VBA macros, forms controls, toolbox controls, Microsoft ExcelS 5.0 dialog boxes, and XLM sheets.
- IRM-protected spreadsheets
- ActiveX controls
- Embedded SmartTags
- Pivot tables based on "multiple consolidation" ranges
- External references (links to other spreadsheets)
- Spreadsheets saved in formula view
- XML expansion packs
- XML maps
- Data validation
- Query tables, SharePoint lists, web queries, and text queries
- Spreadsheets that reference add-ins
- Spreadsheets that use the RTD() function
- Spreadsheets that use spreadsheet and sheet protection
- Embedded pictures or clip art
- Cell and Sheet background pictures
- AutoShapes and WordArt
- Ink annotations
- Organization charts and diagrams.
- DDE links

Other items are not displayed by Excel Services. If a worksheet contains items in the list below, the worksheet is still displayed, but the item in question is ignored.

Items Ignored by Excel Services

- Split and freeze panes
- Headers and footers
- Page layout view
- Cell patterns
- Zoom
- Analysis Services' member properties in ToolTips
- Some cell formatting, such as like diagonal borders and border types not supported by HTML

Viewing the Pivot Table in the Browser

After publishing the file to Excel Services, you can open the workbook with Internet Explorer or Firefox.

Navigation aids in the browser include sheet tabs in the lower-left corner, a filter button to control the pivot table filter fields in cell B1, and a drop-down in cell B3.

The report in Figure 8.9 still looks like a spreadsheet. If you are trying to use spreadsheet logic in a quick application, you might choose to turn off gridlines and row/column headers in the original workbook before publishing to Excel Services.

Figure 8.9
This web page has a surprising amount of spreadsheet-like functionality.

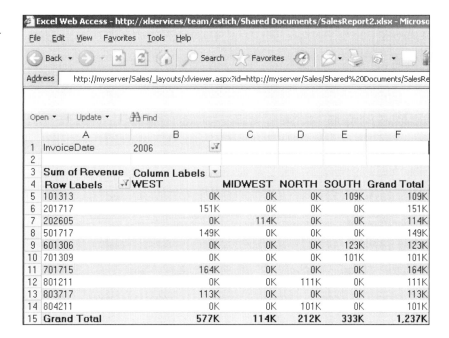

Next Steps

In the next chapter, you learn about running pivot tables on data stored outside Excel, including OLAP data sources and SQL Server.

Working with and Analyzing OLAP Data

9

What Is OLAP?

Online Analytical Processing, or OLAP, is a category of data warehousing that allows you to mine and analyze vast amounts of data with ease and efficiency. Unlike other types of databases, OLAP databases are designed specifically for reporting and data mining. In fact, there are several key differences between your standard transactional databases, such as Access or SQL Server, and OLAP databases.

Records within a transactional database are routinely added, deleted, or updated. OLAP databases, on the other hand, contain only snapshots of data. The data in an OLAP database is typically archived data, stored solely for reporting purposes. Although new data may be appended on a regular basis, existing data is rarely edited or deleted.

Another difference between transactional databases and OLAP databases is structure. Transactional databases typically contain many tables; each table usually contains multiple relationships with other tables. Indeed, some transactional databases contain so many tables that it can be difficult to determine how each table relates to another. In an OLAP database, however, all the relationships between the various data points have been predefined and stored in *OLAP cubes*. These cubes already contain the relationships and hierarchies you need to easily navigate the data within. Consequently, you can build reports without the need to know how the data tables relate to one another.

The biggest difference between OLAP and transactional databases is the way the data is stored. The data in an OLAP cube is rarely stored in raw form. OLAP cubes typically store data in preorganized and preaggregated views. That is, grouping, sorting, and aggregations are all predefined and ready to

IN THIS CHAPTER

What Is OLAP? 201

Connecting to an OLAP Cube 202

Understanding the Structure of an OLAP Cube 205

Understanding Limitations of OLAP Pivot Tables 207

Creating Offline Cubes 207

Breaking Out of the Pivot Table Mold with Cube Functions 211

Next Steps 213

use. This makes querying and browsing for data far more efficient than in a transactional database, where you would have to group, aggregate, and sort records on the fly.

> **NOTE**
> An OLAP database is typically set up and maintained by the database administrator in your IT department. If your organizatoin does not utilize OLAP datbases, you may want to speak with your database administrator to discuss the possiblity of some OLAP reporting solutions.

Connecting to an OLAP Cube

Before you can browse OLAP data, you must first establish a connection to an OLAP cube. Start on the Data tab and select From Other Sources to see the drop-down menu shown in Figure 9.1. Here, you select the From Analysis Services option.

Figure 9.1
Select From Analysis Services.

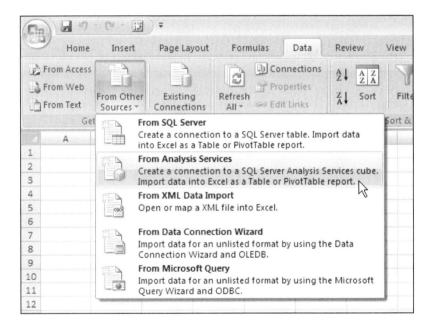

Selecting this option activates the Data Connection Wizard, shown in Figure 9.2. The idea here is that you configure your connection settings so Excel can establish a link to the server.

> **NOTE**
> The examples you see in this chapter have been created using the Analysis Services Tutorial cube that comes with SQL Server Analysis Services 2005. The actions you take to connect to and work with your OLAP database are the same as demonstrated here because the concepts are applicable to any OLAP cube you may be using.

1. The first step in this endeavor is to provide Excel with some authentication information. Enter the name of your server as well as your username and password, as demonstrated in Figure 9.2. Then select Next.

Figure 9.2
Enter your authentication information and select Next.

> **NOTE** If you are typically authenticated via Windows authentication, you simply select the Use Windows Authentication option.

2. Next, you select the database with which you are working from the drop-down box. As Figure 9.3 illustrates, the AdventureWorks database is selected for this scenario. Selecting this database causes all the available OLAP cubes to be exposed in the list of objects below the drop-down menu. Choose the cube you want to analyze and then select Next.

3. The next screen, shown in Figure 9.4, allows you to enter some descriptive information about the connection you've just created.

> **NOTE** All the fields in the screen shown in Figure 9.4 are optional edits only. That is, you can bypass this screen without editing anything, and your connection will work fine.

9

Figure 9.3
Specify your database
and then choose the
OLAP cube you want to
analyze.

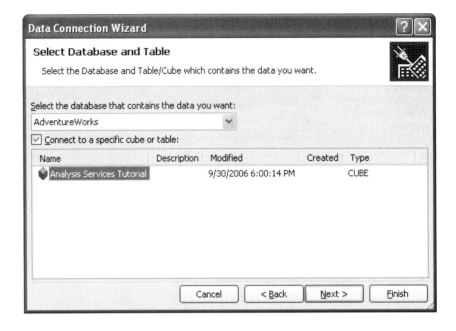

Figure 9.4
Edit descriptive informa-
tion for your connection.

4. Click the Finish button to finalize your connection settings. You immediately see the Import Data dialog box, as shown in Figure 9.5. From here, you select PivotTable Report and then click the OK button to start building your pivot table.

Figure 9.5
When your connection is finalized, you can start building your pivot table.

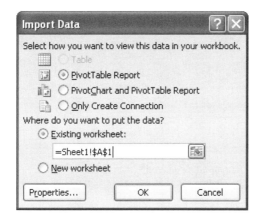

Understanding the Structure of an OLAP Cube

When your pivot table is created, you might notice that the PivotTable Field List looks somewhat different from that of a standard pivot table. The reason is that the PivotTable Field List for an OLAP pivot table is arranged to represent the structure of the OLAP cube you are connected to.

To effectively browse an OLAP cube, you need to understand the component parts of OLAP cubes and the way they interact with one another. Figure 9.6 illustrates the basic structure of a typical OLAP cube.

As you can see, the main components of an OLAP cube are dimensions, hierarchies, levels, members, and measures:

- **Dimensions** are major classifications of data that contain the data items that are analyzed. Some common examples of dimensions are Products dimension, Customer dimension, and Employee dimension. In Figure 9.6, the structure you see is that of the Products dimension.

- **Hierarchies** are predefined aggregations of levels within a particular dimension. A hierarchy enables you to pivot and analyze multiple levels at one time without any previous knowledge of the relationships between the levels. In the example in Figure 9.6, the Products dimension has three levels that are aggregated into one hierarchy called Product Categories.

- **Levels** are categories of data that are aggregated within a hierarchy. You can think of Levels as data fields that can be queried and analyzed individually. In Figure 9.6, note that there are three levels: Category, SubCategory, and Product Name.

Figure 9.6
The basic structure of an OLAP cube.

■ **Members** are the individual data items within in a dimension. Members are typically accessed via the OLAP structure of dimension, hierarchy, level, and member. In the example shown in Figure 9.6, the members you see belong to the Product Name level. The other levels have their own members and are not shown here.

■ **Measures** are the actual data values within the OLAP cube. Measures are stored within their own dimension appropriately called the Measures dimension. The idea is that you can use any combination of dimension, hierarchy, level, and member to query the measures. This is called *slicing the measures*.

Now that you understand how the data in an OLAP cube is structured, take a look at the PivotTable Field List again. The arrangement of the available fields starts to make sense. Figure 9.7 illustrates what the PivotTable Field List for an OLAP pivot table may look like.

As you can see, the measures are listed first under the Sigma icon. These are the only items you can drop in the values area of your pivot table. Next, you see dimensions represented next to the table icon. In this example, you see the Product dimension. Under the Product dimension, you see the Product Categories hierarchy that can be drilled into. Drilling into the Product Categories hierarchy allows you to see the individual levels.

The cool thing is that you are able to browse the entire cube structure by simply navigating through your PivotTable Field List! From here, you can build your OLAP pivot table report just as you would build a standard pivot table.

Figure 9.7
The PivotTable Field List
for an OLAP pivot table.

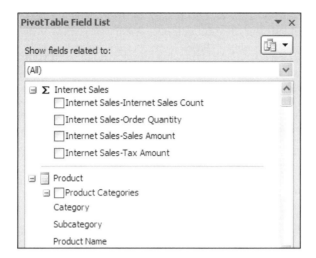

Understanding Limitations of OLAP Pivot Tables

When working with OLAP pivot tables, you must remember that the source data is maintained and controlled in the Analysis Services OLAP environment. This means that every aspect of the cube's behavior, from the dimensions and measures included in the cube to the ability to drill into the details of a dimension, is controlled via Analysis Services. This reality translates into some limitations to the actions you can take with your OLAP pivot tables.

When your pivot table report is based on an OLAP data source

- You cannot place any field other than measures into the values area of the pivot table.
- You cannot change the function used to summarize a data field.
- You cannot create a calculated field or a calculated item.
- Any changes you make to field names are lost when you remove the field from the pivot table.
- The page field settings are not available.
- The Show Pages command is disabled.
- The Show Items with No Data option is disabled.
- The Subtotal Hidden Page Items setting is disabled.
- The Background Query option is not available.
- The Optimize Memory check box in the PivotTable Options dialog box is disabled.

Creating Offline Cubes

With a standard pivot table, the source data is typically stored on your local drive. This way, you can work with and analyze your data while disconnected from the network. However, this is not the case with OLAP pivot tables. With an OLAP pivot table, the pivot cache is never brought to your local drive. This means that while you are disconnected from the network, your pivot table is out of commission. You can't even move a field while disconnected.

If you need to analyze your OLAP data while disconnected from your network, you need to create an offline cube. An *offline cube* is essentially a file that acts as a pivot cache, locally storing OLAP data so that you can browse that data while disconnected from the network.

To create an offline cube, start with an OLAP-based pivot table. Place your cursor anywhere inside the pivot table and click the OLAP Tools drop-down menu button on the PivotTable Tools Options tab. Here, you select Offline OLAP, as demonstrated in Figure 9.8.

Figure 9.8
Select Offline OLAP to start the creation of an offline cube.

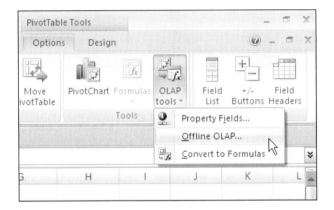

Selecting this option activates the Offline OLAP Settings dialog box, where you click the Create Offline Data File button.

The Create Cube File Wizard, shown in Figure 9.9, activates. Select Next to start the process.

As you can see in Figure 9.10, you first select the dimensions and levels you want included in your offline cube. This dialog box tells Excel which data you wanted imported from the OLAP database. The idea here is to select only the dimensions that you need available to you while disconnected from the server. The more dimensions you select, the more disk space your offline cube file will take up.

Clicking Next moves you to the next dialog box, shown in Figure 9.11. Here, you are given the opportunity to filter out any members or data items that you do not want included. For instance, the Internet Sales-Extended Amount measure is not needed, so the check has been removed from its selection box. Deselecting this box ensures that this measure will not be imported and will not take up unnecessary disk space.

The final step is to specify a name and location for your cube file. In Figure 9.12, the cube file is named **MyOfflineCube.cub**, and it will be placed in a directory called **MyDirectory**.

Figure 9.9
Start the Create Cube File Wizard.

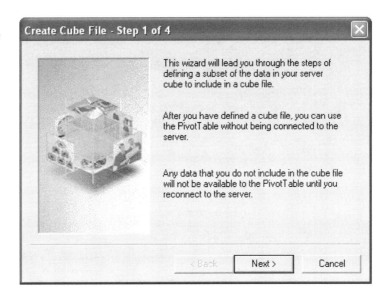

Figure 9.10
Select the dimensions and level you want included in your offline cube.

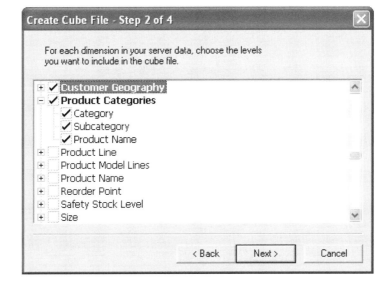

NOTE
The file extension for all offline cubes is `.cub`.

After a few moments of crunching, Excel outputs your offline cube file to your chosen directory. To test it, simply double-click the file to automatically generate an Excel workbook that is linked to the offline cube via a pivot table.

9

Figure 9.11
Deselect any members you do not need to see offline.

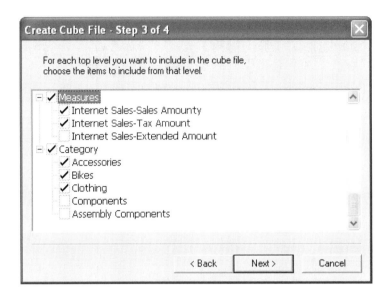

Figure 9.12
Specify a name and location for your cube file.

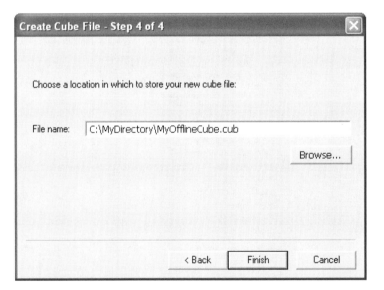

After your offline cube file has been created, you can distribute it to others and use it while disconnected from the network.

TIP

When you're connected to the network, you can open your offline cube file and refresh the pivot table within. This automatically refreshes the data in the cube file. The idea is that you can use the data within the cube file while you are disconnected from the network and can refresh the cube file while a data connection is available. Any attempt to refresh an offline cube while disconnected causes an error.

Breaking Out of the Pivot Table Mold with Cube Functions

Cube functions are Excel functions that can be used to access OLAP data outside a pivot table object. In previous versions of Excel, you could find cube functions only if you installed the Analysis Services Add-In. In Excel 2007, cube functions have been brought into the native Excel environment. To fully understand the benefit of cube functions, take a moment to walk through an example.

One of the easiest ways to start exploring cube functions is to allow Excel to convert your OLAP-based pivot table into cube formulas. Converting a pivot table to cube formulas is a delightfully easy way to create a few cube formulas without doing any of the work yourself. The idea is to tell Excel to replace all cells in the pivot table with a formula that connects back to the OLAP database. Figure 9.13 shows a pivot table connected to an OLAP database.

Figure 9.13
A normal OLAP pivot table.

	A	B	C	D	E
1	Customer Geography	United States			
2					
3	Internet Sales-Sales An				
4			CY 2003	CY 2004	Grand Total
5	⊟ Accessories				
6		⊞ Bike Racks	$7,680	$9,480	$17,160
7		⊞ Bike Stands	$6,996	$6,519	$13,515
8		⊞ Bottles and Cages	$8,292	$12,7⏚	$21,030
9		⊞ Cleaners	$1,240	$1,590	$2,830
10		⊞ Fenders	$8,880	$12,946	$21,826
11		⊞ Helmets	$31,771	$45,522	$77,293
12		⊞ Hydration Packs	$6,049	$9,073	$15,122
13		⊞ Tires and Tubes	$38,001	$51,520	$89,521
14	Accessories Total		$108,909	$149,388	$258,298

With just a few clicks, you can convert any OLAP pivot table into a series of cube formulas. Place the cursor anywhere inside the pivot table and click the OLAP Tools drop-down menu button on the PivotTable Tools Options tab. Here, you select Convert to Formulas, as demonstrated in Figure 9.14.

If your pivot table contains a report filter field, the dialog box shown in Figure 9.15 activates. This dialog box gives you the option of converting your filter drop-down selectors to cube formulas. If you select this option, the drop-down selectors are removed, leaving a static formula. If you need to have your filter drop-down selectors intact so that you may continue to interactively change the selections in the filter field, leave the Convert Report Filters option unchecked.

Figure 9.14
Select Convert to
Formulas to convert your
pivot table to cube for-
mulas.

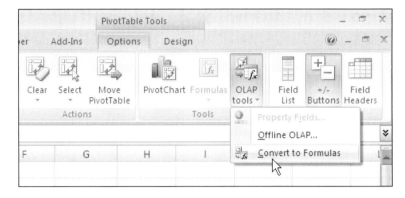

Figure 9.15
Excel gives you the
option of converting
your report filter fields.

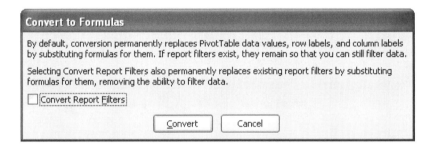

> **NOTE**
> If you are working with a pivot table in compatibility mode, Excel automatically converts the filter
> fields to formulas.

After a second or two, the cells that used to house a pivot table are now homes for cube formulas. Note that, as in Figure 9.16, any styles that you may have applied are removed.

Figure 9.16
Note in the formula bar,
these cells are now a
series of cube formulas!

	A	B	C	D	E
	C6		fx =CUBEVALUE("AdventureWorks OLAP Cube",$B$1,$A$3,$B6,C$4)		
1	Customer Geography	United States			
2					
3	Internet Sales-Sales Amount				
4			CY 2003	CY 2004	Grand Total
5	Accessories				
6		Bike Racks	$7,680.00	$9,480.00	$17,160.00
7		Bike Stands	$6,996.00	$6,519.00	$13,515.00
8		Bottles and Cages	$8,292.26	$12,738.04	$21,030.30
9		Cleaners	$1,240.20	$1,590.00	$2,830.20
10		Fenders	$8,879.92	$12,946.22	$21,826.14
11		Helmets	$31,770.92	$45,521.99	$77,292.91
12		Hydration Packs	$6,048.90	$9,073.35	$15,122.25
13		Tires and Tubes	$38,001.19	$51,519.83	$89,521.02
14	Accessories Total		$108,909.39	$149,388.43	$258,297.82

So why is this capability useful? Well, now that the values you see are no longer part of a pivot table object, you can insert rows and columns, you can add your own calculations, you can combine the data with other external data, and you can modify the report in all sorts of ways by simply moving the formulas around. For instance, Figure 9.17 illustrates a report in which specific data items from Accessories and Bikes have been combined and formatted to create a new Bike Products report. Again, note that all cells displaying values for each product are formulas that read directly from the OLAP cube via the connection you created.

Figure 9.17
A Bike Products report built using cube formulas from a converted OLAP pivot table.

	D6		f_x	=CUBEVALUE("AdventureWorks OLAP Cube",$B$1,$D$1,$A6,D$4)		
	A	B	C	D	E	F
1	Customer Geography	United States ☑		Internet Sales-Sales Amount		
2						
3	**Bike Products**					
4		CY 2003	CY 2004	Grand Total		
5						
6	Bike Racks	$7,680	$9,480	$17,160		
7	Bike Stands	$6,996	$6,519	$13,515		
8	Mountain Bikes	$1,387,330	$1,474,746	$2,862,076		
9	Road Bikes	$862,974	$797,771	$1,660,746		
10	Touring Bikes	$456,283	$849,374	$1,305,657		
11	Helmets	$31,771	$45,522	$77,293		
12	Total	$2,753,034	$3,183,412	$5,936,447		

Next Steps

In the next chapter, you learn how macros can help you enhance your pivot table reports and empower your users to do their own data analysis.

Enhancing Your Pivot Table Reports with Macros

10

Why Use Macros with Your Pivot Table Reports?

Imagine that you could be in multiple locations at one time, with multiple clients at one time, helping them with their pivot table reports. Suppose you could help multiple clients refresh their data, extract top 20 records, group by months, or sort by revenue—all at the same time. The fact is you can do just that by using Excel macros.

A macro is a series of keystrokes that have been recorded and saved. Once saved, the macro can be played back on command. In other words, you can record your actions in a macro, save the macro, and then allow your clients to play back your actions with the touch of a button. It would be as though you were there with them! This functionality is exceptionally useful when you're distributing pivot table reports.

For example, suppose that you want to give your clients the option of grouping their pivot table report by month, by quarter, or by year. Although the process of grouping can be technically performed by anyone, some of your clients may not have a clue how to do it. In this case, you could record a macro to group by month, a macro to group by quarter, and a macro to group by year. Then you could create three buttons, one for each macro. In the end, your clients, having little experience with pivot tables, need only to click a button to group their pivot table report.

A major benefit of using macros with your pivot table reports is the power you can give your clients to easily perform pivot table actions that they would not normally be able to perform on their own, empowering them to more effectively analyze the data you provide.

IN THIS CHAPTER

Why Use Macros with Your Pivot Table Reports? 215

Recording Your First Macro 216

Creating a User Interface with Form Controls 218

Altering a Recorded Macro to Add Functionality 220

Case Study: Synchronizing Two Pivot Tables with One Combo Box 225

Next Steps 229

Recording Your First Macro

Look at the pivot table in Figure 10.1. You know that you can refresh this pivot table by right-clicking inside the pivot table and selecting Refresh Data. Now, if you were to record your actions with a macro while you refreshed your pivot table, you, or anyone else, could replicate your actions and refresh this pivot table by running the macro.

Figure 10.1
This basic pivot table can easily be refreshed by right-clicking and selecting Refresh Data, but if you recorded your actions with a macro, you could also refresh this pivot table simply by running the macro.

	A	B
1	Region	(All)
2		
3	**Row Labels**	**Sum of Sales_Amount**
4	ACASCO Corp.	$675
5	ACECUL Corp.	$593
6	ACEHUA Corp.	$580
7	ACOPUL Corp.	$675
8	ACORAR Corp.	$2,232
9	ACSBUR Corp.	$720
10	ADACEC Corp.	$345
11	ADADUL Corp.	$690
12	ADANAS Corp.	$345
13	ADCOMP Corp.	$553
14	ADDATI Corp.	$379
15	ADDOUS Corp.	$5,209

The first step in recording a macro is to initiate the Record Macro dialog box. Select the Developer tab on the Ribbon and then select Record Macro.

> **TIP**
> Can't find the Developer tab on the Ribbon? Click on the Office icon in the top-left corner of Excel and then select Excel Options. Selecting this option opens the Excel Options dialog box. In the Personalize section, you see an option called Show Developer Tab in the Ribbon. Placing a check next to this option enables the Developer tab.

When the Record Macro dialog box activates, you can fill in a few key pieces of information about the macro:

- **Macro Name**—Enter a name for your macro. You should generally enter a name that describes the action being performed.

- **Shortcut Key**—You can enter any letter into this input box. That letter becomes part of a set of keys on your keyboard that can be pressed to play back the macro. This is optional.

- **Store Macro In**—Specify where you want the macro to be stored. If you are distributing your pivot table report, you should select This Workbook so that the macro is available to your clients.

- **Description**—In this input box, you can enter a few words that give more detail about the macroRecord Macro dialog box. Select the Developer tab on the Ribbon and the.

Because this macro will refresh your pivot table when it is played, name your macro `RefreshData`. Also assign a shortcut key of R. Notice that the dialog box gives you a full key of Ctrl+Shift+R. Keep in mind that you use the full key to play your macro after it is created. Be sure to store the macro in This Workbook. Click OK to continue. When this is done, your dialog box should look like the one shown in Figure 10.2.

Figure 10.2
Fill in the Record Macro dialog box Record Macro dialog box. Select the Developer tab on the Ribbon and theas shown here and then click OK to continue.

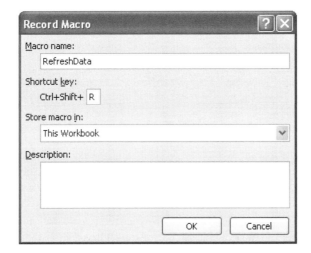

When you click OK in the Record Macro dialog box, you initiate the recording process. At this point, any action you perform is being recorded by Excel. In that case, you want to record the process of refreshing your pivot table.

Right-click anywhere inside the pivot table and select Refresh Data. After you have refreshed your pivot table, you can stop the recording process by going up to the Developer tab and selecting the Stop Recording button.

Congratulations! You have just recorded your first macro. You can now play your macro by pressing Ctrl, Shift, and R on your keyboard at the same time.

A Word on Macro Security

You should be aware that when you record a macro yourself, your macro will run fine on your PC with no security restrictions. However, when you distribute workbooks that contain macros, your clients will have to let Excel know that your workbook is not a security risk, thus allowing your macros to run.

Indeed, you will note that the sample file that comes with this chapter will not run unless you tell Excel to enable the macros within.

The best way to do this is to use the workbook in a *trusted location*, a directory that is deemed a safe zone where only trusted workbooks are placed. A trusted location allows you and your clients to run a macro-enabled workbook with no security restrictions, as long as the workbook is in that location.

To set up a trusted location, follow these steps:

1. Select the Macro Security button on the Developer tab. This activates the Trust Center dialog box.

2. Select the Trusted Locations button.

3. Select Add New Location.

4. Click Browse to specify the directory to be considered a trusted location.

After you specify a trusted location, all workbooks opened from that location are, by default, opened with macros enabled.

> **NOTE**
> For information on macro security in Excel 2007, pick up Que Publishing's Special Edition Using *Excel 2007* by Bill Jelen.

Creating a User Interface with Form Controls

Allowing your clients to run your macro with shortcut keys like Ctrl+Shift+R can be a satisfactory solution if you have only one macro in your pivot table report. However, suppose you want to allow your clients to perform several macro actions. In this case, you should give your clients a clear and easy way to run each macro without having to remember a gaggle of shortcut keys. A basic user interface provides the perfect solution. You can think of a user interface as a set of controls such as buttons, scrollbars, and other devices that allow users to run macros with a simple click of the mouse.

In fact, Excel offers a set of controls designed specifically for creating user interfaces directly on a spreadsheet. These controls are called *form controls*. The general idea behind form controls is that you can place one on a spreadsheet and then assign a macro to it—meaning a macro you have already recorded. After a macro is assigned to the control, that macro is executed, or played, when the control is clicked.

Form controls can be found in the Controls group on the Developer tab. To get to the form controls, simply select the Insert icon in the Controls group, as demonstrated in Figure 10.3.

> **NOTE**
> Notice that there are form controls and ActiveX controls. Although they look similar, they are quite different. Form controls, with their limited overhead and easy configuration settings, are designed specifically for use on a spreadsheet. Meanwhile, ActiveX controls are typically used on Excel userforms. As a general rule, you always want to use form controls when working on a spreadsheet.

Here, you can select the control that best suits your needs. In this example, you want your clients to be able to refresh their pivot table with the click of a button. Click on the Button control to select it and then drop the control onto your spreadsheet by clicking the location you would like to place the button.

Figure 10.3
To see the available form controls, click Insert in the Controls group on the Developer tab.

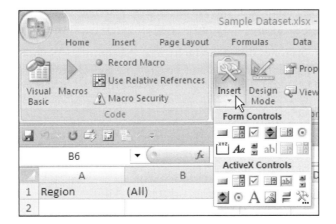

After you drop the button control onto your spreadsheet, the Assign Macro dialog box, shown in Figure 10.4, opens and asks you to assign a macro to this button. Select the macro you want to assign to the button, in this case RefreshData, and then click OK.

Figure 10.4
Select the macro you want to assign to the button and then click OK. In this case, you want to select RefreshData.

> N O T E Keep in mind that all the controls in the Forms toolbar work in the same way as the command button, in that you assign a macro to run when the control is selected.

As you can see in Figure 10.5, you can assign each macro in your workbook to a different form control and then name the controls to distinguish between them.

Figure 10.6 demonstrates that after you have all the controls you need for your pivot table report, you can format the controls and surrounding spreadsheet to create a basic interface.

Figure 10.5
You can create a different button for each one of your macros.

Figure 10.6
You can easily create the feeling of an interface with a handful of macros, a few form controls, and a little formatting.

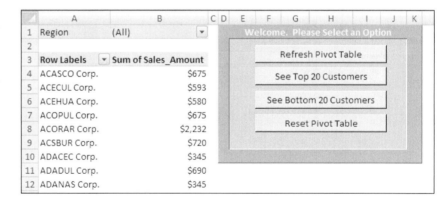

Altering a Recorded Macro to Add Functionality

When you record a macro, Excel creates a module that stores the recorded steps of your actions. These recorded steps are actually lines of VBA code that make up your macro. You can add some interesting functionality to your pivot table reports by tweaking your macro's VBA code to achieve various effects.

To get a better understanding of how this process works, start by creating a new macro that will extract the top five records by customer. Go to the Developer tab and select Record Macro. Set up the Record Macro dialog box as shown in Figure 10.7. Name your new macro **TopNthCusts** and specify that you want to store the macro in This Workbook. Click OK to start recording.

Figure 10.7
Name your new macro and specify where you want to store it.

Record Macro

Macro name:
TopNthCusts

Shortcut key:
Ctrl+ [ ]

Store macro in:
This Workbook

Description:

[OK]   [Cancel]

After you have started recording, right-click on the Customer field and select Filter. Then select Top 10. Selecting this option opens the Filter dialog box, where you specify that you want to see the top five customers by sales amount. Enter the settings shown in Figure 10.8 and then click OK.

Figure 10.8
Enter the settings you see here to get the top five customers by revenue.

Top 10 Filter (Customer_Name)

Show

Top ▼ 5 ▲▼ Items ▼ by Sum of Sales_Amount ▼

[OK]   [Cancel]

After successfully recording the steps to extract the top five customers by revenue, select Stop Recording from the Developer tab.

You now have a macro that, when played, will filter your pivot table to the top 5 customers by revenue. The plan is to tweak this macro to respond to a scrollbar. That is, you force the macro to base the number used to filter the pivot table on the number represented by a scrollbar in your user interface. In other words, a user can get the top 5, top 8, or top 32 simply by moving a scrollbar up or down.

To get a scrollbar onto your spreadsheet, select the Insert icon on Developer tab; then select the scrollbar control from the form controls. Place the scrollbar control onto your spreadsheet.

Right-click on the scrollbar and select Format Control. This activates the Format Object dialog box. Here, you make the following setting changes: Set Minimum Level to 1 so the scrollbar cannot go below 1, set Maximum Level to 200 so the scrollbar cannot go above

200, and set Cell Link to $M$2 so that the number represented by the scrollbar will output to cell M2. After you have completed these steps, your dialog box should look like the one shown in Figure 10.9.

Figure 10.9
After you have placed a scrollbar on your spreadsheet, configure the scrollbar as shown here.

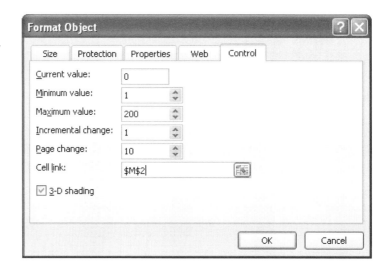

Next, assign the TopNthCusts macro you just recorded to your scrollbar, as demonstrated in Figure 10.10. Right-click on the scrollbar and select Assign Macro. Select the TopNthCusts macro from the list and then click OK. Assigning this macro ensures that it will play each time the scrollbar is clicked.

At this point, test your scrollbar by clicking on it. When you click on your scrollbar, two things should happen: The TopNthCusts macro should play, and the number in cell M2 should change to reflect your scrollbar's position. The number in cell M2 is important because that is the number you are going to reference in your TopNthCusts macro.

The only thing left to do is to tweak your macro to respond to the number in cell M2, effectively tying it to your scrollbar. To do this, you have to get to the VBA code that makes up the macro. There are several ways to get there, but for the purposes of this example, go to the Developer tab and select Macros. Selecting this option opens the Macro dialog box, exposing several options. From here, you can run, delete, step into, or edit a selected macro. To get to the VBA code that makes up your macro, select the macro and then select Edit, as demonstrated in Figure 10.11.

The Visual Basic Editor opens with a detailed view of all the VBA code that makes up this macro (see Figure 10.12). Notice that the number 5 is hard-coded as part of your macro. The reason is that you originally recorded your macro to filter the top five customers by revenue. Your goal here is to replace the hard-coded number 5 with the value in cell M2, which is tied to your scrollbar.

Figure 10.10
Select the macro from the list.

Figure 10.11
To get to the VBA code that makes up the TopNthCusts macro, select the macro and then select Edit.

You delete the number 5 and replace it with the following:

```
ActiveSheet.Range("M2").Value
```

Your macro's code should now look similar to the code shown in Figure 10.13.

Figure 10.12
Your goal is to replace the hard-coded number 5, as specified when you originally recorded your macro, with the value in cell M2.

```
Ln 59, Col 69                                                      TopIthCusts

(General)                                                          TopIthCusts

    Sub TopNthCusts()
    '
    ' TopNthCusts Macro
    '

    '
        Range("A4").Select
        ActiveSheet.PivotTables("PivotTable1").PivotFields("Customer_Name").ClearAllFilters

        ActiveSheet.PivotTables("PivotTable1").PivotFields("Customer_Name"). _
            PivotFilters.Add Type:=xlTopCount, DataField:=ActiveSheet.PivotTables( _
            "PivotTable1").PivotFields("Sum of Sales_Amount"), Value1:=5

    End Sub
```

Figure 10.13
Simply delete the hard-coded number 5 and replace it with a reference to cell M2.

```
Ln 59, Col 68                                                      TopIthCusts

(General)                                                          TopIthCusts

    Sub TopNthCusts()
    '
    ' TopNthCusts Macro
    '

    '
        Range("A4").Select
        ActiveSheet.PivotTables("PivotTable1").PivotFields("Customer_Name").ClearAllFilters

        ActiveSheet.PivotTables("PivotTable1").PivotFields("Customer_Name"). _
            PivotFilters.Add Type:=xlTopCount, DataField:=ActiveSheet.PivotTables( _
            "PivotTable1").PivotFields("Sum of Sales_Amount"), Value1:=ActiveSheet.Range("M2").Value

    End Sub
```

Close the Visual Basic Editor to get back to your pivot table report. Test your scrollbar by setting the scrollbar to 11. Your macro should play and filter out the Top 11 customers by revenue, as shown in Figure 10.14.

Figure 10.14
After a little formatting, you have a clear and easy way for your clients to get the top customers by revenue.

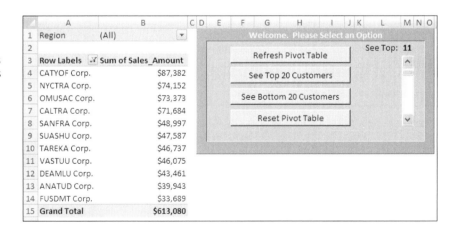

	A	B	C	D	E	F	G	H	I	J	K	L	M	N	O
1	Region	(All)						Welcome. Please Select an Option							
2													See Top:	11	
3	Row Labels	Sum of Sales_Amount					Refresh Pivot Table								
4	CATYOF Corp.	$87,382													
5	NYCTRA Corp.	$74,152					See Top 20 Customers								
6	OMUSAC Corp.	$73,373													
7	CALTRA Corp.	$71,684					See Bottom 20 Customers								
8	SANFRA Corp.	$48,997													
9	SUASHU Corp.	$47,587					Reset Pivot Table								
10	TAREKA Corp.	$46,737													
11	VASTUU Corp.	$46,075													
12	DEAMLU Corp.	$43,461													
13	ANATUD Corp.	$39,943													
14	FUSDMT Corp.	$33,689													
15	**Grand Total**	**$613,080**													

Synchronizing Two Pivot Tables with One Combo Box

The report in Figure 10.15 contains two pivot tables. Each pivot table has a filter field for allowing you to select a market. The problem is that every time you select a market from the filter field in one pivot table, you have to select the same market from the filter field in the other pivot table to ensure you are analyzing the correct Units Sold versus Revenue.

Not only is it a bit of a hassle to have to synchronize both pivot tables every time you want to analyze a new market's data, but there is a chance you, or your clients, may forget to do so.

Figure 10.15
This pivot table report contains two pivot tables with filter fields that filter out a market. The issue is that you have to synchronize the two pivot tables when analyzing data for a particular market.

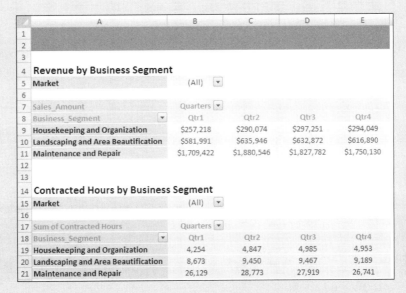

One way to synchronize these pivot tables is to use a combo box. The idea is to record a macro that selects a market from the Market field of both tables. Then you can create a combo box and fill it with the market names that exist in your two pivot tables. Finally, you can alter your macro to filter both pivot tables, using the value from your combo box. To do so, follow these steps:

1. Create a new macro and call it **SynchMarkets**. When recording starts, select the California market from the Market field in both pivot tables; then stop recording.

2. Activate the Forms toolbar and place a combo box onto your spreadsheet.

3. Create a hard-coded list of all the markets that exist in your pivot table. Note that the first entry in your list is (All). You must include this entry if you want to be able to select all markets with your combo box.

   As you can see in Figure 10.16, you place the combo box and your list of markets directly in your spreadsheet.

4. Right-click on your combo box and select Format Control to perform the initial setup.

Figure 10.16
At this point, you should have all the tools you need: a macro that changes the Market field of both pivot tables, a combo box on your spreadsheet, and a list of all the markets that exist in your pivot table.

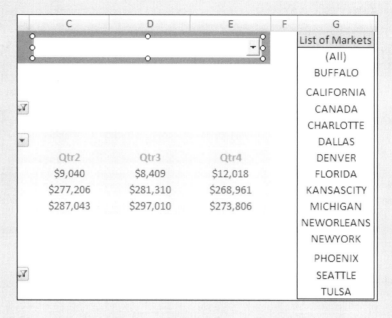

First, specify an input range for the list you are using to fill your combo box. In this case, this means the market list you created in step 3. Next, specify a cell link—that is, the cell that will show the index number of the item you select (cell H1 is the cell link in this example). After you have configured your combo box, your dialog box should look similar to the one shown in Figure 10.17.

Figure 10.17
The settings for your combo box should reference your market list as the input range and specify a cell link close to your market list. In this case, the cell link is cell H1.

At this point, you should now be able to select a market from your combo box and see the associated index number in cell H1. Why an index number instead of the name of the selected market? Well, the only output of a combo box form control is an index number. This is the position number of the selected item. For instance, in Figure 10.18, the selection of Charlotte from the combo box results in the number 5 in cell H1. This means that Charlotte was the fifth item in the combo box.

Figure 10.18
Your combo box, now filled with market names, will output an index number in cell H1 when a market is selected.

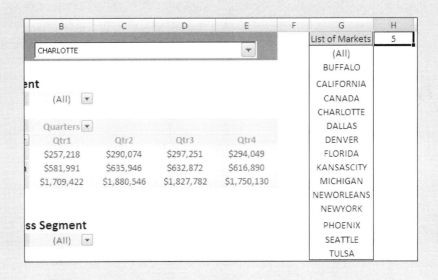

To make use of this index number, you have to pass it through the INDEX function. The INDEX function converts an index number to a value that can be recognized.

5. Enter an INDEX function that converts the index number in cell H1 to a value.

   An INDEX function requires two arguments to work properly. The first argument is the range of the list you are working with. In most cases, you use the same range that is feeding your combo box. The second argument is the index number. If the index number is in a cell (like in cell H1), you can simply reference the cell.

Figure 10.19
The index function in cell I1 converts the index number in cell H1 to a value. You will eventually use the value in cell I1 to alter your macro.

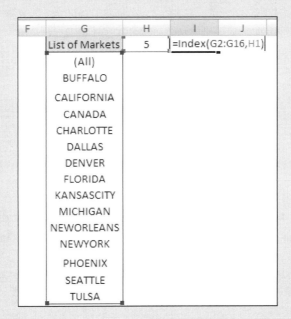

6. Edit the SynchMarkets macro using the value in cell I1, instead of a hard-coded value.

To get to the VBA code that makes up your macro, click the Macros button on the Developer tab. This activates the Macro dialog box, shown in Figure 10.20. From here, select the SynchMarkets macro and then select Edit.

Figure 10.20
In the Macro dialog box, select the SynchMarkets macro and select Edit.

When you recorded your macro originally, you selected the California market from the Market field in both pivot tables. As you can see in Figure 10.21, California is hard-coded in your macro's VBA code.

Figure 10.21
The California market is hard-coded in your macro's VBA code.

Replace `California` with `ActiveSheet.Range("I1").Value`, as demonstrated in Figure 10.22. This code references the value in cell I1. After you have edited the macro, close the Visual Basic Editor to get back to the spreadsheet.

7. All that is left to do is ensure that the macro will play when you select a market from the combo box. Right-click on the combo box and select Assign Macro. Select the SynchMarkets macro and then click OK.

Figure 10.22
Replace `California` with `ActiveSheet. Range("I1"). Value` and then close the Visual Basic Editor.

```
(General)                                                    SynchMarkets

    Option Explicit

    Sub SynchMarkets()

        ActiveSheet.PivotTables("PivotTable1").PivotFields("Market").ClearAllFilters
        ActiveSheet.PivotTables("PivotTable1").PivotFields("Market").CurrentPage = ActiveSheet.Range("I1").Value

        ActiveSheet.PivotTables("PivotTable2").PivotFields("Market").ClearAllFilters
        ActiveSheet.PivotTables("PivotTable2").PivotFields("Market").CurrentPage = ActiveSheet.Range("I1").Value

    End Sub
```

8. Clean up the formatting on your newly created report by hiding the rows and columns that hold the filter fields in your pivot tables, the market list you created, and any unseemly formulas.

As you can see in Figure 10.23, this setup provides your clients with an attractive interface that allows them to make selections in multiple pivot tables using one control.

Figure 10.23
Your pivot table report is ready to use!

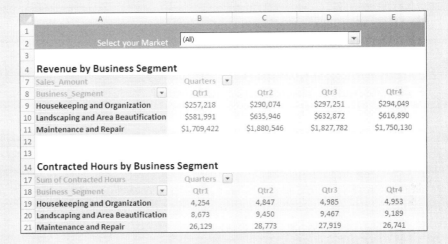

	A	B	C	D	E
1					
2	Select your Market	(All)			▼
3					
4	**Revenue by Business Segment**				
7	Sales_Amount	Quarters ▼			
8	Business_Segment ▼	Qtr1	Qtr2	Qtr3	Qtr4
9	**Housekeeping and Organization**	$257,218	$290,074	$297,251	$294,049
10	**Landscaping and Area Beautification**	$581,991	$635,946	$632,872	$616,890
11	**Maintenance and Repair**	$1,709,422	$1,880,546	$1,827,782	$1,750,130
12					
13					
14	**Contracted Hours by Business Segment**				
17	Sum of Contracted Hours	Quarters ▼			
18	Business_Segment ▼	Qtr1	Qtr2	Qtr3	Qtr4
19	**Housekeeping and Organization**	4,254	4,847	4,985	4,953
20	**Landscaping and Area Beautification**	8,673	9,450	9,467	9,189
21	**Maintenance and Repair**	26,129	28,773	27,919	26,741

TIP
When you select a new item from your combo box, the pivot tables automatically adjust the columns to fit the data. This behavior can be annoying when you have a formatted template. You can suppress this behavior by right-clicking on each pivot table and selecting Table Options. Selecting this option activates the PivotTable Options dialog box, where you can remove the check next to the Autofit Column Widths on Update selection.

Next Steps

In the next chapter, you go beyond recording macros. Chapter 11 shows how to utilize Visual Basic for Applications to create powerful, behind-the-scenes processes and calculations using pivot tables.

Using VBA to Create Pivot Tables

11

Introducing VBA

Version 5 of Excel introduced a powerful new macro language called Visual Basic for Applications (VBA). Every copy of Excel shipped since 1993 has had a copy of the powerful VBA language hiding behind the worksheets. VBA allows you to perform steps that you normally perform in Excel, but to perform them very very quickly and flawlessly. I've seen a VBA program take a process that would take days each month and turn it into a single button click and a minute of processing time.

Don't be intimidated by VBA. The VBA macro recorder tool will get you 90% of the way to a useful macro and I will get you the rest of the way there using examples in this chapter.

Every example in this chapter is available for download from http://www.mrexcel.com/pivot2007data.html/.

Enabling VBA in Your Copy of Excel

By default, VBA is disabled in Office 2007. Before you can start using VBA, you need to enable macros in the Trust Center. From the Office icon menu, choose Excel Options, Trust Center, Trust Center Settings, Macro Settings.

Choose one of the options below.

- Disable all macros with notification—this setting is equivalent to medium macro security in Excel 2003. When you open a workbook that contains macros, a message will appear alerting that there are macros in the workbook. If you expect macros to be in the workbook, you simply click Options, Enable to allow the macros to run. This is the safest setting, as it forces you to explicitly enable macros in each workbook.

IN THIS CHAPTER

Introducing VBA 231

Learning Tricks of the Trade 234

Understanding Versions 236

Building a Pivot Table in Excel VBA 239

Creating a Report Showing Revenue by Product 246

Handling Additional Annoyances When Creating Your Final Report 250

Addressing Issues with Two or More Data Fields 257

Summarizing Date Fields with Grouping ...263

Using Advanced Pivot Table Techniques 267

Controlling the Sort Order Manually 276

Using Sum, Average, Count, Min, Max, and More 276

Creating Report Percentages 277

Using New Pivot Table Features in Excel 2007 279

Next Steps 289

■ Enable all macros (not recommended; potentially dangerous code can run)—this setting is equivalent to low macros security in Excel 2003. Because it could allow rogue macros to run in files that are sent to you by others, Microsoft recommends that you do not use this setting.

> **TIP**
>
> If you have previously enabled the Developer tab of the Ribbon, you can use the Macro Security icon to jump quickly to the Trust Center dialog box.

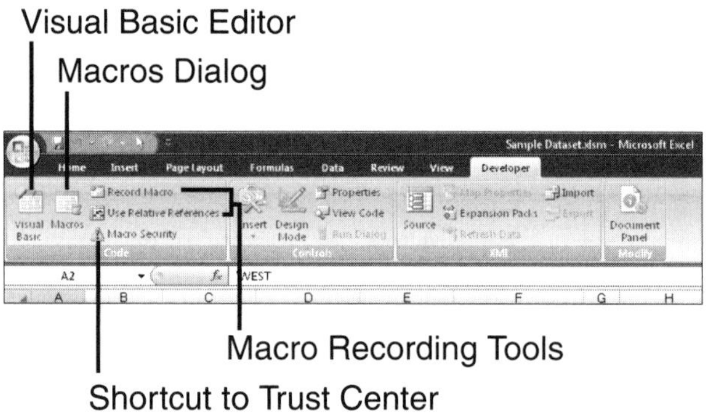

Visual Basic Editor
Macros Dialog

Figure 11.1
Enable the Developer tab to access the VBA tools.

Macro Recording Tools
Shortcut to Trust Center

Further, when you save your files, you have to save the files as Excel 2007 macro-enabled workbooks with the `.xlsm` extension.

Enabling the Developer Ribbon

Most of the VBA tools are located on a Developer tab of the Excel 2007 Ribbon. By default, this tab is not displayed. To enable it, from the Office icon menu, select Excel Options, Popular. Then choose Show Developer Tab in the Ribbon.

As shown in Figure 11.1, the Code group on the Developer tab of the Ribbon offers icons for accessing the Visual Basic Editor, Macros dialog box, macro recording tools, and Macro Security setting.

Visual Basic Editor

From Excel, press Alt+F11 or choose Developer, Code, Visual Basic to open the Visual Basic Editor, as shown in Figure 11.2. The three main sections of the VBA Editor are described here. If this is your first time using VBA, some of these items may be disabled. Follow the instructions given in the following list to make sure that each is enabled:

■ **Project Explorer**—This pane displays a hierarchical tree of all open workbooks. Expand the tree to see the worksheets and code modules present in the workbook. If the Project Explorer is not visible, enable it by pressing Ctrl+R.

Project Explorer   Code window

Figure 11.2
The Visual Basic Editor
window is lurking
behind every copy of
Excel shipped since 1993.

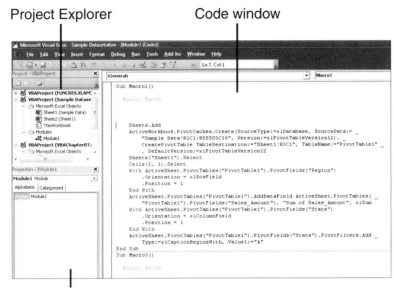

Properties window

- **Properties window**—The Properties window is important when you begin to program user forms. It has some use when you're writing normal code, so enable it by pressing F4.

- **Code window**—This is the area where you write your code. Code is stored in one or more code modules attached to your workbook. To add a code module to a workbook, select Insert, Code Module from the application menu.

Visual Basic Tools

Visual Basic is a powerful development environment. Although this chapter cannot offer a complete course on VBA, if you are new to VBA, you should take advantage of these important tools:

- As you begin to type code, Excel may offer a drop-down with valid choices. This feature, known as AutoComplete, allows you to type code faster and eliminate typing mistakes.

- For assistance on any keyword, put the cursor in the keyword and press F1. You might need your installation CDs because the VBA help file can be excluded from the installation of Office 2007.

- Excel checks each line of code as you finish it. Lines in error appear in red. Comments appear in green. You can add a comment by typing a single apostrophe. Use lots of comments so you can remember what each section of code is doing.

11

- Despite the aforementioned error checking, Excel may still encounter an error at run-time. If this happens, click the Debug button. The line that caused the error is high-lighted in yellow. Hover your mouse cursor over any variable to see the current value of the variable.

- When you are in Debug mode, use the Debug menu to step line by line through code. You can toggle back and forth between Excel and VBA to see the effect of running a line of code on the worksheet.

- Other great debugging tools are breakpoints, the Watch window, the Object Browser, and the Immediate window. Read about these tools in the Excel VBA Help menu.

The Macro Recorder

Excel offers a macro recorder that is about 90% perfect. Unfortunately, the last 10% is frus-trating. Code that you record to work with one dataset is hard-coded to work only with that dataset. This behavior might work fine if your transactional database occupies cells A1:K415501 every single day, but if you are pulling in a new invoice register every day, it is unlikely that you will have the same number of rows each day. Given that you might need to work with other data, it would be a lot better if Excel could record selecting cells using the End key. This is one of the shortcomings of the macro recorder.

In reality, Excel pros use the macro recorder to record code but then expect to have to clean up the recorded code.

Understanding Object-Oriented Code

VBA is an object-oriented language. Most lines of VBA code follow the *Noun.Verb* syntax. However, in VBA, it is called *Object.Method*. Objects can be workbooks, worksheets, cells, or ranges of cells. Methods can be typical Excel actions, such as `.Copy`, `.Paste`, and `.PasteSpecial`.

Many methods allow adverbs—parameters you use to specify how to perform the method. If you see a construct with a colon/equal sign, you know that the macro recorder is describing how the method should work.

You also might see the type of code in which you assign a value to the adjectives of an object. In VBA, adjectives are called *properties*. If you set `ActiveCell.Font.ColorIndex = 3`, you are setting the font color of the active cell to red. Note that when you are dealing with properties, there is only an equal sign, not a colon/equal sign.

Learning Tricks of the Trade

You need to master a few simple techniques to be able to write efficient VBA code. These techniques will help you make the jump to writing effective code.

Writing Code to Handle Any Size Data Range

The macro recorder hard-codes the fact that your data is in a range, such as A1:K415501. Although this hard-coding works for today's dataset, it may not work as you get new datasets. You need to write code that can deal with different size datasets.

The macro recorder uses syntax such as `Range("H12")` to refer to a cell. However, it is more flexible to use `Cells(12, 8)` to refer to the cell in row 12, column 8. Similarly, the macro recorder refers to a rectangular range as `Range("A1:K415501")`. However, it is more flexible to use the `Cells` syntax to refer to the upper-left corner of the range and then use the `Resize()` syntax to refer to the number of rows and columns in the range. The equivalent way to describe the preceding range is `Cells(1, 1).Resize(415501,11)`. This approach is more flexible because you can replace any of the numbers with a variable.

In the Excel user interface, you can use the End key on the keyboard to jump to the end of a range of data. If you move the cell pointer to the final row on the worksheet and press the End key followed by the up-arrow key, the cell pointer jumps to the last row with data. The equivalent of doing this in VBA is to use the following code:

```
Range("A1048576").End(xlUp).Select
```

You don't need to select this cell; you just need to find the row number that contains the last row. The following code locates this row and saves the row number to a variable named `FinalRow`:

```
FinalRow = Range("A1048576").End(xlUp).Row
```

There is nothing magic about the variable name `FinalRow`. You could call this variable x or y, or even your dog's name. However, because VBA allows you to use meaningful variable names, you should use something such as `FinalRow` to describe the final row.

> **NOTE**
> Excel 2007 offers 1,048,576 rows and 16,384 columns. Excel 97 through Excel 2003 offered 65,536 rows and 256 columns. To make your code flexible enough to handle any versions of Excel, you can use `Rows.Count` to learn the total number of rows in this version of Excel. The preceding code could then be generalized like so:
>
> ```
> FinalRow = Cells(Rows.Count, 1).End(xlUp).Row
> ```

You also can find the final column in a dataset. If you are relatively sure that the dataset begins in row 1, you can use the End key in combination with the left-arrow key to jump from cell XFD1 to the last column with data. To generalize for the possibility that the code is running in earlier versions of Excel, you can use the following code:

```
FinalCol = Cells(1, Columns.Count).End(xlToLeft).Column
```

End+Down Versus End+Up

You might be tempted to find the final row by starting in cell A1 and using the End key in conjunction with the down-arrow key. Avoid this approach. Data coming from another system is imperfect. If your program will import 500,000 rows from a legacy computer system every day for the next five years, a day will come when someone manages to key a null value into the dataset. This value will cause a blank cell or even a blank row to appear in the middle of your dataset. Using `Range("A1").End(xlDown)` will stop prematurely at the blank cell instead of including all your data. This blank cell will cause that day's report to miss thousands of rows of data, a potential disaster that will call into question the credibility of your report. Take the extra step of starting at the last row in the worksheet to greatly reduce the risk of problems.

Using Super-Variables: Object Variables

In typical programming languages, a variable holds a single value. You might use `x = 4` to assign a value of 4 to the variable `x`.

Think about a single cell in Excel. Many properties describe a cell. A cell might contain a value such as 4, but the cell also has a font size, a font color, a row, a column, possibly a formula, possibly a comment, a list of precedents, and more. It is possible in VBA to create a super-variable that contains all the information about a cell or about any object. A statement to create a typical variable such as `x = Range("A1")` assigns the current value of A1 to the variable `x`.

However, you can use the `Set` keyword to create an object variable:

```
Set x = Range("A1")
```

You've now created a super-variable that contains all the properties of the cell. Instead of having a variable with only one value, you have a variable in which you can access the value of many properties associated with that variable. You can reference `x.Formula` to learn the formula in A1 or `x.Font.ColorIndex` to learn the color of the cell.

Understanding Versions

Pivot tables have been evolving. They were introduced in Excel 5 and perfected in Excel 97. In Excel 2000, pivot table creation in VBA was dramatically altered. Some new parameters were added in Excel 2002. A few new properties such as `PivotFilters` and `TableStyle2` were added in Excel 2007. Therefore, you need to be extremely careful when writing code in Excel 2007 that might be run in Excel 2003 or Excel 2000 or Excel 97.

Just a few simple tweaks make 2003 code run in 2000, but a major overhaul is required to make any code run in Excel 97. Because it has been 10 years since the release of Excel 97 (and because Microsoft has not supported that product for 5+ years), this chapter focuses on using only the pivot cache method introduced in Excel 2000. At the end of the chapter, you briefly learn the PivotTable Wizard method, which is your only option if you need code to run in Excel 97.

New in Excel 2007

Although the basic concept of pivot tables is the same in Excel 2007 as it was in Excel 2003, several new features are available in Excel 2007 pivot tables. The entire Design ribbon is new, including the concepts of subtotals at the top, the report layout options, blank rows, and the new PivotTable styles. Excel 2007 offers better filters than previous versions. It also makes the expand and collapse functionality more apparent by adding buttons to the pivot table grid. Every new feature adds one or more methods or properties to VBA.

If you are hoping to share your pivot table macro with people running prior versions of Excel, you need to avoid these methods. Your best bet is to open an Excel 2003 workbook in compatibility mode and record the macro while the workbook is in compatibility mode. If you are using the macro only in Excel 2007 or later, you can use any of these new features.

Table 11.1 shows the methods that are new in Excel 2007. If you record a macro that uses these methods, you cannot share the macro with someone using Excel 2003 or earlier.

Table 11.1   Methods New in Excel 2007

Method	Description
ClearAllFilters	Clears all filters in the pivot table.
ClearTable	Removes all fields from the pivot table but keeps the pivot table intact.
ConvertToFormulas	Converts a pivot table to cube formulas. This method is valid only for pivot tables based on OLAP data sources.
DisplayAllMemberPropertiesInTooltip	Equivalent to Options, Display, Show Properties in ToolTips.
RowAxisLayout	Changes the layout for all fields in the row area. Valid values are xlCompactRow, xlTabularRow, or xlOutlineRow.
SubtotalLocation	Controls whether subtotals appear at the top or bottom of each group. Valid arguments are xlAtTop or xlAtBottom.

Table 11.2 lists the properties that are new in Excel 2007. If you record a macro that refers to these properties, you cannot share the macro with someone using Excel 2003 or earlier.

Table 11.2   Properties New in Excel 2007

Property	Description
ActiveFilters	Indicates the active filters in the pivot table; this is a read-only property.

continues

Table 11.2 Continued

Property	Description
AllowMultipleFilters	Indicates whether a pivot field can have multiple filters applied to it at the same time.
CompactLayoutColumnHeader	Specifies the caption that is displayed in the column header of a pivot table when in compact row layout form.
CompactLayoutRowHeader	Specifies the caption that is displayed in the row header of a pivot table when in compact row layout form.
CompactRowIndent	Indicates the indent increment for pivot items when compact row layout form is turned on.
DisplayContextTooltips	Controls whether ToolTips are displayed for pivot table cells.
DisplayFieldCaptions	Controls whether filter buttons and pivot field captions for rows and columns are displayed in the grid.
DisplayMemberPropertyTooltips	Controls whether to display member properties in ToolTips.
FieldListSortAscending	Controls the sort order of fields in the PivotTable Field List. When this property is True, the fields are sorted in alphabetical order. When it is set to False, the fields are presented in the same sequence as the data source columns.
InGridDropZones	Controls whether you can drag and drop fields onto the grid. Changing the pivot table layout also changes this property. Changing this property forces the layout back to a table layout.
LayoutRowDefault	Specifies the layout settings for pivot fields when they are added to the pivot table for the first time. Valid values are xlCompactRow, xlTabularRow, or xlOutlineRow.
PivotColumnAxis	Returns a PivotAxis object representing the entire column axis.
PivotRowAxis	Returns a PivotAxis object representing the entire row axis.
PrintDrillIndicators	Specifies whether drill indicators are printed with the pivot table.

Property	Description
ShowDrillIndicators	Specifies whether drill indicators are shown in the pivot table.
ShowTableStyleColumnHeaders	Controls whether table style 2 should affect the column headers.
ShowTableStyleColumnStripes	Controls whether table style 2 should show banded columns.
ShowTableStyleLastColumn	Controls whether table style 2 should format the final column.
ShowTableStyleRowHeaders	Controls whether table style 2 should affect the row headers.
ShowTableStyleRowStripes	Controls whether table style 2 should show banded columns.
SortUsingCustomLists	Controls whether custom lists are used for sorting items of fields, both initially and later when applying a sort. Setting this property to False can optimize performance for fields with many items and allows you to avoid using custom-list based sorting.
TableStyle2	Specifies the pivot table style currently applied to the pivot table. Note that previous versions of Excel offered a weak AutoFormat option. That feature's settings were held in the TableStyle property, so Microsoft had to use TableStyle2 as the property name for the new pivot table styles. The property might have a value such as PivotStyleLight17.

Building a Pivot Table in Excel VBA

In this chapter, we do not mean to imply that you use VBA to build pivot tables to give to your clients. Rather, the purpose of this chapter is to remind you that pivot tables can be used as a means to an end; you can use a pivot table to extract a summary of data and then use that summary elsewhere.

> **TIP**
>
> The code listings from this chapter are available for download at http://www.MrExcel.com/pivot2007data.html.

11

> **CAUTION**
>
> Although the Excel user interface has new names for the various sections of a pivot table, VBA code will continue to refer to the old names. Microsoft had to use this choice, otherwise millions of lines of code would stop working in Excel 2007 when they referred to a page field instead of a filter field. While the four sections of a pivot table in the Excel user interface are Report Filter, Column Labels, Row Labels, and Values, VBA continues to use the old terms of Page fields, Column fields, Row fields, and Data fields.

In Excel 2000 and newer, you first build a pivot cache object to describe the input area of the data:

```
Dim WSD As Worksheet
Dim PTCache As PivotCache
Dim PT As PivotTable
Dim PRange As Range
Dim FinalRow As Long
Dim FinalCol As Long
Set WSD = Worksheets("PivotTable")

' Delete any prior pivot tables
For Each PT In WSD.PivotTables
    PT.TableRange2.Clear
Next PT

' Define input area and set up a Pivot Cache
FinalRow = WSD.Cells(Rows.Count, 1).End(xlUp).Row
FinalCol = WSD.Cells(1, Columns.Count).End(xlToLeft).Column
Set PRange = WSD.Cells(1, 1).Resize(FinalRow, FinalCol)
Set PTCache = ActiveWorkbook.PivotCaches.Add(SourceType:=xlDatabase, _
    SourceData:=PRange)
```

After defining the pivot cache, use the `CreatePivotTable` method to create a blank pivot table based on the defined pivot cache:

```
Set PT = PTCache.CreatePivotTable(TableDestination:=WSD.Cells(2, FinalCol + 2), _
    TableName:="PivotTable1")
```

In the `CreatePivotTable` method, you specify the output location and optionally give the table a name. After running this line of code, you have a strange-looking blank pivot table, like the one shown in Figure 11.3. You now have to use code to drop fields onto the table.

If you choose the Defer Layout Update setting in the user interface to build the pivot table, Excel does not recalculate the pivot table after you drop each field onto the table. By default in VBA, Excel calculates the pivot table as you execute each step of building the table. This could require the pivot table to be executed a half-dozen times before you get to the final result. To speed up your code execution, you can temporarily turn off calculation of the pivot table by using the `ManualUpdate` property:

```
PT.ManualUpdate = True
```

Figure 11.3
Immediately after you use the `CreatePivotTable` method, Excel gives you a four-cell blank pivot table that is not very useful.

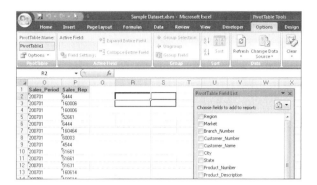

You can now run through the steps needed to lay out the pivot table. In the `.AddFields` method, you can specify one or more fields that should be in the row, column, or filter area of the pivot table.

The `RowFields` parameter enables you to define fields that appear in the Row Labels layout area of the PivotTable Field List. The `ColumnFields` parameter corresponds to the Column Labels layout area. The `PageFields` parameter corresponds to the Report Filter layout area.

The following line of code will populate a pivot table with two fields in the row area and one field in the column area.

```
' Set up the row & column fields
PT.AddFields RowFields:=Array("Business Segment", "Product"), _
    ColumnFields:="Region"
```

To add a field such as Revenue to the values area of the table, you change the `Orientation` property of the field to be `xlDataField`.

Getting a Sum Instead of a Count

Excel is smart. When you build a report with revenue, it assumes you want to sum the revenue. But there is a problem. Say that one of the revenue cells is blank. When you build the pivot table, even though 99.9% of fields are numeric, Excel assumes you have alphanumeric data and offers to count this field. This is annoying. It seems to be an anomaly that, on one hand, you are expected to make sure that 100% of your cells have numeric data, but on the other hand, the results of the pivot table are often filled with non-numeric blank cells.

When you build the pivot table in the Excel interface, you should take care in the Values drop zone to notice that the field reads Count of Revenue instead of Sum of Revenue. At that point, the right course of action is to go back and fix the data, but what people usually do is double-click the Count of Revenue button and change it to Sum of Revenue.

In VBA, you should always explicitly define that you are creating a sum of revenue by explicitly setting the `Function` property to `xlSum`:

```
' Set up the data fields
With PT.PivotFields("Revenue")
    .Orientation = xlDataField
    .Function = xlSum
    .Position = 1
End With
```

At this point, you've given VBA all the settings required to correctly generate the pivot table. If you set `ManualUpdate` to `False`, Excel calculates and draws the pivot table. You can immediately thereafter set this back to `True`:

```
' Calc the pivot table
PT.ManualUpdate = False
PT.ManualUpdate = True
```

Your pivot table inherits the table style settings selected as the default on whatever computer happens to run the code. If you would like control over the final format, you can explicitly choose a table style. The following code applies banded rows and a medium table style:

```
' Format the pivot table
PT.ShowTableStyleRowStripes = True
PT.TableStyle2 = "PivotStyleMedium10"
```

At this point, you have a complete pivot table like the one shown in Figure 11.4.

11

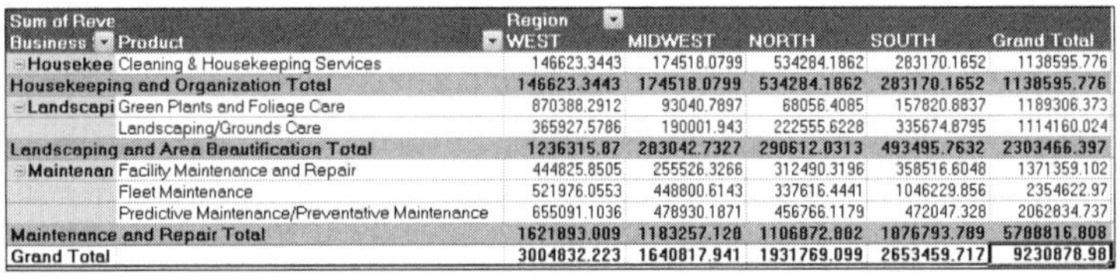

Sum of Reve		Region				
Business	Product	WEST	MIDWEST	NORTH	SOUTH	Grand Total
Housekee	Cleaning & Housekeeping Services	146623.3443	174518.0799	534284.1862	283170.1652	1138595.776
Housekeeping and Organization Total		146623.3443	174518.0799	534284.1862	283170.1652	1138595.776
Landscapi	Green Plants and Foliage Care	870388.2912	93040.7897	68056.4085	157820.8837	1189306.373
	Landscaping/Grounds Care	365927.5786	190001.943	222555.6228	335674.8795	1114160.024
Landscaping and Area Beautification Total		1236315.87	283042.7327	290612.0313	493495.7632	2303466.397
Maintenan	Facility Maintenance and Repair	444825.8505	255526.3266	312490.3196	358516.6048	1371359.102
	Fleet Maintenance	521976.0553	448800.6143	337616.4441	1046229.856	2354622.97
	Predictive Maintenance/Preventative Maintenance	655091.1036	478930.1871	456766.1179	472047.328	2062834.737
Maintenance and Repair Total		1621893.009	1183257.128	1106872.882	1876793.789	5788816.808
Grand Total		3004832.223	1640817.941	1931769.099	2653459.717	9230878.98

Figure 11.4
Fewer than 50 lines of code create this pivot table in less than a second.

Listing 11.1 shows the complete code used to generate the pivot table.

Listing 11.1 Code to Generate a Pivot Table

```
Sub CreatePivot()
    Dim WSD As Worksheet
    Dim PTCache As PivotCache
    Dim PT As PivotTable
    Dim PRange As Range
    Dim FinalRow As Long
    Dim FinalCol As Long
    Set WSD = Worksheets("PivotTable")

    ' Delete any prior pivot tables
    For Each PT In WSD.PivotTables
        PT.TableRange2.Clear
    Next PT

    ' Define input area and set up a Pivot Cache
    FinalRow = WSD.Cells(Rows.Count, 1).End(xlUp).Row
    FinalCol = WSD.Cells(1, Columns.Count). _
        End(xlToLeft).Column
```

```
    Set PRange = WSD.Cells(1, 1).Resize(FinalRow, FinalCol)
    Set PTCache = ActiveWorkbook.PivotCaches.Add(SourceType:= _
        xlDatabase, SourceData:=PRange)

    ' Create the Pivot Table from the Pivot Cache
    Set PT = PTCache.CreatePivotTable(TableDestination:=WSD. _
        Cells(2, FinalCol + 2), TableName:="PivotTable1")

    ' Turn off updating while building the table
    PT.ManualUpdate = True

    ' Set up the row & column fields
    PT.AddFields RowFields:=Array("Business Segment", "Product"), _
        ColumnFields:="Region"

    ' Set up the data fields
    With PT.PivotFields("Revenue")
        .Orientation = xlDataField
        .Function = xlSum
        .Position = 1
    End With

    ' Calc the pivot table
    PT.ManualUpdate = False
    PT.ManualUpdate = True

' Format the pivot table
PT.ShowTableStyleRowStripes = True
PT.TableStyle2 = "PivotStyleMedium10"

End Sub
```

Learning Why You Cannot Move or Change Part of a Pivot Report

Although pivot tables are incredible, they have annoying limitations. You cannot move or change just part of a pivot table. For example, try to run a macro that would delete column X, which contains the Grand Total column of the pivot table. The macro comes to a screeching halt with an error 1004, as shown in Figure 11.5. To get around this limitation, you can change the summary from a pivot table to just values using the PasteSpecial method described below.

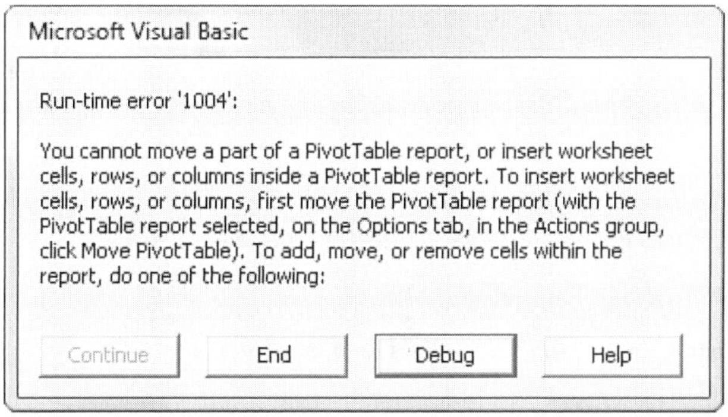

Figure 11.5
You cannot delete just part of a pivot table.

Microsoft Visual Basic

Run-time error '1004':

You cannot move a part of a PivotTable report, or insert worksheet cells, rows, or columns inside a PivotTable report. To insert worksheet cells, rows, or columns, first move the PivotTable report (with the PivotTable report selected, on the Options tab, in the Actions group, click Move PivotTable). To add, move, or remove cells within the report, do one of the following:

| Continue | End | Debug | Help |

Determining Size of a Finished Pivot Table

Knowing the size of a pivot table in advance is difficult. If you run a report of transactional data on one day, you may or may not have sales from the West region, for example. This could cause your table to be either six or seven columns wide. Therefore, you should use the special property `TableRange2` to refer to the entire resultant pivot table.

Because of the limitations of pivot tables, you should generally copy the results of a pivot table to a new location on the worksheet and then delete the original pivot table. The code in `CreateSummaryReportUsingPivot()` creates a small pivot table. Note that you can set the `ColumnGrand` and `RowGrand` properties of the table to `False` to prevent the totals from being added to the table.

`PT.TableRange2` includes the entire pivot table. In this case, this includes the extra row at the top with the button Sum of Revenue. To eliminate that row, the code copies `PT.TableRange2` but offsets this selection by one row by using `.Offset(1, 0)`. Depending on the nature of your pivot table, you might need to use an offset of two or more rows to get rid of extraneous information at the top of the pivot table.

The code copies `PT.TableRange2` and uses `PasteSpecial` on a cell five rows below the current pivot table. At that point in the code, your worksheet appears as shown in Figure 11.6. The table in R2 is a live pivot table, and the table in R10 is just the copied results.

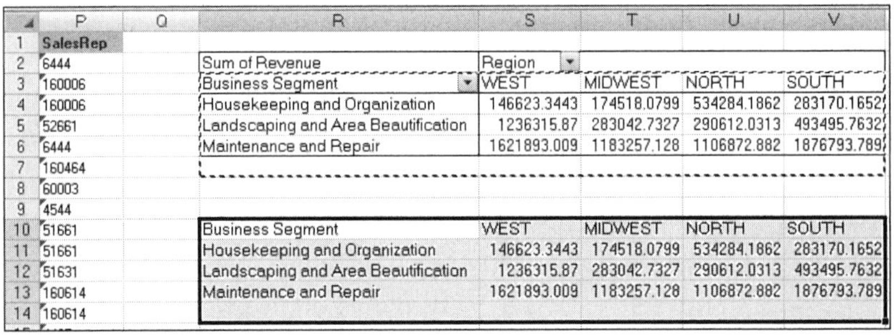

	P	Q	R	S	T	U	V
1	SalesRep						
2	6444		Sum of Revenue	Region			
3	160006		Business Segment	WEST	MIDWEST	NORTH	SOUTH
4	160006		Housekeeping and Organization	146623.3443	174518.0799	534284.1862	283170.1652
5	52661		Landscaping and Area Beautification	1236315.87	283042.7327	290612.0313	493495.7632
6	6444		Maintenance and Repair	1621893.009	1183257.128	1106872.882	1876793.789
7	160464						
8	60003						
9	4544						
10	51661		Business Segment	WEST	MIDWEST	NORTH	SOUTH
11	51661		Housekeeping and Organization	146623.3443	174518.0799	534284.1862	283170.1652
12	51631		Landscaping and Area Beautification	1236315.87	283042.7327	290612.0313	493495.7632
13	160614		Maintenance and Repair	1621893.009	1183257.128	1106872.882	1876793.789
14	160614						

Figure 11.6
An intermediate result of the macro. Only the summary in R10:V14 will remain after the macro finishes.

You can then totally eliminate the pivot table by applying the `Clear` method to the entire table. If your code is then going on to do additional formatting, you should remove the pivot cache from memory by setting `PTCache` equal to `Nothing`.

The following code will use a pivot table to produce a summary from the underlying data. At the end of the code, the pivot table will be copied to static values and the pivot table will be cleared.

Listing 11.2 Code to Produce a Static Summary from a Pivot Table

```
Sub CreateSummaryReportUsingPivot()
    ' Use a Pivot Table to create a static summary report
    ' with model going down the rows and regions across
    Dim WSD As Worksheet
    Dim PTCache As PivotCache
```

```
Dim PT As PivotTable
Dim PRange As Range
Dim FinalRow As Long
Set WSD = Worksheets("PivotTable")

' Delete any prior pivot tables
For Each PT In WSD.PivotTables
    PT.TableRange2.Clear
Next PT
WSD.Range("R1:AZ1").EntireColumn.Clear

' Define input area and set up a Pivot Cache
FinalRow = WSD.Cells(Rows.Count, 1).End(xlUp).Row
FinalCol = WSD.Cells(1, Columns.Count). _
    End(xlToLeft).Column
Set PRange = WSD.Cells(1, 1).Resize(FinalRow, FinalCol)
Set PTCache = ActiveWorkbook.PivotCaches.Add(SourceType:= _
    xlDatabase, SourceData:=PRange.Address)

' Create the Pivot Table from the Pivot Cache
Set PT = PTCache.CreatePivotTable(TableDestination:=WSD. _
    Cells(2, FinalCol + 2), TableName:="PivotTable1")

' Turn off updating while building the table
PT.ManualUpdate = True

' Set up the row fields
PT.AddFields RowFields:="Business Segment", ColumnFields:="Region"

' Set up the data fields
With PT.PivotFields("Revenue")
    .Orientation = xlDataField
    .Function = xlSum
    .Position = 1
End With

With PT
    .ColumnGrand = False
    .RowGrand = False
    .NullString = "0"
End With

' Calc the pivot table
PT.ManualUpdate = False
PT.ManualUpdate = True

' PT.TableRange2 contains the results. Move these to R10
' as just values and not a real pivot table.
PT.TableRange2.Offset(1, 0).Copy
WSD.Cells(5 + PT.TableRange2.Rows.Count, FinalCol + 2). _
    PasteSpecial xlPasteValues

' At this point, the worksheet looks like Figure 11.6


' Delete the original Pivot Table & the Pivot Cache
PT.TableRange2.Clear
Set PTCache = Nothing
```

continues

Listing 11.2 Continued

```
    WSD.Activate
    Range("R1").Select
End Sub
```

The preceding code creates the pivot table. It then copies the results as values and pastes them as values in R10:V13. Figure 11.6 shows an intermediate result just before the original pivot table is cleared.

So far, this chapter has walked you through building the simplest of pivot table reports. Pivot tables offer far more flexibility. Read on for more complex reporting examples.

Creating a Report Showing Revenue by Product

A typical report might provide a list of markets by product with revenue by year. This report could be given to product line managers to show them which markets are selling well. In this example, you want to show the markets in descending order by revenue with years going across the columns. A sample report is shown in Figure 11.7.

Figure 11.7
A typical request is to take transactional data and produce a summary by product for product line managers. You can use a pivot table to get 90% of this report and then a little formatting to finish it.

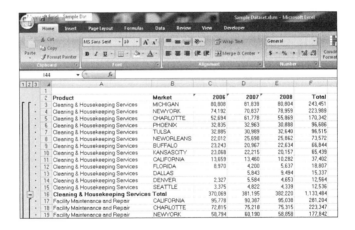

The key to producing this data quickly is to use a pivot table. Although pivot tables are incredible for summarizing data, they are quirky and their presentation is downright ugly. The final result is rarely formatted in a manner that is acceptable to line managers. There is not a good way to insert page breaks between each product in the pivot table.

To create this report, start with a pivot table that has Product and Market as row fields, Invoice Date grouped by year as a column field, and Sum of Revenue as the data field. Figure 11.8 shows the default pivot table created with these settings.

Figure 11.8
Use the power of the pivot table to get the summarized data, but then use your own common sense in formatting the report.

▲	R	S	T
2	Sum of Rev		InvoiceDate ▼
3	Product ▼	Market ▼	2006
4	⊟Cleaning	BUFFALO	23243.2381
5		CALIFORNIA	13659.459
6		CHARLOTTE	52694.0799
7		DALLAS	8970.1623
8		DENVER	2326.6595
9		FLORIDA	
10		KANSASCITY	23068.2759
11		MICHIGAN	80808.0588
12		NEWORLEANS	22011.5508
13		NEWYORK	74192.2907
14		PHOENIX	32834.6763
15		SEATTLE	3375.0822
16		TULSA	32885.3702
17	Cleaning & Housekeeping S		370068.9037
18	⊟Facility M	BUFFALO	23912.3083
19		CALIFORNIA	95778.1248

Here are just a few of the annoyances that most pivot tables present in their default state:

- The Outline view is horrible. In Figure 11.8, the value Cleaning & Housekeeping Services appears in the product column only once and is followed by 12 blank cells. This is the worst feature of pivot tables, and there is absolutely no way to correct it. Although humans can understand that this entire section is for Cleaning sales, it is radically confusing if your Cleaning section spills to a second or third page. Page 2 starts without any indication that the report is for Cleaning sales. If you intend to repurpose the data, you need the Cleaning sales value to be on every row.

- The report contains blank cells instead of zeros. In Figure 11.8, the Florida market had no cleaning sales in 2006. Excel produces a pivot table where cell T9 is blank instead of zero. This is simply bad form. Excel experts rely on being able to "ride the range," using the End and arrow keys. Blank cells ruin this ability.

- The title is boring. Most people would agree that Sum of Revenue is an annoying title.

- Some captions are extraneous. Invoice Date floating in cell T2 of Figure 11.8 really does not belong in a report.

- The default alphabetical sort order is rarely useful. Product line managers are going to want the top markets at the top of the list. It would be helpful to have the report sorted in descending order by revenue.

- The borders are ugly. Excel draws in a myriad of borders that really make the report look awful.

- The default number format is General. It would be better to set this up as data with commas to serve as thousands separators, or perhaps even data in thousands or millions.

- Pivot tables offer no intelligent page break logic. If you want to be able to produce one report for each Line of Business manager, there is no fast method for indicating that each product should be on a new page.

11

- Because of the page break problem, you may find it is easier to do away with the pivot table's subtotal rows and have the `Subtotal` method add subtotal rows with page breaks. You need a way to turn off the pivot table subtotal rows offered for Product in Figure 11.8. These rows show up automatically whenever you have two or more row fields. If you had four row fields, you would want to turn off the automatic subtotals for the three outermost row fields.

Even with all these problems in default pivot tables, they are still the way to go. You can overcome each complaint, either by using special settings within the pivot table or by entering a few lines of code after the pivot table is created and then copied to a regular dataset.

Eliminating Blank Cells in the Values Area

People started complaining about the blank cells immediately when pivot tables were first introduced. Anyone using Excel 97 or later can easily replace blank cells with zeros. In the user interface, you can find the setting on the Layout & Format tab of the PivotTable Options dialog box. Choose the For Empty Cells, Show option and type **0** in the box.

The equivalent operation in VBA is to set the `NullString` property for the pivot table to `"0"`.

> **NOTE**   Although the proper code is to set this value to a text zero, Excel actually puts a real zero in the empty cells.

Ensuring Table Layout Is Utilized

In previous versions of Excel, multiple row fields appeared in multiple columns. Three layouts are now available. The Compact layout squeezes all the row fields into a single column.

To prevent this outcome and ensure that your pivot table is in the classic table layout, use this code:

```
PT.RowAxisLayout xlTabularRow
```

Controlling the Sort Order with AutoSort

The Excel user interface offers an AutoSort option that enables you to show markets in descending order based on revenue. The equivalent code in VBA to sort the product field by descending revenue uses the `AutoSort` method:

```
PT.PivotFields("Market").AutoSort Order:=xlDescending, _
    Field:="Sum of Revenue"
```

Changing Default Number Format

To change the number format in the user interface, choose a revenue field, click PivotTable Tools Options, Active Field, Field Settings, Number Format. Then choose an appropriate number format.

When you have large numbers, displaying the thousands separator helps the person reading the report. To set up this format in VBA code, use the following:

```
PT.PivotFields("Sum of Revenue").NumberFormat = "#,##0"
```

Some companies have customers who typically buy thousands or millions of dollars' worth of goods. You can display numbers in thousands by using a single comma after the number format. Of course, you need to include a K abbreviation to indicate that the numbers are in thousands:

```
PT.PivotFields("Sum of Revenue").NumberFormat = "#,##0,K"
```

Of course, local custom dictates the thousands abbreviation. If you are working for a relatively young computer company where everyone uses K for the thousands separator, you're in luck because Microsoft makes it easy to use this abbreviation. However, if you work at a 100+ year-old soap company where you use M for thousands and MM for millions, you have a few more hurdles to jump. You are required to prefix the M character with a backslash to have it work:

```
PT.PivotFields("Sum of Revenue").NumberFormat = "#,##0,\M"
```

Alternatively, you can surround the M character with double quotation marks. To put double quotation marks inside a quoted string in VBA, you must put two sequential quotation marks. To set up a format in tenths of millions that uses the #,##0.0,,"MM" format, you would use this line of code:

```
PT.PivotFields("Sum of Revenue").NumberFormat = "#,##0.0,, ""M"""
```

Here, the format is quotation mark, pound, comma, pound, pound, zero, period, zero, comma, comma, quotation mark, quotation mark, M, quotation mark, quotation mark, quotation mark. The three quotation marks at the end are correct. You use two quotation marks to simulate typing one quotation mark in the custom number format box and a final quotation mark to close the string in VBA.

Suppressing Subtotals for Multiple Row Fields

As soon as you have more than one row field, Excel automatically adds subtotals for all but the innermost row field. However, you may want to suppress subtotals for any number of reasons. Although accomplishing this task manually may be relatively simple, the VBA code to suppress subtotals is surprisingly complex.

You must set the Subtotals property equal to an array of 12 False values. Read the VBA help for all the gory details, but it goes something like this: The first False turns off automatic subtotals, the second False turns off the Sum subtotal, the third False turns off the Count subtotal, and so on. It is interesting that you have to turn off all 12 possible subtotals, even though Excel displays only one subtotal. This line of code suppresses the Product subtotal:

```
PT.PivotFields("Product").Subtotals = Array(False, False, False, False, _
    False, False, False, False, False, False, False, False)
```

A different technique is to turn on the first subtotal. This method automatically turns off the other 11 subtotals. You can then turn off the first subtotal to make sure that all subtotals are suppressed:

```
PT.PivotFields("Product").Subtotals(1) = True
PT.PivotFields("Product").Subtotals(1) = False
```

Suppressing Grand Total for Rows

Because you are going to be using VBA code to add automatic subtotals, you can get rid of the Grand Total row. If you turn off Grand Total for Rows, you delete the column called Grand Total. Thus, to get rid of the Grand Total row, you must uncheck Grand Total for Columns. This is handled in the code with the following line:

```
PT.ColumnGrand = False
```

Handling Additional Annoyances When Creating Your Final Report

You've reached the end of the adjustments that you can make to the pivot table. To achieve the final report, you have to make the remaining adjustments after converting the pivot table to regular data.

Figure 11.9 shows the pivot table with all the adjustments described in the preceding sections and with `PT.TableRange2` selected.

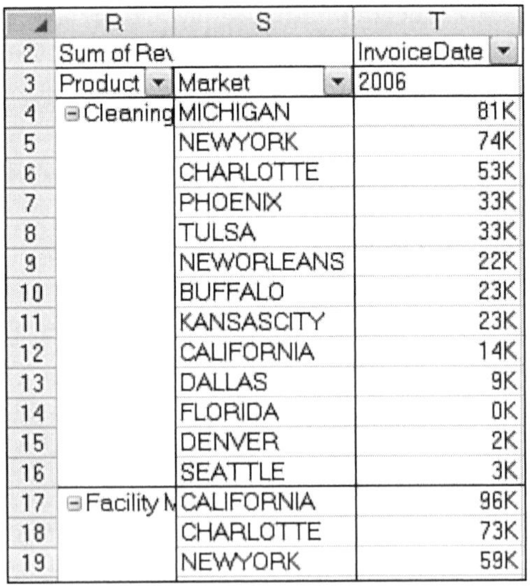

Figure 11.9
Getting 90% of the way to the final report took less than one second and fewer than 30 lines of code. To solve the last five annoying problems, you have to change this data from a pivot table to regular data.

	R	S	T
2	Sum of Rev		InvoiceDate
3	Product	Market	2006
4	Cleaning	MICHIGAN	81K
5		NEWYORK	74K
6		CHARLOTTE	53K
7		PHOENIX	33K
8		TULSA	33K
9		NEWORLEANS	22K
10		BUFFALO	23K
11		KANSASCITY	23K
12		CALIFORNIA	14K
13		DALLAS	9K
14		FLORIDA	0K
15		DENVER	2K
16		SEATTLE	3K
17	Facility M	CALIFORNIA	96K
18		CHARLOTTE	73K
19		NEWYORK	59K

Creating a New Workbook to Hold the Report

Say you want to build the report in a new workbook so that it can be easily mailed to the product managers. Doing this is fairly easy. To make the code more portable, assign object variables to the original workbook, new workbook, and first worksheet in the new workbook. At the top of the procedure, add these statements:

```
Dim WSR As Worksheet
Dim WBO As Workbook
Dim WBN As Workbook
Set WBO = ActiveWorkbook
Set WSD = Worksheets("Pivot Table")
```

After the pivot table has been successfully created, build a blank Report workbook with this code:

```
' Create a New Blank Workbook with one Worksheet
Set WBN = Workbooks.Add(xlWorksheet)
Set WSR = WBN.Worksheets(1)
WSR.Name = "Report"
' Set up Title for Report
With WSR.Range("A1")
    .Value = "Revenue by Market and Year"
    .Font.Size = 14
End With
```

Creating a Summary on a Blank Report Worksheet

Imagine that you have submitted the pivot table in Figure 11.9, and your manager hates the borders, hates the title, and hates the words "Invoice Date" in cell T2. You can solve all three of these problems by excluding the first row(s) of `PT.TableRange2` from the `.Copy` method and then using `PasteSpecial(xlPasteValuesAndNumberFormats)` to copy the data to the report sheet.

<table>
<tr><td>

CAUTION

In Excel 2000 and earlier, `xlPasteValuesAndNumberFormats` was not available. You had to use Paste Special twice: once as `xlPasteValues` and once as `xlPasteFormats`.

</td></tr>
</table>

In the current example, the `.TableRange2` property includes only one row to eliminate, row 2, as shown in Figure 11.9. If you had a more complex pivot table with several column fields and/or one or more page fields, you would have to eliminate more than just the first row of the report. It helps to run your macro to this point, look at the result, and figure out how many rows you need to delete. You can effectively not copy these rows to the report by using the `Offset` property. Copy the `TableRange2` property, offset by one row. Purists will note that this code copies one extra blank row from below the pivot table, but this really does not matter because the row is blank. After copying, you can erase the original pivot table and destroy the pivot cache:

```
' Copy the Pivot Table data to row 3 of the Report sheet
' Use Offset to eliminate the title row of the pivot table
PT.TableRange2.Offset(1, 0).Copy
WSR. Range("A3").PasteSpecial Paste:=xlPasteValuesAndNumberFormats
PT.TableRange2.Clear
Set PTCache = Nothing
```

Note that you use the Paste Special option to paste just values and number formats. This gets rid of both borders and the pivot nature of the table. You might be tempted to use the All Except Borders option under Paste, but this keeps the data in a pivot table, and you won't be able to insert new rows in the middle of the data.

Filling the Outline View

The report is almost complete. You are nearly a Data, Subtotals command away from having everything you need. Before you can use the Subtotals command, however, you need to fill in all the blank cells in the Outline view of column A.

Fixing the Outline view requires just a few obscure steps. Here are the steps in the user interface:

1. Select all the cells in column A that make up the report.

2. Select Home, Editing, Find & Select, Go To Special to bring up the Go To Special dialog box. Select Blanks to select only the blank cells.

3. Enter an R1C1-style formula to fill the blank with the cell above it. This formula is =R[1]C. In the user interface, you would type an equal sign, press the up-arrow key, and then press Ctrl+Enter.

4. Reselect all the cells in column A that make up the report. This step is necessary because the Paste Special step cannot work with noncontiguous selections.

5. Copy the formulas in column A and convert them to values by choosing Home, Clipboard, Paste, Paste Values.

Fixing the Outline view in VBA requires fewer steps. The equivalent VBA logic is shown here:

1. Find the last row of the report.

2. Enter the formula =R[-1]C in the blank cells in A.

3. Change those formulas to values. The code to do this follows:

```
Dim FinalReportRow as Long
    ' Fill in the Outline view in column A
    ' Look for last row in column B since many rows
    ' in column A are blank
FinalReportRow = WSR.Cells(Rows.Count, 2).End(xlUp).Row
With Range("A3").Resize(FinalReportRow - 2, 1)
    With .SpecialCells(xlCellTypeBlanks)
        .FormulaR1C1 = "=R[-1]C"
    End With
    .Value = .Value
End With
```

Handling Final Formatting

The last steps for the report involve some basic formatting tasks and then adding the subtotals. You can bold and right-justify the headings in row 3. Set up rows 1–3 so that the top three rows print on each page:

```
' Do some basic formatting
' Autofit columns, bold the headings, right-align
Selection.Columns.AutoFit
Range("A3").EntireRow.Font.Bold = True
Range("A3").EntireRow.HorizontalAlignment = xlRight
Range("A3:B3").HorizontalAlignment = xlLeft

' Repeat rows 1-3 at the top of each page
WSR.PageSetup.PrintTitleRows = "$1:$3"
```

Adding Subtotals

Automatic subtotals are a powerful feature found on the Data menu. Figure 11.10 shows the Subtotal dialog box. Note the option Page Break Between Groups.

If you were sure that you would always have three years and a total, the code to add subtotals for each Line of Business group would be the following:

```
' Add Subtotals by Product.
' Be sure to add a page break at each change in product
Selection.Subtotal GroupBy:=1, Function:=xlSum, TotalList:=Array(3, 4, 5, 6), _
    PageBreaks:=True
```

Figure 11.10
Use automatic subtotals because doing so enables you to add a page break after each product. Using this feature ensures that each product manager has a clean report with only her product on it.

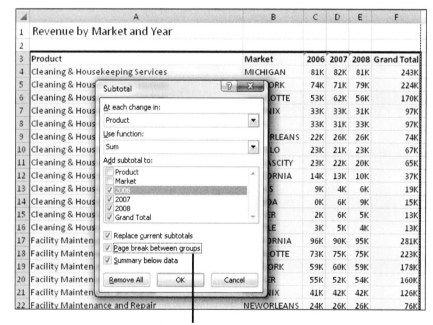

Add page breaks

However, this code fails if you have more or less than three years. The solution is to use the following convoluted code to dynamically build a list of the columns to total, based on the number of columns in the report:

```
Dim TotColumns()
Dim I as Integer
FinalCol = Cells(3, Columns.Count).End(xlToLeft).Column
ReDim Preserve TotColumns(1 To FinalCol - 2)
For i = 3 To FinalCol
    TotColumns(i - 2) = i
Next i
Selection.Subtotal GroupBy:=1, Function:=xlSum, TotalList:=TotColumns,_
    Replace:=True, PageBreaks:=True, SummaryBelowData:=True
```

Finally, with the new totals added to the report, you need to autofit the numeric columns again with this code:

```
Dim GrandRow as Long
' Make sure the columns are wide enough for totals
GrandRow = Cells(Rows.Count, 1).End(xlUp).Row
Cells(3, 3).Resize(GrandRow - 2, FinalCol - 2).Columns.AutoFit
Cells(GrandRow, 3).Resize(1, FinalCol - 2).NumberFormat = "#,##0,K"
' Add a page break before the Grand Total row, otherwise
' the product manager for the final Line will have two totals
WSR.HPageBreaks.Add Before:=Cells(GrandRow, 1)
```

Putting It All Together

Listing 11.3 produces the product line manager reports in a few seconds.

Listing 11.3   Code That Produces the Product Line Report in Figure 11.11

```
Sub ProductLineReport()
    ' Product and Market as Row
    ' Years as Column
    Dim WSD As Worksheet
    Dim PTCache As PivotCache
    Dim PT As PivotTable
    Dim PRange As Range
    Dim FinalRow As Long
    Dim TotColumns()

    Set WSD = Worksheets("PivotTable")
    Dim WSR As Worksheet
    Dim WBO As Workbook
    Dim WBN As Workbook
    Set WBO = ActiveWorkbook

    ' Delete any prior pivot tables
    For Each PT In WSD.PivotTables
        PT.TableRange2.Clear
    Next PT
    WSD.Range("R1:AZ1").EntireColumn.Clear

    ' Define input area and set up a Pivot Cache
    FinalRow = WSD.Cells(Rows.Count, 1).End(xlUp).Row
    FinalCol = WSD.Cells(1, Columns.Count). _
        End(xlToLeft).Column
    Set PRange = WSD.Cells(1, 1).Resize(FinalRow, FinalCol)
    Set PTCache = ActiveWorkbook.PivotCaches.Add(SourceType:= _
        xlDatabase, SourceData:=PRange.Address)
```

```vba
' Create the Pivot Table from the Pivot Cache
Set PT = PTCache.CreatePivotTable(TableDestination:=WSD. _
    Cells(2, FinalCol + 2), TableName:="PivotTable1")

' Turn off updating while building the table
PT.ManualUpdate = True

' Set up the row fields
PT.AddFields RowFields:=Array("Product", "Market"), _
    ColumnFields:="InvoiceDate"
' Ensure table layout, with each row field in a new column
PT.RowAxisLayout xlTabularRow


' Set up the data fields
With PT.PivotFields("Revenue")
    .Orientation = xlDataField
    .Function = xlSum
    .Position = 1
    .NumberFormat = "#,##0,K"
End With

' Calc the pivot table
PT.ManualUpdate = False
PT.ManualUpdate = True

' Group by Year
WSD.Activate
Cells(3, FinalCol + 4).Group Start:=True, End:=True, _
    Periods:=Array(False, False, False, False, False, False, True)

' Replace blanks with zero
PT.NullString = "0"

' Remove subtotals by product
PT.PivotFields("Product").Subtotals(1) = True
PT.PivotFields("Product").Subtotals(1) = False
PT.ColumnGrand = False

' Sort descending by revenue
PT.PivotFields("Market").AutoSort Order:=xlDescending, _
    Field:="Sum of Revenue"

' Calc the pivot table
PT.ManualUpdate = False
PT.ManualUpdate = True

'   PT.TableRange2.Select

' Create a New Blank Workbook with one Worksheet
Set WBN = Workbooks.Add(xlWBATWorksheet)
Set WSR = WBN.Worksheets(1)
WSR.Name = "Report"
' Set up Title for Report
With WSR.[A1]
    .Value = "Revenue by Market and Year"
```

11

continues

Listing 11.3 Continued

```
        .Font.Size = 14
    End With

    ' Copy the Pivot Table data to row 3 of the Report sheet
    ' Use Offset to eliminate the title row of the pivot table
    PT.TableRange2.Offset(1, 0).Copy
    WSR.[A3].PasteSpecial Paste:=xlPasteValuesAndNumberFormats
    PT.TableRange2.Clear
    Set PTCache = Nothing

    ' Fill in the Outline view in column A
    ' Look for last row in column B since many rows
    ' in column A are blank
    FinalReportRow = WSR.Cells(Rows.Count, 2).End(xlUp).Row
    With Range("A3").Resize(FinalReportRow - 2, 1)
        With .SpecialCells(xlCellTypeBlanks)
            .FormulaR1C1 = "=R[-1]C"
        End With
        .Value = .Value
    End With

    ' Do some basic formatting
    ' Autofit columns, bold the headings, right-align
    Selection.Columns.AutoFit
    Range("A3").EntireRow.Font.Bold = True
    Range("A3").EntireRow.HorizontalAlignment = xlRight
    Range("A3:B3").HorizontalAlignment = xlLeft

    ' Repeat rows 1-3 at the top of each page
    WSR.PageSetup.PrintTitleRows = "$1:$3"

    ' Add subtotals
    FinalCol = Cells(3, Columns.Count).End(xlToLeft).Column
    ReDim Preserve TotColumns(1 To FinalCol - 2)
    For i = 3 To FinalCol
        TotColumns(i - 2) = i
    Next i
    Selection.Subtotal GroupBy:=1, Function:=xlSum, _
        TotalList:=TotColumns, Replace:=True, _
        PageBreaks:=True, SummaryBelowData:=True

    ' Make sure the columns are wide enough for totals
    GrandRow = WSR.Cells(Rows.Count, 1).End(xlUp).Row
    Cells(3, 3).Resize(GrandRow - 2, FinalCol - 2).Columns.AutoFit
    Cells(GrandRow, 3).Resize(1, FinalCol - 2).NumberFormat = "#,##0,K"
    ' Add a page break before the Grand Total row, otherwise
    ' the product manager for the final Line will have two totals
    WSR.HPageBreaks.Add Before:=Cells(GrandRow, 1)

End Sub
```

Figure 11.11 shows the report produced by this code.

	A	B	C	D	E	F
1	Revenue by Market and Year					
2						
3	Product	Market	2006	2007	2008	Grand Total
4	Cleaning & Housekeeping Services	MICHIGAN	81K	82K	81K	243K
5	Cleaning & Housekeeping Services	NEWYORK	74K	71K	79K	224K
6	Cleaning & Housekeeping Services	CHARLOTTE	53K	62K	56K	170K
7	Cleaning & Housekeeping Services	PHOENIX	33K	33K	31K	97K
8	Cleaning & Housekeeping Services	TULSA	33K	31K	33K	97K
9	Cleaning & Housekeeping Services	NEWORLEANS	22K	26K	26K	74K
10	Cleaning & Housekeeping Services	BUFFALO	23K	21K	23K	67K
11	Cleaning & Housekeeping Services	KANSASCITY	23K	22K	20K	65K
12	Cleaning & Housekeeping Services	CALIFORNIA	14K	13K	10K	37K
13	Cleaning & Housekeeping Services	DALLAS	9K	4K	6K	19K
14	Cleaning & Housekeeping Services	FLORIDA	0K	6K	9K	15K
15	Cleaning & Housekeeping Services	DENVER	2K	6K	5K	13K
16	Cleaning & Housekeeping Services	SEATTLE	3K	5K	4K	13K
17	Cleaning & Housekeeping Services Total		370K	381K	382K	1,133K
18	Facility Maintenance and Repair	CALIFORNIA	96K	90K	95K	281K
19	Facility Maintenance and Repair	CHARLOTTE	73K	75K	75K	223K

Figure 11.11
Converting 50,000 rows of transactional data to this useful report takes less than two seconds if you use the code that produced this example. Without pivot tables, the code would be far more complex.

Addressing Issues with Two or More Data Fields

So far, you have built some powerful summary reports, but you've touched only a portion of the powerful features available in pivot tables. The preceding example produced a report but had only one data field. It is possible to have multiple fields in the Σ Values section of a pivot report. The data in this example includes not just revenue, but also a count of customers.

When you have two or more data fields, you have a choice of placing the data fields in one of four locations. By default, Excel builds the pivot report with the data field as the innermost column field. It is often preferable to have the data field as the outermost row field.

When a pivot table is going to have more than one data field, you have a virtual field named Σ Values in the drop zones of the PivotTable Field List. In VBA, this equivalent virtual field is named Data.

Where you place the data field in the `.AddFields` method determines which view of the data you get. The default setup, with the data fields arranged as the innermost column field, as shown in Figure 11.12, would have this `AddFields` line:

```
PT.AddFields ColumnFields:=Array("Region", "Data")
```

The view shown in Figure 11.13 would use this code:

```
PT.AddFields RowFields:=Array("Data", "Product"")
```

One view that would make sense would have Data as the only column field:

```
PT.AddFields RowFields:="Product", ColumnFields:="Data"
```

After adding a column field called Data, you would then go on to define two data fields:

```
' Set up the data fields
With PT.PivotFields("Revenue")
    .Orientation = xlDataField
    .Function = xlSum
    .Position = 1
    .NumberFormat = "#,##0,K"
End With
```

```
With PT.PivotFields("Units")
    .Orientation = xlDataField
    .Function = xlSum
    .Position = 2
    .NumberFormat = "#,##0"
End With
```

Figure 11.12
The default pivot table report has multiple data fields as the innermost column field.

Figure 11.13
By moving the data field to the first row field, you can obtain this view of the multiple data fields.

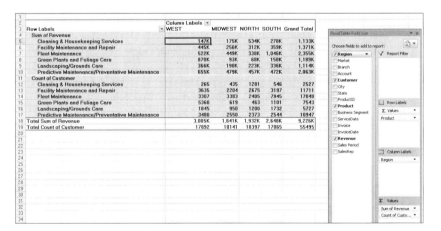

Calculated Data Fields

Pivot tables offer two types of formulas. The most useful type defines a formula for a calculated field. This adds a new field to the pivot table. Calculations for calculated fields are always done at the summary level. If you define a calculated field for average price as Revenue divided by Units Sold, Excel first adds the total revenue and total quantity, and then it does the division of these totals to get the result. In many cases, this is exactly what you need. If your calculation does not follow the associative law of mathematics, it might not work as you expect.

To set up a calculated field, use the Add method with the CalculatedFields object. You have to specify a field name and a formula. Note that if you create a field called Average Price, the default pivot table produces a field called Sum of Average Price. This title is misleading and downright silly. What you have is actually the average of the sums of prices. The solution is to use the Name property when defining the data field to replace Sum of Average Price with something such as Avg Price. Note that this name must be different from the name for the calculated field.

Listing 11.4 produces the report shown in Figure 11.14.

Listing 11.4   Code That Calculates an Average Price Field as a Second Data Field

```
Sub TwoDataFields()
    ' Listing 11.4
    Dim WSD As Worksheet
    Dim PTCache As PivotCache
    Dim PT As PivotTable
    Dim PRange As Range
    Dim FinalRow As Long

    Set WSD = Worksheets("PivotTable")
    Dim WSR As Worksheet
    Dim WBO As Workbook
    Dim WBN As Workbook
    Set WBO = ActiveWorkbook

    ' Delete any prior pivot tables
    For Each PT In WSD.PivotTables
        PT.TableRange2.Clear
    Next PT
    WSD.Range("R1:AZ1").EntireColumn.Clear

    ' Define input area and set up a Pivot Cache
    FinalRow = WSD.Cells(Rows.Count, 1).End(xlUp).Row
    FinalCol = WSD.Cells(1, Columns.Count). _
        End(xlToLeft).Column
    Set PRange = WSD.Cells(1, 1).Resize(FinalRow, FinalCol)
    Set PTCache = ActiveWorkbook.PivotCaches.Add(SourceType:= _
        xlDatabase, SourceData:=PRange.Address)

    ' Create the Pivot Table from the Pivot Cache
    Set PT = PTCache.CreatePivotTable(TableDestination:=WSD. _
        Cells(2, FinalCol + 2), TableName:="PivotTable1")

    ' Turn off updating while building the table
    PT.ManualUpdate = True
```

continues

Listing 11.4   Continued

```
' Set up the row fields
PT.AddFields RowFields:="Product", ColumnFields:="Data"

' Define Calculated Fields
PT.CalculatedFields.Add Name:="AveragePrice", Formula:="=Revenue/Units"

' Set up the data fields
With PT.PivotFields("Revenue")
    .Orientation = xlDataField
    .Function = xlSum
    .Position = 1
    .NumberFormat = "$#,##0,K"
End With

With PT.PivotFields("Units")
    .Orientation = xlDataField
    .Function = xlSum
    .Position = 2
    .NumberFormat = "#,##0"
End With

With PT.PivotFields("AveragePrice")
    .Orientation = xlDataField
    .Function = xlSum
    .Position = 3
    .NumberFormat = "$#,##0.00"
    .Name = "Avg Price"
End With

' Ensure that we get zeros instead of blanks in the data area
PT.NullString = "0"

' Calc the pivot table
PT.ManualUpdate = False
PT.ManualUpdate = True

WSD.Activate
Range("R1").Select

End Sub
```

Calculated Items

Say that in your company one manager is responsible for Landscaping/Grounds Care and Green Plants and Foliage Care. The idea behind a calculated item is that you can define a new item along the Product field to calculate the total of these two items. Listing 11.5 produces the report shown in Figure 11.15.

Figure 11.14

The virtual Data dimension contains two fields from your dataset plus a calculation. It is shown along the column area of the report.

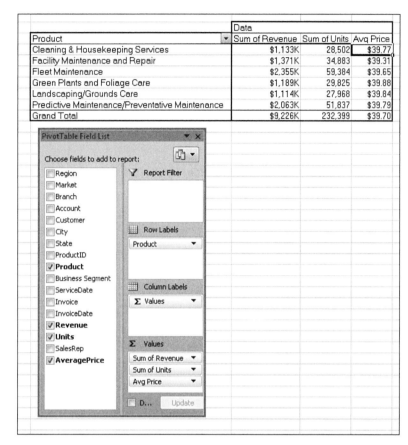

Listing 11.5   Code That Adds a New Item Along the Product Dimension

```
Sub CalcItemsProblem()
    ' Listing 11.5
    Dim WSD As Worksheet
    Dim PTCache As PivotCache
    Dim PT As PivotTable
    Dim PRange As Range
    Dim FinalRow As Long

    Set WSD = Worksheets("PivotTable")
    Dim WSR As Worksheet

    ' Delete any prior pivot tables
    For Each PT In WSD.PivotTables
        PT.TableRange2.Clear
    Next PT
    WSD.Range("R1:AZ1").EntireColumn.Clear
```

continues

Listing 11.5   Continued

```
' Define input area and set up a Pivot Cache
FinalRow = WSD.Cells(Rows.Count, 1).End(xlUp).Row
FinalCol = WSD.Cells(1, Columns.Count). _
    End(xlToLeft).Column
Set PRange = WSD.Cells(1, 1).Resize(FinalRow, FinalCol)
Set PTCache = ActiveWorkbook.PivotCaches.Add(SourceType:= _
    xlDatabase, SourceData:=PRange.Address)

' Create the Pivot Table from the Pivot Cache
Set PT = PTCache.CreatePivotTable(TableDestination:=WSD. _
    Cells(2, FinalCol + 2), TableName:="PivotTable1")

' Turn off updating while building the table
PT.ManualUpdate = True

' Set up the row fields
PT.AddFields RowFields:="Product"

' Define calculated item along the product dimension
PT.PivotFields("Product").CalculatedItems _
    .Add "Plants Group", _
    "='Landscaping/Grounds Care'+'Green Plants and Foliage Care'"

' Resequence so that the report Landscaping First
PT.PivotFields("Product"). _
    PivotItems("Landscaping/Grounds Care").Position = 1
PT.PivotFields("Product"). _
    PivotItems("Green Plants and Foliage Care").Position = 2
PT.PivotFields("Product"). _
    PivotItems("Plants Group").Position = 3

' Set up the data fields
With PT.PivotFields("Revenue")
    .Orientation = xlDataField
    .Function = xlSum
    .Position = 1
    .NumberFormat = "#,##0"
End With

' Ensure that we get zeros instead of blanks in the data area
PT.NullString = "0"

' Calc the pivot table
PT.ManualUpdate = False
PT.ManualUpdate = True
WSD.Activate
Range("R1").Select

End Sub
```

Figure 11.15
Unless you love restating numbers to the Securities and Exchange Commission, avoid using calculated items.

Sum of Revenue	
Product ▼	Total
Landscaping/Grounds Care	1,114,160
Green Plants and Foliage Care	1,189,306
Plants Group	2,303,466
Cleaning & Housekeeping Services	1,133,484
Facility Maintenance and Repair	1,371,359
Fleet Maintenance	2,354,623
Predictive Maintenance/Preventative Maintenance	2,062,835
Grand Total	11,529,233

Look closely at the results shown in Figure 11.15. The calculation for Plants Group is correct. The approximate $2.3 million for the Plants Group is the sum of $1.1 million of landscaping and $1.2 million of Green Plants. However, the grand total should be about $9.2 million. Instead, Excel gives you a grand total of $11.6 million. The total revenue for the company just increased by $2.3 million. Excel gives the wrong grand total when a field contains both regular and calculated items. The only plausible method for dealing with this situation is to attempt to hide the products that make up the Plants Group:

```
With PT.PivotFields("Product")
    .PivotItems("Landscaping/Grounds Care").Visible = False
    .PivotItems("Green Plants and Foliage Care").Visible = False
End With
```

The results are shown in Figure 11.16.

Figure 11.16
After the components that make up the calculated Plants Group item are hidden, the total revenue for the company is again correct. However, it would be easier to add a new field to the original data with a Responsibility field.

Sum of Revenue	
Product ▼	Total
Plants Group	2,303,466
Cleaning & Housekeeping Services	1,133,484
Facility Maintenance and Repair	1,371,359
Fleet Maintenance	2,354,623
Predictive Maintenance/Preventative Maintenance	2,062,835
Grand Total	9,225,767

Summarizing Date Fields with Grouping

With transactional data, you often find your date-based summaries having one row per day. Although daily data might be useful to a plant manager, many people in the company want to see totals by month or quarter and year.

The great news is that Excel handles the summarization of dates in a pivot table with ease. For anyone who has ever had to use the arcane formula =A2+1-Day(A2) to change daily dates into monthly dates, you will appreciate the ease with which you can group transactional data into months or quarters.

Creating a group with VBA is a bit quirky. The .Group method can be applied to only a single cell in the pivot table, and that cell must contain a date or the Date field label. This is the first example in this chapter where you must allow VBA to calculate an intermediate pivot table result.

You must define a pivot table with Invoice Date in the row field. Turn off ManualCalculation to allow the Date field to be drawn. You can then use the LabelRange property to locate the date label and group from there. Figure 11.17 shows the result of Listing 11.6.

Figure 11.17

The In Balance Date field is now composed of three fields in the pivot table, representing year, quarter, and month.

Sum of Revenue				Region ▼	
Years ▼	Quarters ▼	InvoiceDate ▼		WEST	MIDWEST N
⊟2006	⊟Qtr1	Jan		67,576	30,920
		Feb		104,759	59,787
		Mar		65,539	34,845
	⊟Qtr2	Apr		87,919	51,608
		May		89,887	51,192
		Jun		82,794	44,692
	⊟Qtr3	Jul		92,481	50,590
		Aug		93,391	45,958
		Sep		78,439	42,088

11

Listing 11.6   Code That Uses the Group Feature to Roll Daily Dates Up to Monthly Dates

```
Sub ReportByMonth()
    ' Listing 11.6
    Dim WSD As Worksheet
    Dim PTCache As PivotCache
    Dim PT As PivotTable
    Dim PRange As Range
    Dim FinalRow As Long

    Set WSD = Worksheets("PivotTable")
    Dim WSR As Worksheet

    ' Delete any prior pivot tables
    For Each PT In WSD.PivotTables
        PT.TableRange2.Clear
    Next PT
    WSD.Range("R1:AZ1").EntireColumn.Clear

    ' Define input area and set up a Pivot Cache
    FinalRow = WSD.Cells(Rows.Count, 1).End(xlUp).Row
    FinalCol = WSD.Cells(1, Columns.Count). _
        End(xlToLeft).Column
    Set PRange = WSD.Cells(1, 1).Resize(FinalRow, FinalCol)
    Set PTCache = ActiveWorkbook.PivotCaches.Add(SourceType:= _
        xlDatabase, SourceData:=PRange.Address)

    ' Create the Pivot Table from the Pivot Cache
    Set PT = PTCache.CreatePivotTable(TableDestination:=WSD. _
        Cells(2, FinalCol + 2), TableName:="PivotTable1")

    ' Turn off updating while building the table
    PT.ManualUpdate = True
```

```
    ' Set up the row fields
    PT.AddFields RowFields:="InvoiceDate", ColumnFields:="Region"

    ' Set up the data fields
    With PT.PivotFields("Revenue")
        .Orientation = xlDataField
        .Function = xlSum
        .Position = 1
        .NumberFormat = "#,##0"
    End With

    ' Ensure that we get zeros instead of blanks in the data area
    PT.NullString = "0"

    ' Calc the pivot table to allow the date label to be drawn
    PT.ManualUpdate = False
    PT.ManualUpdate = True
    WSD.Activate

    ' Group ShipDate by Month, Quarter, Year
    PT.PivotFields("InvoiceDate").LabelRange.Group Start:=True, _
        End:=True, Periods:= _
        Array(False, False, False, False, True, True, True)

    ' Calc the pivot table
    PT.ManualUpdate = False
    PT.ManualUpdate = True
    WSD.Activate
    Range("R1").Select

End Sub
```

Group by Week

You probably noticed that Excel allows you to group by day, month, quarter, and year. There is no standard grouping for week. You can, however, define a group that bunches groups of seven days.

By default, Excel starts the week based on the first date found in the data. This means that the default week would run from Thursday, January 5, 2006, through Wednesday, December 31, 2008. You can override this by changing the Start parameter from True to an actual date. Use the WeekDay function to determine how many days to adjust the start date.

There is one limitation to grouping by week. When you group by week, you cannot also group by any other measure. Grouping by week and quarter is not valid.

Listing 11.7 creates the report shown in Figure 11.18.

Figure 11.18
Use the Number of Days setting to group by week.

Sum of Revenue	Region ▼	
InvoiceDate ▼	WEST	MIDWEST
1/2/2006 – 1/8/2006	9,828	5,513
1/9/2006 – 1/15/2006	20,405	9,189
1/16/2006 – 1/22/2006	14,013	8,017
1/23/2006 – 1/29/2006	15,758	5,563
1/30/2006 – 2/5/2006	18,759	9,025
2/6/2006 – 2/12/2006	29,668	16,976
2/13/2006 – 2/19/2006	26,972	14,577
2/20/2006 – 2/26/2006	26,097	15,591

Listing 11.7   Code That Uses the Group Feature to Roll Daily Dates Up to Weekly Dates

```
Sub ReportByWeek()
    ' Listing 11.7
    Dim WSD As Worksheet
    Dim PTCache As PivotCache
    Dim PT As PivotTable
    Dim PRange As Range
    Dim FinalRow As Long

    Set WSD = Worksheets("PivotTable")
    Dim WSR As Worksheet

    ' Delete any prior pivot tables
    For Each PT In WSD.PivotTables
        PT.TableRange2.Clear
    Next PT
    WSD.Range("R1:AZ1").EntireColumn.Clear

    ' Define input area and set up a Pivot Cache
    FinalRow = WSD.Cells(Rows.Count, 1).End(xlUp).Row
    FinalCol = WSD.Cells(1, Columns.Count). _
        End(xlToLeft).Column
    Set PRange = WSD.Cells(1, 1).Resize(FinalRow, FinalCol)
    Set PTCache = ActiveWorkbook.PivotCaches.Add(SourceType:= _
        xlDatabase, SourceData:=PRange.Address)

    ' Create the Pivot Table from the Pivot Cache
    Set PT = PTCache.CreatePivotTable(TableDestination:=WSD. _
        Cells(2, FinalCol + 2), TableName:="PivotTable1")

    ' Turn off updating while building the table
    PT.ManualUpdate = True

    ' Set up the row fields
    PT.AddFields RowFields:="InvoiceDate", ColumnFields:="Region"

    ' Set up the data fields
    With PT.PivotFields("Revenue")
        .Orientation = xlDataField
        .Function = xlSum
        .Position = 1
        .NumberFormat = "#,##0"
    End With
```

```
    ' Ensure that we get zeros instead of blanks in the data area
    PT.NullString = "0"

    ' Calc the pivot table to allow the date label to be drawn
    PT.ManualUpdate = False
    PT.ManualUpdate = True
    WSD.Activate

    ' Group Date by Week.
    'Figure out the first Monday before the minimum date
    FirstDate = Application.Min(PT.PivotFields("InvoiceDate").DataRange)
    WhichDay = Application.WorksheetFunction.Weekday(FirstDate, 3)
    StartDate = FirstDate - WhichDay
    PT.PivotFields("InvoiceDate").LabelRange.Group _
        Start:=StartDate, End:=True, By:=7, _
        Periods:=Array(False, False, False, True, False, False, False)

    ' Calc the pivot table
    PT.ManualUpdate = False
    PT.ManualUpdate = True
    WSD.Activate
    Range("R1").Select

End Sub
```

Using Advanced Pivot Table Techniques

You may be a pivot table pro and never have run into some of the really advanced techniques available with pivot tables. The following sections discuss such techniques.

Using AutoShow to Produce Executive Overviews

If you are designing an executive dashboard utility, you might want to spotlight the top five markets.

As with the AutoSort option, you could be a pivot table pro and never have stumbled across the AutoShow feature in Excel. This setting lets you select either the top or bottom *n* records based on any data field in the report.

The code to use AutoShow in VBA uses the `.AutoShow` method:

```
' Show only the top 5 Markets
PT.PivotFields("Market").AutoShow Top:=xlAutomatic, Range:=xlTop, _
    Count:=5, Field:= "Sum of Revenue"
```

When you create a report using the `.AutoShow` method, it is often helpful to copy the data and then go back to the original pivot report to get the totals for all markets. In the following code, this is achieved by removing the Market field from the pivot table and copying the grand total to the report. Listing 11.8 produces the report shown in Figure 11.19.

Figure 11.19
The Top 5 Markets report contains two pivot tables.

	A	B	C	D	E	F	G	H
1	Top 5 Markets							
2								
3	Market	Cleaning & Housekeeping Services	Facility Maintenance and Repair	Fleet Maintenance	Green Plants and Foliage Care	Landscaping/ Grounds Care	Predictive Maintenance /Preventative Maintenance	Grand Total
4	CALIFORNIA	37,402	281,204	337,225	830,422	248,343	520,156	2,254,752
5	FLORIDA	15,337	0	556,004	85,134	153,011	225,761	1,035,246
6	CHARLOTTE	170,342	223,347	245,120	46,483	80,240	124,983	890,514
7	NEWYORK	223,989	177,842	184,747	24,049	75,804	187,150	873,581
8	DENVER	12,564	160,325	170,188	42,408	73,622	186,477	645,584
9	Top 5 Total	459,633	842,718	1,493,284	1,028,496	631,020	1,244,527	5,699,677
10								
11	Total Company	1,133,484	1,371,359	2,354,623	1,189,306	1,114,160	2,062,835	9,225,767

Listing 11.8   Code Used to Create the Top 5 Markets Report

```
Sub Top5Markets()
    ' Listing 11.8
    ' Produce a report of the top 5 markets
    Dim WSD As Worksheet
    Dim WSR As Worksheet
    Dim WBN As Workbook
    Dim PTCache As PivotCache
    Dim PT As PivotTable
    Dim PRange As Range
    Dim FinalRow As Long
    Set WSD = Worksheets("PivotTable")

    ' Delete any prior pivot tables
    For Each PT In WSD.PivotTables
        PT.TableRange2.Clear
    Next PT
    WSD.Range("R1:AZ1").EntireColumn.Clear

    ' Define input area and set up a Pivot Cache
    FinalRow = WSD.Cells(Rows.Count, 1).End(xlUp).Row
    FinalCol = WSD.Cells(1, Columns.Count). _
        End(xlToLeft).Column
    Set PRange = WSD.Cells(1, 1).Resize(FinalRow, FinalCol)
    Set PTCache = ActiveWorkbook.PivotCaches.Add(SourceType:= _
        xlDatabase, SourceData:=PRange.Address)

    ' Create the Pivot Table from the Pivot Cache
    Set PT = PTCache.CreatePivotTable(TableDestination:=WSD. _
        Cells(2, FinalCol + 2), TableName:="PivotTable1")

    ' Turn off updating while building the table
    PT.ManualUpdate = True

    ' Set up the row fields
    PT.AddFields RowFields:="Market", ColumnFields:="Product"

    ' Set up the data fields
    With PT.PivotFields("Revenue")
        .Orientation = xlDataField
        .Function = xlSum
```

```
        .Position = 1
        .NumberFormat = "#,##0"
        .Name = "Total Revenue"
    End With

    ' Ensure that we get zeros instead of blanks in the data area
    PT.NullString = "0"

    ' Sort markets descending by sum of revenue
    PT.PivotFields("Market").AutoSort Order:=xlDescending, _
        Field:="Total Revenue"

    ' Show only the top 5 markets
    PT.PivotFields("Market").AutoShow Type:=xlAutomatic, Range:=xlTop, _
        Count:=5, Field:="Total Revenue"

    ' Calc the pivot table to allow the date label to be drawn
    PT.ManualUpdate = False
    PT.ManualUpdate = True

    ' Create a new blank workbook with one worksheet
    Set WBN = Workbooks.Add(xlWBATWorksheet)
    Set WSR = WBN.Worksheets(1)
    WSR.Name = "Report"
    ' Set up title for report
    With WSR.[A1]
        .Value = "Top 5 Markets"
        .Font.Size = 14
    End With

    ' Copy the pivot table data to row 3 of the report sheet
    ' Use offset to eliminate the title row of the pivot table
    PT.TableRange2.Offset(1, 0).Copy
    WSR.[A3].PasteSpecial Paste:=xlPasteValuesAndNumberFormats
    LastRow = WSR.Cells(65536, 1).End(xlUp).Row
    WSR.Cells(LastRow, 1).Value = "Top 5 Total"

    ' Go back to the pivot table to get totals without the AutoShow
    PT.PivotFields("Market").Orientation = xlHidden
    PT.ManualUpdate = False
    PT.ManualUpdate = True
    PT.TableRange2.Offset(2, 0).Copy
    WSR.Cells(LastRow + 2, 1).PasteSpecial Paste:=xlPasteValuesAndNumberFormats
    WSR.Cells(LastRow + 2, 1).Value = "Total Company"

    ' Clear the pivot table
    PT.TableRange2.Clear
    Set PTCache = Nothing

    ' Do some basic formatting
    ' Autofit columns, bold the headings, right-align
    WSR.Range(WSR.Range("A3"), WSR.Cells(LastRow + 2, 10)).Columns.AutoFit
    Range("A3").EntireRow.Font.Bold = True
    Range("A3").EntireRow.HorizontalAlignment = xlRight
    Range("A3").HorizontalAlignment = xlLeft

    Range("A2").Select
    MsgBox "CEO Report has been Created"
End Sub
```

The Top 5 Markets report actually contains two snapshots of a pivot table. After using the AutoShow feature to grab the top five markets with their totals, the macro went back to the pivot table, removed the AutoShow option, and grabbed the total of all markets to produce the Total Company row.

Using `ShowDetail` to Filter a Recordset

Take any pivot table in the Excel user interface. Double-click any number in the table. Excel inserts a new sheet in the workbook and copies all the source records that represent that number. In the Excel user interface, this is a great way to perform a drill-down query into a dataset.

The equivalent VBA property is `ShowDetail`. By setting this property to `True` for any cell in the pivot table, you generate a new worksheet with all the records that make up that cell:

```
PT.TableRange2.Offset(2, 1).Resize(1, 1).ShowDetail = True
```

Listing 11.9 produces a pivot table with the total revenue for the top three stores and `ShowDetail` for each of those stores. This is an alternative method to using the Advanced Filter report. The results of this macro are three new sheets. Figure 11.20 shows the first sheet created.

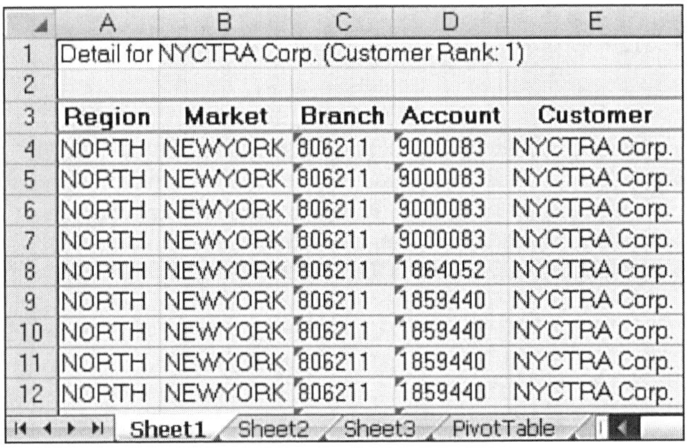

Figure 11.20
Pivot table applications are incredibly diverse. This macro created a pivot table of the top three stores and then used the `ShowDetail` property to retrieve the records for each of those stores.

	A	B	C	D	E
1	Detail for NYCTRA Corp. (Customer Rank: 1)				
2					
3	**Region**	**Market**	**Branch**	**Account**	**Customer**
4	NORTH	NEWYORK	806211	9000083	NYCTRA Corp.
5	NORTH	NEWYORK	806211	9000083	NYCTRA Corp.
6	NORTH	NEWYORK	806211	9000083	NYCTRA Corp.
7	NORTH	NEWYORK	806211	9000083	NYCTRA Corp.
8	NORTH	NEWYORK	806211	1864052	NYCTRA Corp.
9	NORTH	NEWYORK	806211	1859440	NYCTRA Corp.
10	NORTH	NEWYORK	806211	1859440	NYCTRA Corp.
11	NORTH	NEWYORK	806211	1859440	NYCTRA Corp.
12	NORTH	NEWYORK	806211	1859440	NYCTRA Corp.

Sheet1 / Sheet2 / Sheet3 / PivotTable

Listing 11.9   Code Used to Create a Report for Each of the Top 3 Customers

```
Sub RetrieveTop3CustomerDetail()
    ' Listing 11.9
    ' Retrieve Details from Top 3 Stores
    Dim WSD As Worksheet
    Dim WSR As Worksheet
    Dim WBN As Workbook
    Dim PTCache As PivotCache
    Dim PT As PivotTable
    Dim PRange As Range
    Dim FinalRow As Long
    Set WSD = Worksheets("PivotTable")
```

```
' Delete any prior pivot tables
For Each PT In WSD.PivotTables
    PT.TableRange2.Clear
Next PT
WSD.Range("R1:AZ1").EntireColumn.Clear

' Define input area and set up a Pivot Cache
FinalRow = WSD.Cells(Rows.Count, 1).End(xlUp).Row
FinalCol = WSD.Cells(1, Columns.Count). _
    End(xlToLeft).Column
Set PRange = WSD.Cells(1, 1).Resize(FinalRow, FinalCol)
Set PTCache = ActiveWorkbook.PivotCaches.Add(SourceType:= _
    xlDatabase, SourceData:=PRange.Address)

' Create the Pivot Table from the Pivot Cache
Set PT = PTCache.CreatePivotTable(TableDestination:=WSD. _
    Cells(2, FinalCol + 2), TableName:="PivotTable1")

' Turn off updating while building the table
PT.ManualUpdate = True

' Set up the row fields
PT.AddFields RowFields:="Customer", ColumnFields:="Data"

' Set up the data fields
With PT.PivotFields("Revenue")
    .Orientation = xlDataField
    .Function = xlSum
    .Position = 1
    .NumberFormat = "#,##0"
    .Name = "Total Revenue"
End With

' Sort Stores descending by sum of revenue
PT.PivotFields("Customer").AutoSort Order:=xlDescending, _
    Field:="Total Revenue"

' Show only the top 3 stores
PT.PivotFields("Customer").AutoShow Type:=xlAutomatic, Range:=xlTop, _
    Count:=3, Field:="Total Revenue"

' Ensure that we get zeros instead of blanks in the data area
PT.NullString = "0"

' Calc the pivot table to allow the date label to be drawn
PT.ManualUpdate = False
PT.ManualUpdate = True

' Produce summary reports for each customer
For i = 1 To 3
    PT.TableRange2.Offset(i + 1, 1).Resize(1, 1).ShowDetail = True
    ' The active sheet has changed to the new detail report
    ' Add a title
    Range("A1:A2").EntireRow.Insert
    Range("A1").Value = "Detail for " & _
        PT.TableRange2.Offset(i + 1, 0).Resize(1, 1).Value & _
        " (Customer Rank: " & i & ")"
Next i
```

11

continues

Listing 11.9   Continued

```
    MsgBox "Detail reports for top 3 customers have been created."
End Sub
```

Creating Reports for Each Region or Model

A pivot table can have one or more Report Filter fields. A Report Filter field goes in a separate set of rows above the pivot report. It can serve to filter the report to a certain region, certain model, or certain combination of region and model.

In VBA, Report Filter fields are called *page fields*.

To set up a page field in VBA, add the `PageFields` parameter to the `AddFields` method. The following line of code creates a pivot table with Region in the page field:

```
PT.AddFields RowFields:= "Product", ColumnFields:= "Data", PageFields:= "Region"
```

The preceding line of code sets up the Region page field with the value (All), which returns all regions. To limit the report to just the North region, use the `CurrentPage` property:

```
PT.PivotFields("Region").CurrentPage = "North"
```

One use of a page field is to build a user form in which someone can select a particular region or particular product. You then use this information to set the `CurrentPage` property and display the results of the user form.

Another interesting use is to loop through all `PivotItems` and display them one at a time in the page field. You can quickly produce top 10 reports for each region using this method.

To determine how many regions are available in the data, use `PT.PivotFields("Region").PivotItems.Count`. Either of these loops would work:

```
For i = 1 To PT.PivotFields("Region").PivotItems.Count
    PT.PivotFields("Region").CurrentPage = _
            PT.PivotFields("Region").PivotItems(i).Name
    PT.ManualUpdate = False
    PT.ManualUpdate = True
Next i

For Each PivItem In PT.PivotFields("Region").PivotItems
    PT.PivotFields("Region").CurrentPage = PivItem.Name
    PT.ManualUpdate = False
    PT.ManualUpdate = True
Next PivItem
```

Of course, in both of these loops, the three region reports fly by too quickly to see. In practice, you would want to save each report while it is displayed.

So far in this chapter, you have been using `PT.TableRange2` when copying the data from the pivot table. The `TableRange2` property includes all rows of the pivot table, including the page fields. There is also a `.TableRange1` property, which excludes the page fields. You can use either statement to get the detail rows:

```
PT.TableRange2.Offset(3, 0)
PT.TableRange1.Offset(1, 0)
```

Which you use is your preference, but if you use `TableRange2`, you won't have problems when you try to delete the pivot table with `PT.TableRange2.Clear`. If you were to accidentally attempt to clear `TableRange1` when there are page fields, you would end up with the dreaded "Cannot move or change part of a pivot table" error.

Listing 11.10 produces a new workbook for each region, as shown in Figure 11.21.

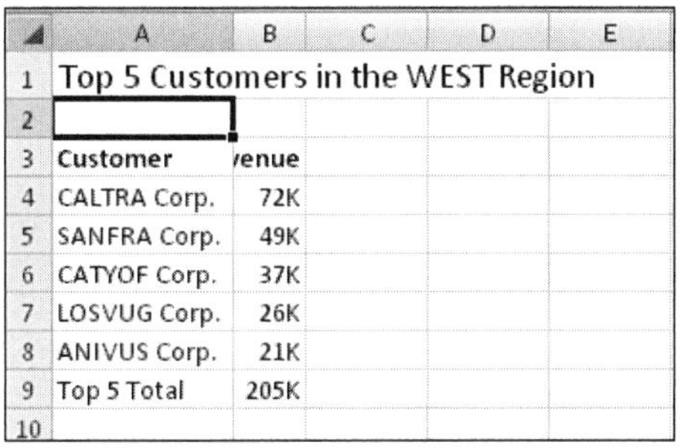

Figure 11.21
By looping through all items found in the Region page field, the macro produced one workbook for each regional manager.

▲	A	B	C	D	E
1	Top 5 Customers in the WEST Region				
2					
3	Customer	/enue			
4	CALTRA Corp.	72K			
5	SANFRA Corp.	49K			
6	CATYOF Corp.	37K			
7	LOSVUG Corp.	26K			
8	ANIVUS Corp.	21K			
9	Top 5 Total	205K			
10					

Listing 11.10   Code That Creates a New Workbook per Region

```
Sub Top5ByRegionReport()
    ' Listing 11.10
    ' Produce a report of top 5 customers for each region
    Dim WSD As Worksheet
    Dim WSR As Worksheet
    Dim WBN As Workbook
    Dim PTCache As PivotCache
    Dim PT As PivotTable
    Dim PRange As Range
    Dim FinalRow As Long

    Set WSD = Worksheets("PivotTable")

    ' Delete any prior pivot tables
    For Each PT In WSD.PivotTables
        PT.TableRange2.Clear
    Next PT
    WSD.Range("R1:AZ1").EntireColumn.Clear

    ' Define input area and set up a Pivot Cache
    FinalRow = WSD.Cells(Rows.Count, 1).End(xlUp).Row
    FinalCol = WSD.Cells(1, Columns.Count). _
        End(xlToLeft).Column
    Set PRange = WSD.Cells(1, 1).Resize(FinalRow, FinalCol)
    Set PTCache = ActiveWorkbook.PivotCaches.Add(SourceType:= _
        xlDatabase, SourceData:=PRange.Address)

    ' Create the Pivot Table from the Pivot Cache
    Set PT = PTCache.CreatePivotTable(TableDestination:=WSD. _
        Cells(2, FinalCol + 2), TableName:="PivotTable1")
```

continues

Listing 11.10   Continued

```vba
' Turn off updating while building the table
PT.ManualUpdate = True

' Set up the row fields
PT.AddFields RowFields:="Customer", ColumnFields:="Data", _
    PageFields:="Region"

' Set up the data fields
With PT.PivotFields("Revenue")
    .Orientation = xlDataField
    .Function = xlSum
    .Position = 1
    .NumberFormat = "#,##0,K"
    .Name = "Total Revenue"
End With

' Sort customers descending by sum of revenue
PT.PivotFields("Customer").AutoSort Order:=xlDescending, _
    Field:="Total Revenue"

' Show only the top 5 stores
PT.PivotFields("Customer").AutoShow Type:=xlAutomatic, Range:=xlTop, _
    Count:=5, Field:="Total Revenue"

' Ensure that we get zeros instead of blanks in the data area
PT.NullString = "0"

' Calc the pivot table
PT.ManualUpdate = False
PT.ManualUpdate = True
Ctr = 0

' Loop through each region
For Each PivItem In PT.PivotFields("Region").PivotItems
    Ctr = Ctr + 1
    PT.PivotFields("Region").CurrentPage = PivItem.Name
    PT.ManualUpdate = False
    PT.ManualUpdate = True

    ' Create a new blank workbook with one worksheet
    Set WBN = Workbooks.Add(xlWBATWorksheet)
    Set WSR = WBN.Worksheets(1)
    WSR.Name = PivItem.Name
    ' Set up Title for Report
    With WSR.[A1]
        .Value = "Top 5 Customers in the " & PivItem.Name & " Region"
        .Font.Size = 14
    End With

    ' Copy the pivot table data to row 3 of the report sheet
    ' Use offset to eliminate the page & title rows of the pivot table
    PT.TableRange2.Offset(3, 0).Copy
    WSR.[A3].PasteSpecial Paste:=xlPasteValuesAndNumberFormats
    LastRow = WSR.Cells(65536, 1).End(xlUp).Row
```

```
       WSR.Cells(LastRow, 1).Value = "Top 5 Total"

       ' Do some basic formatting
       ' Autofit columns, bold the headings, right-align
       WSR.Range(WSR.Range("A2"), WSR.Cells(LastRow, 8)).Columns.AutoFit
       Range("A3").EntireRow.Font.Bold = True
       Range("A3").EntireRow.HorizontalAlignment = xlRight
       Range("A3").HorizontalAlignment = xlLeft
       Range("B3").Value = "Revenue"

       Range("A2").Select

   Next PivItem

   ' Clear the pivot table
   PT.TableRange2.Clear
   Set PTCache = Nothing

   MsgBox Ctr & " Region reports have been created"

End Sub
```

Manually Filtering Two or More Items in a PivotField

In addition to setting up a calculated pivot item to display the total of a couple of products that make up a dimension, you can manually filter a particular PivotField.

For example, you have one client who sells shoes. In the report showing sales of sandals, he wants to see just the stores that are in warm-weather states. The code to hide a particular store is

```
PT.PivotFields("Store").PivotItems("Minneapolis").Visible = False
```

You need to be very careful never to set all items to False; otherwise, the macro ends with an error. This tends to happen more than you would expect. An application may first show products A and B and then on the next loop show products C and D. If you attempt to make A and B not visible before making C and D visible, no products will be visible along the PivotField, which causes an error. To correct this, always loop through all PivotItems, making sure to turn them back to visible before the second pass through the loop.

This process is easy in VBA. After building the table with Product in the page field, loop through to change the Visible property to show only the total of certain products:

```
   ' Make sure all PivotItems along line are visible
   For Each PivItem In _
       PT.PivotFields("Product").PivotItems
       PivItem.Visible = True
   Next PivItem

   ' Now - loop through and keep only certain items visible
   For Each PivItem In _
       PT.PivotFields("Product").PivotItems
       Select Case PivItem.Name
           Case "Landscaping/Grounds Care", _
               "Green Plants and Foliage Care"
```

11

```
                        PivItem.Visible = True
                Case Else
                        PivItem.Visible = False
            End Select
        Next PivItem
```

Controlling the Sort Order Manually

If your company has been reporting regions in the sequence South, North, West forever, it is an uphill battle getting managers to accept seeing the report ordered North, South, West just because this is the default alphabetical order offered by pivot tables.

Strangely enough, Microsoft offers a bizarre method for handling a custom sort order in a pivot table. It's called a *manual sort order*. To change the sort order in the user interface, you simply go to a cell in the pivot table that contains North, type the word **South**, and press Enter. As if by magic, North and South switch places. Of course, all the numbers for North move to the appropriate column.

The VBA code to do a manual sort involves setting the Position property for a specific PivotItem. This is somewhat dangerous because you don't know whether the underlying fields will have data for South on any given day. Be sure to set error checking to resume in case South doesn't exist today:

```
On Error Resume Next
PT.PivotFields("Region").PivotItems("South").Position = 1
On Error GoTo 0
```

Using Sum, Average, Count, Min, Max, and More

So far, every example in this chapter has involved summing data. It is also possible to get an average, minimum, or maximum of data. In VBA, change the Function property of the data field and give the data field a unique name. For example, the following code fragment produces five different summaries of the revenue field, each with a unique name:

```
' Set up the data fields
With PT.PivotFields("Revenue")
    .Orientation = xlDataField
    .Function = xlSum
    .Position = 1
    .NumberFormat = "#,##0,K"
    .Name = "Total Revenue"
End With

With PT.PivotFields("Revenue")
    .Orientation = xlDataField
    .Function = xlCount
    .Position = 2
    .NumberFormat = "#,##0"
    .Name = "Number Orders"
End With

With PT.PivotFields("Revenue")
    .Orientation = xlDataField
```

```
      .Function = xlAverage
      .Position = 3
      .NumberFormat = "#,##0"
      .Name = "Average Revenue"
End With

With PT.PivotFields("Revenue")
      .Orientation = xlDataField
      .Function = xlMin
      .Position = 4
      .NumberFormat = "#,##0"
      .Name = "Smallest Order"
End With

With PT.PivotFields("Revenue")
      .Orientation = xlDataField
      .Function = xlMax
      .Position = 5
      .NumberFormat = "#,##0"
      .Name = "Largest Order"
End With
```

The resultant pivot table provides a number of statistics about the average revenue, largest order, smallest order, and so on.

Creating Report Percentages

In addition to the available choices, such as Sum, Min, Max, and Average, you can use another set of pivot table options called the *calculation options*. They allow you to show a particular field as a percentage of the total, a percentage of the row, a percentage of the column, or as the percent difference from the previous or next item. All these settings are controlled through the .Calculation property of the page field.

The valid properties for .Calculation are xlPercentOf, xlPercentOfColumn, xlPercentOfRow, xlPercentOfTotal, xlRunningTotal, xlPercentDifferenceFrom, xlDifferenceFrom, xlIndex, and xlNoAdditionalCalculation. Each has its own unique set of rules. Some require that you specify a BaseField, and others require that you specify both a BaseField and BaseItem. The following sections provide some specific examples.

Percentage of Total

To get the percentage of the total, specify xlPercentOfTotal as the .Calculation property for the page field:

```
' Set up a percentage of total
With PT.PivotFields("Revenue")
      .Orientation = xlDataField
      .Caption = "PctOfTotal"
      .Function = xlSum
      .Position = 2
      .NumberFormat = "#0.0%"
      .Calculation = xlPercentOfTotal
End With
```

Percentage Growth from Previous Month

With ship months going down the columns, you might want to see the percentage of revenue growth from month to month. You can set up this arrangement with the `xlPercentDifferenceFrom` setting. In this case, you must specify that the `BaseField` is `"Invoice Date"` and that the `BaseItem` is something called `"(previous)"`:

```
' Set up % change from prior month
With PT.PivotFields("Revenue")
    .Orientation = xlDataField
    .Function = xlSum
    .Caption = "%Change"
    .Calculation = xlPercentDifferenceFrom
    .BaseField = "Invoice Date"
    .BaseItem = "(previous)"
    .Position = 3
    .NumberFormat = "#0.0%"
End With
```

Note that with positional calculations, you cannot us the AutoShow or AutoSort method. This is too bad; it would be interesting to sort the customers high to low and to see their sizes in relation to each other.

Percentage of a Specific Item

You can use the `xlPercentDifferenceFrom` setting to express revenues as a percentage of the California market sales:

```
' Show revenue as a percentage of California
With PT.PivotFields("Revenue")
    .Orientation = xlDataField
    .Function = xlSum
    .Caption = "% of California"
    .Calculation = xlPercentDifferenceFrom
    .BaseField = "Market"
    .BaseItem = "California"
    .Position = 3
    .NumberFormat = "#0.0%"
End With
```

Running Total

Setting up a running total is not intuitive; to do this, you must define a `BaseField`. In this example, Invoice Date runs down the column. To define a running total column for revenue, you must specify that `BaseField` is `"Invoice Date"`:

```
' Set up Running Total
With PT.PivotFields("Revenue")
    .Orientation = xlDataField
    .Function = xlSum
    .Caption = "YTD Total"
    .Calculation = xlRunningTotal
    .Position = 4
    .NumberFormat = "#,##0,K"
    .BaseField = "Invoice Date"
End With
```

Figure 11.22 shows the results of a pivot table with three custom calculation settings, as discussed earlier.

Figure 11.22
This pivot table presents four views of Sum of Revenue. Column T is the normal calculation. Column U is % of Total. Column V is % change from previous month. Column W is the running total.

	R	S	T	U	V	W
1						
2			Data			
3	Years ▼	InvoiceDate ▼	Sum of Revenue	PctOfTotal	%Change	YTD Total
4	⊟2006	Jan	197K	2.1%		197K
5		Feb	313K	3.4%	58.7%	510K
6		Mar	200K	2.2%	-36.1%	710K
7		Apr	269K	2.9%	34.8%	979K
8		May	278K	3.0%	3.0%	1,257K
9		Jun	252K	2.7%	-9.3%	1,509K
10		Jul	276K	3.0%	9.6%	1,784K
11		Aug	275K	3.0%	-0.4%	2,059K
12		Sep	237K	2.6%	-13.8%	2,296K
13		Oct	284K	3.1%	20.0%	2,580K
14		Nov	266K	2.9%	-6.3%	2,847K
15		Dec	213K	2.3%	-20.1%	3,060K

Using New Pivot Table Features in Excel 2007

Pivot tables offer a variety of new features in Excel 2007. The new label and value filters, conditional formatting, table formatting, and layout views are significant improvements to the pivot table environment.

If you want to utilize any of these features, the pivot table must exist in a file that is stored in Excel 2007 file format. If your file is in compatibility mode, none of the new features are available in the user interface nor in VBA.

Similarly, if you use any of these features, the code runs only in Excel 2007. There is no hope of going backward to share the code with someone using Excel 2003.

Using the New Filters

In previous versions of Excel, the filtering feature allowed you to choose one or more pivot items from a drop-down list. The only conceptual filter was the top 10 AutoShow filter.

Excel 2007 offers new conceptual filters that are easy to access. In the PivotTable Field List, hover the mouse cursor over any active field in the field list portion of the dialog box. In the drop-down that appears, you can choose either Label Filters, Date Filters, or Value Filters.

In Figure 11.23, the flyout menu shows the list of Label filters available for the Branch field.

To apply a label filter in VBA, use the `PivotFilters.Add` method. The following code filters to the Branches that start with 1:

```
PT.PivotFields("Branch").PivotFilters.Add _
    Type:=xlCaptionBeginsWith, Value1:="1"
```

11

Figure 11.23
You can easily choose all the Branch items that meet your criteria.

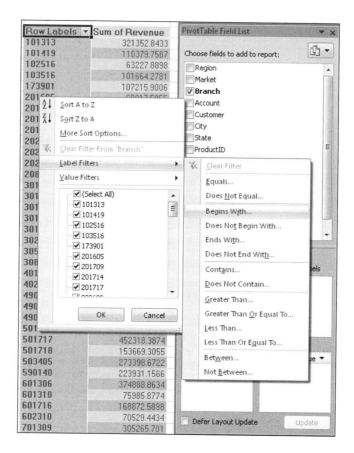

To clear the filter from the Branch field, use the `ClearAllFilters` method:

```
PT.PivotFields("Branch").ClearAllFilters
```

To apply a date filter to the invoice date field to find records from this week, use this code:

```
PT.PivotFields("InvoiceDate").PivotFilters.Add Type:=xlThisWeek
```

The value filters allow you to filter one field based on the value of another field. For example, to find all the branches where the total revenue is over $100,000, you would use this code:

```
PT.PivotFields("Branch").PivotFilters.Add _
    Type:=xlValueIsGreaterThan, _
    DataField:=PT.PivotFields("Sum of Revenue"), _
    Value1:=100000
```

Other value filters might allow you to specify that you want branches where the revenue is between $50,000 and $100,000. In this case, you would specify one limit as `Value1` and the second limit as `Value2`:

```
PT.PivotFields("Branch").PivotFilters.Add _
    Type:=xlValueIsBetween, _
    DataField:=PT.PivotFields("Sum of Revenue"), _
    Value1:=50000, Value2:=100000
```

Table 11.3 lists all the possible filter types.

Table 11.3   Filter Types

Filter Type	Description
xlBefore	Filters for all dates before a specified date
xlBeforeOrEqualTo	Filters for all dates on or before a specified date
xlAfter	Filters for all dates after a specified date
xlAfterOrEqualTo	Filters for all dates on or after a specified date
xlAllDatesInPeriodJanuary	Filters for all dates in January
xlAllDatesInPeriodFebruary	Filters for all dates in February
xlAllDatesInPeriodMarch	Filters for all dates in March
xlAllDatesInPeriodApril	Filters for all dates in April
xlAllDatesInPeriodMay	Filters for all dates in May
xlAllDatesInPeriodJune	Filters for all dates in June
xlAllDatesInPeriodJuly	Filters for all dates in July
xlAllDatesInPeriodAugust	Filters for all dates in August
xlAllDatesInPeriodSeptember	Filters for all dates in September
xlAllDatesInPeriodOctober	Filters for all dates in October
xlAllDatesInPeriodNovember	Filters for all dates in November
xlAllDatesInPeriodDecember	Filters for all dates in December
xlAllDatesInPeriodQuarter1	Filters for all dates in Quarter 1
xlAllDatesInPeriodQuarter2	Filters for all dates in Quarter 2
xlAllDatesInPeriodQuarter3	Filters for all dates in Quarter 3
xlAllDatesInPeriodQuarter4	Filters for all dates in Quarter 4
xlBottomCount	Filters for the specified number of values from the bottom of a list
xlBottomPercent	Filters for the specified percentage of values from the bottom of a list
xlBottomSum	Sums the values from the bottom of the list
xlCaptionBeginsWith	Filters for all captions beginning with the specified string

continues

Table 11.3   Continued

Filter Type	Description
`xlCaptionContains`	Filters for all captions that contain the specified string
`xlCaptionDoesNotBeginWith`	Filters for all captions that do not begin with the specified string
`xlCaptionDoesNotContain`	Filters for all captions that do not contain the specified string
`xlCaptionDoesNotEndWith`	Filters for all captions that do not end with the specified string
`xlCaptionDoesNotEqual`	Filters for all captions that do not match the specified string
`xlCaptionEndsWith`	Filters for all captions that end with the specified string
`xlCaptionEquals`	Filters for all captions that match the specified string
`xlCaptionIsBetween`	Filters for all captions that are between a specified range of values
`xlCaptionIsGreaterThan`	Filters for all captions that are greater than the specified value
`xlCaptionIsGreaterThanOrEqualTo`	Filters for all captions that are greater than or match the specified value
`xlCaptionIsLessThan`	Filters for all captions that are less than the specified value
`xlCaptionIsLessThanOrEqualTo`	Filters for all captions that are less than or match the specified value
`xlCaptionIsNotBetween`	Filters for all captions that are not between a specified range of values
`xlDateBetween`	Filters for all dates that are between a specified range of dates
`xlDateLastMonth`	Filters for all dates that apply to the previous month
`xlDateLastQuarter`	Filters for all dates that apply to the previous quarter
`xlDateLastWeek`	Filters for all dates that apply to the previous week
`xlDateLastYear`	Filters for all dates that apply to the previous year

Filter Type	Description
xlDateNextMonth	Filters for all dates that apply to the next month
xlDateNextQuarter	Filters for all dates that apply to the next quarter
xlDateNextWeek	Filters for all dates that apply to the next week
xlDateNextYear	Filters for all dates that apply to the next year
xlDateThisMonth	Filters for all dates that apply to the current month
xlDateThisQuarter	Filters for all dates that apply to the current quarter
xlDateThisWeek	Filters for all dates that apply to the current week
xlDateThisYear	Filters for all dates that apply to the current year
xlDateToday	Filters for all dates that apply to the current date
xlDateTomorrow	Filters for all dates that apply to the next day
xlDateYesterday	Filters for all dates that apply to the previous day
xlNotSpecificDate	Filters for all dates that do not match a specified date
xlSpecificDate	Filters for all dates that match a specified date
xlTopCount	Filters for the specified number of values from the top of a list
xlTopPercent	Filters for the specified percentage of values from a list
xlTopSum	Sums the values from the top of the list
xlValueDoesNotEqual	Filters for all values that do not match the specified value
xlValueEquals	Filters for all values that match the specified value
xlValueIsBetween	Filters for all values that are between a specified range of values
xlValueIsGreaterThan	Filters for all values that are greater than the specified value
xlValueIsGreaterThanOrEqualTo	Filters for all values that are greater than or match the specified value
xlValueIsLessThan	Filters for all values that are less than the specified value
xlValueIsLessThanOrEqualTo	Filters for all values that are less than or match the specified value

11

continues

Table 11.3   Continued

Filter Type	Description
xlValueIsNotBetween	Filters for all values that are not between a specified range of values
xlYearToDate	Filters for all values that are within one year of a specified date

Applying a Table Style

The Design ribbon offers two groups dedicated to formatting the pivot table, as shown in Figure 11.24. The PivotTable Style Options group has four check boxes that modify the styles in the PivotTable Styles Gallery.

Figure 11.24
The four check boxes and gallery of styles offer many variations for formatting the pivot table.

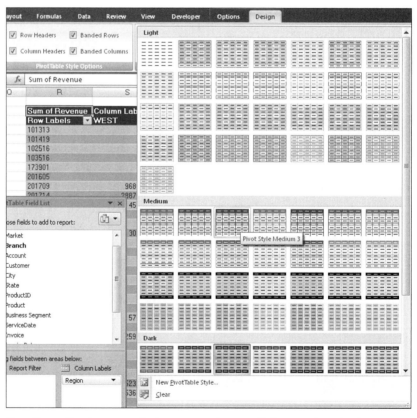

The following four lines of code are equivalent to turning on all four settings in the PivotTable Style Options group:

```
PT.ShowTableStyleRowHeaders = True
PT.ShowTableStyleColumnHeaders = True
PT.ShowTableStyleRowStripes = True
PT.ShowTableStyleColumnStripes = True
```

To apply a table style from the gallery, use the `TableStyle2` property. If you want to get the correct name, it might be best to record a macro:

```
' Format the pivot table
PT.ShowTableStyleRowStripes = True
PT.TableStyle2 = "PivotStyleMedium3"
```

In Figure 11.24, the ToolTip shows a style named Pivot Style Medium 3.

> **NOTE**
>
> Previous versions of Excel offered an AutoFormat feature for pivot tables. This feature was annoying because it actually changed the layout of your pivot table. That obsolete command used the `TableStyle` property; hence, Excel 2007 had to use `TableStyle2` as the property name for the new style tables.

> **CAUTION**
>
> It is possible to create custom table styles. If you have a custom table style named `MyStyle44` and use this name in a macro, the macro will run fine on your computer but may not run on anyone else's computer. To alleviate the chance of a runtime error, you use `On Error Resume Next` before applying `TableStyle2`.

Changing the Layout

The Layout group of the Design ribbon contains four drop-downs. These drop-downs control the location of subtotals (top or bottom), the presence of grand totals, the report layout, and the presence of blank rows.

Subtotals can appear either at the top or bottom of a group of pivot items. The `SubtotalLocation` property applies to the entire pivot table; valid values are `xlAtBottom` or `xlAtTop`:

```
PT.SubtotalLocation:=xlAtTop
```

Grand totals can be turned on or off for rows or columns. The following code turns them off for both:

```
PT.ColumnGrand = False
PT.RowGrand = False
```

There are three settings for the report layout. The Tabular layout is similar to the default layout in Excel 2003. The Outline layout was optionally available in Excel 2003. The Compact layout is new in Excel 2007.

Excel can remember the last layout used and will apply it to additional pivot tables created in the same Excel session. For this reason, you should always explicitly choose the layout that you want. Use the `RowAxisLayout` method; valid values are `xlTabularRow`, `xlOutlineRow`, or `xlCompactRow`:

```
PT.RowAxisLayout xlTabularRow
PT.RowAxisLayout xlOutlineRow
PT.RowAxisLayout = xlCompactRow
```

In Excel 2007, you can add a blank line to the layout after each group of pivot items. Although the Design ribbon offers a single setting to affect the entire pivot table, the setting is actually applied to each individual pivot field individually. The macro recorder responds by recording a dozen lines of code for a pivot table with 12 fields. You can intelligently add a single line of code for the outer row field(s):

```
PT.PivotFields("Region").LayoutBlankLine = True
```

Applying a Data Visualization

Excel 2007 offers fantastic new data visualizations such as icon sets, color gradients, and in-cell data bars. When you apply a visualization to a pivot table, you should exclude the total rows from the visualization.

If you have 30 branches that average $50,000 in revenue each, the total for the 30 branches is $1.5 million. If you include the total in the data visualization, the total gets the largest bar, and all the branch records have tiny bars.

In the Excel user interface, you always want to use the Add Rule or Edit Rule choice to choose the option All Cells Showing "Sum of Revenue" for "Branch," as shown in Figure 11.25.

Figure 11.25
To create meaningful visualizations in your pivot table, exclude the totals by choosing the third option at the top of this dialog box.

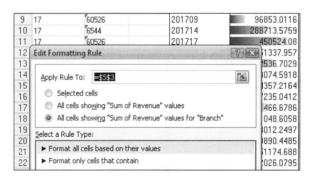

The code in Listing 11.11 adds a pivot table and applies a data bar to the revenue field.

Listing 11.11   Code That Creates a Pivot Table with Data Bars

```
Sub CreatePivotDataBar()
    ' Listing 11.11
    Dim WSD As Worksheet
    Dim PTCache As PivotCache
    Dim PT As PivotTable
    Dim PRange As Range
    Dim FinalRow As Long
    Set WSD = Worksheets("PivotTable")
```

```
' Delete any prior pivot tables
For Each PT In WSD.PivotTables
    PT.TableRange2.Clear
Next PT
WSD.Range("R1:AZ1").EntireColumn.Clear

' Define input area and set up a Pivot Cache
FinalRow = WSD.Cells(Rows.Count, 1).End(xlUp).Row
FinalCol = WSD.Cells(1, Columns.Count). _
    End(xlToLeft).Column
Set PRange = WSD.Cells(1, 1).Resize(FinalRow, FinalCol)
Set PTCache = ActiveWorkbook.PivotCaches.Add(SourceType:= _
    xlDatabase, SourceData:=PRange.Address)

' Create the Pivot Table from the Pivot Cache
Set PT = PTCache.CreatePivotTable(TableDestination:=WSD. _
    Cells(2, FinalCol + 2), TableName:="PivotTable1")

' Turn off updating while building the table
PT.ManualUpdate = True

' Set up the row & column fields
PT.AddFields RowFields:="Branch", _
    ColumnFields:="Data"

' Set up the data fields
With PT.PivotFields("Revenue")
    .Orientation = xlDataField
    .Function = xlSum
    .Position = 1
End With

' Calc the pivot table
PT.ManualUpdate = False
PT.ManualUpdate = True

' Apply a Databar
PT.TableRange2.Cells(3, 2).Select
Selection.FormatConditions.AddDatabar
Selection.FormatConditions(1).ShowValue = True
Selection.FormatConditions(1).SetFirstPriority
With Selection.FormatConditions(1)
    .MinPoint.Modify newtype:=xlConditionValueLowestValue
    .MaxPoint.Modify newtype:=xlConditionValueHighestValue
End With
With Selection.FormatConditions(1).BarColor
    .ThemeColor = xlThemeColorAccent3
    .TintAndShade = -0.499984740745262
End With
Selection.FormatConditions(1).ScopeType = xlFieldsScope

WSD.Activate
Range("R1").Select

End Sub
```

Understanding Special Considerations for Excel 97

Pivot tables and VBA took a radical turn in Excel 2000. In Excel 2000, Microsoft introduced the `PivotCache` object. This object allows you to define one pivot cache and then build many pivot reports from the pivot cache.

Officially, Microsoft quit supporting Excel 97 a few years ago. But, in practical terms, many companies are still using Excel 97. If you need your code to work on a legacy platform, you should be aware of the way pivot tables were created in Excel 97.

In Excel 97, you used the `PivotTableWizard` method. Take a look at the code for building a simple pivot table showing revenue by region and product. Where current code uses two steps (add `PivotCache` and then use `CreatePivotTable`), Excel 97 used just one step, using the `PivotTableWizard` method to create the table:

```
Sub PivotExcel97Compatible()
    ' Pivot Table Code for Excel 97 Users
    Dim WSD As Worksheet
    Dim PT As PivotTable
    Dim PRange As Range
    Dim FinalRow As Long

    Set WSD = Worksheets("PivotTable")

    ' Delete any prior pivot tables
    For Each PT In WSD.PivotTables
        PT.TableRange2.Clear
    Next PT

    ' Define input area
    FinalRow = WSD.Cells(Rows.Count, 1).End(xlUp).Row
    FinalCol = WSD.Cells(1, Columns.Count). _
        End(xlToLeft).Column
    Set PRange = WSD.Cells(1, 1).Resize(FinalRow, FinalCol)

    ' Create pivot table using PivotTableWizard
    Set PT = WSD.PivotTableWizard(SourceType:=xlDatabase, _
        SourceData:=PRange.Address, _
        TableDestination:="R2C18", TableName:="PivotTable1")

    PT.ManualUpdate = True
    ' Set up the row fields
    PT.AddFields RowFields:="Region", ColumnFields:="Product"

    ' Set up the data fields
    With PT.PivotFields("Revenue")
        .Orientation = xlDataField
        .Function = xlSum
        .Position = 1
        .NumberFormat = "#,##0,K"
        .Name = "Total Revenue"
    End With

    PT.ManualUpdate = False
    PT.ManualUpdate = True
End Sub
```

Next Steps

In the next chapter, you learn a myriad of techniques for handling common questions and issues with pivot tables.

11

Common Pivot Table Issues and Questions

In this chapter, you get quick solutions to the most common pivot table issues. You also find the answers to the most commonly asked pivot table questions. Take some time to glance at the topics covered here. Who knows? You may find the answer to *your* question!

Troubleshooting Common Pivot Table Issues

I keep getting the error "The PivotTable field name is not valid."

Problem:

When you try to create a pivot table, you get the following error message:

```
The PivotTable field name is not valid. To
create a PivotTable report,
you must use data that is organized as a list
with labeled columns.
If you are changing the name of a PivotTable
field, you must type
a new name for the field.
```

Solution:

This message means that one or more columns in your data source do not have a header name. To correct this problem, go to the dataset you are using to create the pivot table and make sure that all columns have a header name.

When I refreshed my pivot table, my data disappeared.

Problem:

After you refresh your pivot table, the field you placed into the values area disappears, effectively removing the data in your pivot table.

IN THIS CHAPTER

Troubleshooting Common Pivot
Table Issues 291

Common Pivot Table Questions 297

Solution:

You run into this behavior when you change the name of the field you placed into the values area. For example, if you create a pivot table and place a field called Revenue into the values area, your pivot table shows revenue numbers in the values area. If you go to your source data and change the Revenue column heading name to Dollars and then refresh your pivot table, the numbers in the values area disappear. The reason is that your pivot table took a new snapshot of your data source when you refreshed and determined that there is no longer a field called Revenue; therefore, it cannot calculate a field that is not there.

To resolve this issue, open your PivotTable Field List and simply drag your new field into the values area.

My pivot table always uses Count instead of Sum.

Problem:

You have a column in your data source that contains numbers. Furthermore, you have explicitly formatted that column to be a number field. Nevertheless, each time you try to add it to your pivot table, Excel automatically tries to use Count on the field instead of Sum. This leaves you manually changing the calculation method to Sum.

Solution:

If there are any text values in a source column, Excel automatically applies Count to the data field for that column. Similarly, even one blank cell causes Excel to apply Count.

It is likely that in your source column, you have either a text value or a blank. To alleviate this problem, simply remove both text and blank values from the source column and refresh the pivot table.

My pivot table constantly adjusts the columns in my workbook to autofit the headings.

Problem:

When you refresh your pivot table or choose a new data item in the filter field, the columns containing headings automatically adjust to fit the column headings. This can be quite annoying when you have a formatted report that needs to stay relatively unchanged.

Solution:

You can easily resolve this problem by using one of those handy PivotTable Options:

1. Right-click on your pivot table and select PivotTable Options.
2. In the activated dialog box, select the Layout & Format tab.
3. Remove the check next to Autofit Column Widths on Update.

The Defer Layout Update option locked me out of other functionality such as sorting, filtering, and grouping.

Problem:

You built your pivot table using the Defer Layout Update option, and now all most functionality is disabled.

Solution:

Remove the check from the Defer Layout Update check box. Leaving this box checked results in your pivot table remaining in a state of manual updates, preventing you from using the other features of the pivot table (such as sorting, filtering, and grouping).

Older versions of Excel do not open my pivot table properly.

Problem:

You built your pivot table report using Excel 2007, and now each time your report is opened in a previous version of Excel, all pivot table functionality is gone.

Solution:

Compatibility issues between the different versions of Excel most often cause this problem. Excel 2007 comes with a substantial increase in the volume of data a pivot table can handle. This increase allows you to build pivot tables that far exceed the limitations of the previous versions.

For example, imagine that you build a pivot table that contains more than 32,500 unique data items (the limit in Excel 2002 and 2003). In addition, imagine that you also include other functionalities that are unique to Excel 2007, such as data bars and conditional icons. Should someone with a previous version of Excel open your Excel 2007 .xlsx file, she will see only hard values. That is, the data in the pivot table is converted to hard-coded data, and the pivot cache is lost, along with the pivot table object and your formatting.

To avoid this problem, you can build your pivot table reports in compatibility mode. Compatibility mode allows you to use Excel 2007 as if it were an Excel 2003 workbook. That is, it artificially takes on the limitations of Excel 2003, preventing you from unwittingly creating a pivot table that is not compatible with previous versions of Excel. Follow these steps when you want to build your pivot tables in compatibility mode:

1. Start a new workbook.
2. Save the empty workbook as an Excel 97–2003 Workbook. Selecting this option saves your workbook as an .xls file.
3. Open your newly created .xls file.

When you open the empty .xls file, Excel automatically enters compatibility mode. From here, you can create your pivot table reports as if you were working in Excel 2003. You can rest assured that while in compatibility mode, you cannot exceed any of the Excel 2003 pivot table limitations.

12

TIP
Review Chapter 1,"Pivot Table Fundamentals," to get a refresher on the limitations of pivot tables in the various versions of Excel.

When I try to group a field, I get an error message.

Problem:

When you try to group a field in your pivot table, you get the following error message: `Cannot group that selection`.

Solution:

One of the following scenarios can trigger this error message:

- The field you are trying to group is a text field.
- The field you are trying to group is a date field but contains text or blank cells.
- The field you are trying to group is a date field but is being recognized by Excel as text.
- The field you are trying to group is in the report filter area of your pivot table.

To resolve this issue, take the following steps:

1. Go to your data source and make sure the field you are trying to group is formatted as date and does not contain blanks cells or cells with text in them. Remove all text, format the cells in the field as date, and fill in all blank cells with a dummy date.
2. Highlight the column that contains the field you are trying to group. Go up to the Ribbon and select the Data tab; then select the Convert Text to Table button. This activates the Text to Columns Wizard. All you have to do in this wizard is select Finish.
3. Go back to your pivot table, right-click, and select Refresh Data.
4. If the field you are trying to group is in the filter area of your pivot table, move the field to the row or column area.
5. At this point, you can group the data items in your field. After the field is grouped, you can move it back to the filter area if needed.

My pivot table shows the same data item twice.

Problem:

Your pivot table shows the same data item two times, effectively treating each instance of the data item as a separate entity. Figure 12.1 demonstrates an example of this error.

Notice that 1/26/2007 is shown in the pivot table twice. There is something wrong here. If these dates are the same, they should be grouped together to give you one calculation, not two.

Figure 12.1
The two occurrences of 1/26/2007 should be grouped together to give you one calculation, not two.

	A	B	C	D	E	F	G
1							
2							
3	Sum of Sales_Amount	Invoice_Date					
4	Sales_Rep	1/26/2007	1/20/2007	1/22/2007	1/23/2007	1/26/2007	1/27/2007	1/28
5	1336	$86	$86			$86	
6	54564				$86		$86
7	55662		$86	$86			$86	$
8	60224		$86		$259		
9	Grand Total	$86	$259	$86	$345	$86	$173	$
10							

Solution:

To solve this problem, follow these steps:

1. Go to your data source and sort your table on the problem field. In this example, the problem field is the Date field.

2. Find all instances of the problem data item (1/26/2007 in this case) and make sure they are all the same. You can do this by copying the first instance of the data item and pasting over the other instances.

3. Highlight the column that contains the field you are trying to group. Go up to the Ribbon and select the Data tab; then select the Convert Text to Table button. Selecting this button activates the Text to Columns Wizard. All you have to do in this wizard is select Finish.

4. Go back to your pivot table, right-click, and select Refresh.

Deleted data items still show up in the filter area.

Problem:

You deleted a data item from your data source and refreshed your pivot table. However, the data item still appears in your pivot table. In the example shown in Figure 12.2, you see five regions, including Southwest, in the filter field.

The issue here is that the Southwest region does not exist any longer, and your data source does not have records tagged as Southwest. Your pivot table is holding onto this data item in its pivot cache.

Solution:

Excel retains data items in a filter field by design. This ensures that selections that are only temporarily missing are not left out of the filter field. For instance, suppose you have a filter field that holds the values YES and NO. There may come a time when your dataset will temporarily have zero records that contain the value NO. Excel, by default, keeps the NO value as a selection in the filter field, anticipating its return.

To clear these phantom data items from your pivot table, completely remove the field that contains the old items (in this example Region) from the pivot table. Refresh the pivot table and then drag the field back to its original position. The phantom data items are now gone.

Figure 12.2
Your pivot table is retaining deleted data items in its pivot cache.

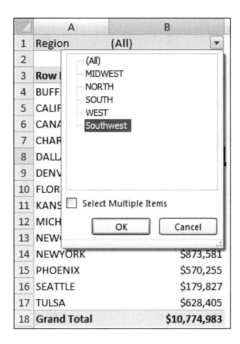

Although this behavior could be useful in some scenarios, it is unwanted behavior in most situations. You can tell Excel to suppress this behavior in the future by following these steps:

1. Right-click on your pivot table and select PivotTable Options.
2. In the activated dialog box, select the Data tab.
3. Change the Number of Items to Retain Per Field property to None.

I refreshed my pivot table, and now my calculated fields are displayed as error values.

Problem:

You have a calculated field in your pivot table that previously worked properly but no longer does. The field now displays an error message.

Solution:

You have either renamed or deleted a field used in your calculated field. To fix this issue, simply edit the calculated field to reflect the changes in your source data.

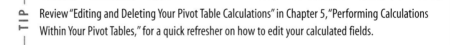

TIP

Review "Editing and Deleting Your Pivot Table Calculations" in Chapter 5, "Performing Calculations Within Your Pivot Tables," for a quick refresher on how to edit your calculated fields.

Common Pivot Table Questions

How do I make my pivot table refresh automatically?

In some situations you may need to have your pivot tables refresh themselves automatically. For instance, suppose you created a pivot table report for your manager. You may not be able to trust that he will refresh the pivot table when needed.

You can force each pivot table to automatically refresh when the workbook opens by following these steps:

1. Right-click on your pivot table and select PivotTable Options.
2. In the activated dialog box, select the Data tab.
3. Place a check next to Refresh Data When Opening the File property.

When this property is activated, the pivot table refreshes itself each time the workbook in which it's located is opened.

> **NOTE** The Refresh Data When Opening the File property must be set for each pivot table individually.

How do I refresh all pivot tables in a workbook at the same time?

When you have multiple pivot tables in a workbook, refreshing all of them can be bothersome. There are several ways to avoid the hassle of manually refreshing multiple pivot tables. Here are a few options.

Option 1: You can configure each pivot table in your workbook to automatically refresh when the workbook opens. To do so, right-click on your pivot table and select PivotTable Options. This activates the PivotTable Options dialog box. Here, select the Data tab and place a check next to Refresh Data When Opening the File property. After you have configured all pivot tables in the workbook, they will automatically refresh when the workbook is opened.

Option 2: You can create a macro to refresh each pivot table in the workbook. This option is ideal when you need to refresh your pivot tables on demand, rather than only when the workbook opens. The idea is to start recording a macro. While the macro is recording, simply go to each pivot table in your workbook and refresh. After all pivot tables are refreshed, stop recording. The result is a macro that can be fired any time you need to refresh all pivot tables.

12

> **TIP** Revisit Chapter 10, "Enhancing Your Pivot Table Reports with Macros," to get more detail on using macros with pivot tables.

Option 3: You can use VBA to refresh all pivot tables in the workbook on demand. This option can be used when it is impractical to record and maintain macros that refresh all pivot tables. This approach entails the use of the `RefreshAll` method of the `Workbook` object.

To employ this technique, start a new module and enter the following code:

```
Sub Refresh_All()
ThisWorkbook.RefreshAll
End Sub
```

You can now call this procedure any time you want to refresh all pivot tables within your workbook.

> **NOTE**
> Keep in mind that the `RefreshAll` method refreshes all external data ranges along with pivot tables. This means that if your workbook contains data from external sources, such as databases and external files, that data is refreshed along with your pivot tables.

How can I sort data items in a unique order that is not ascending or descending?

Figure 12.3 shows the default sequence of regions in a pivot table report. Alphabetically, the regions are shown in sequence of Midwest, North, South, West. If your company is based in California, company traditions might dictate that the West region should be shown first, followed by Midwest, North, and South. Unfortunately, neither an ascending sort order nor a descending sort order can help you.

Figure 12.3
Company traditions dictate that the Region field should be in West, Midwest, North, South sequence.

	A	B	C	D	E	F
1						
2						
3	Sum of Sales_Amount	Region				
4	Product_Description	MIDWEST	NORTH	SOUTH	WEST	Grand Total
5	Cleaning & Housekeeping Services	$174,518	$534,282	$283,170	$146,623	$1,138,593
6	Facility Maintenance and Repair	$463,077	$606,747	$846,515	$444,820	$2,361,158
7	Fleet Maintenance	$448,800	$610,791	$1,046,231	$521,976	$2,627,798
8	Green Plants and Foliage Care	$93,562	$155,021	$157,821	$870,379	$1,276,783
9	Landscaping/Grounds Care	$190,003	$299,309	$335,676	$365,928	$1,190,915
10	Predictive Maintenance/Preventative Maintenance	$478,928	$572,860	$472,045	$655,092	$2,178,925
11	Grand Total	$1,848,887	$2,779,009	$3,141,458	$3,004,818	$10,774,172

You can rearrange data items in your pivot table manually by simply typing the exact name of the data item where you would like to see its data. You can also drag the data item where you want it.

To solve the problem in this example, you simply type the word **West** in cell B4 and then press Enter. The pivot table responds by resequencing the regions. The $3 million in sales for the West region automatically moves from column E to column B. The remaining regions move over to the next two columns.

How do I turn my pivot table into hard data?

You created your pivot table only to summarize and shape your data. You do not want to keep the source data, nor do you want to keep the pivot table with all its overhead.

Turning your pivot table into hard data allows you to utilize the results of the pivot table without having to deal with the source data or a pivot cache. How you turn your pivot table into hard data depends on how much of your pivot table you are going to copy.

If you are copying just a portion of your pivot table, do the following:

1. Select the data you want to copy from the pivot table. Then right-click and select Copy.
2. Right-click anywhere on a spreadsheet and select Paste.

If you are copying your entire pivot table, follow these steps:

1. Select the entire pivot table, right-click, and select Copy.
2. Right-click anywhere on a spreadsheet and select Paste Special.
3. Select Values and then click OK.

> **TIP**
>
> You may want to consider removing any subtotals before turning your pivot table into hard data. Subtotals typically aren't very useful when you are creating a standalone dataset.
>
> To remove the subtotals from your pivot table, first identify the field for which subtotals are being calculated. Then right-click on the field's header (either in the pivot table itself or in the PivotTable Field List) and select Field Settings. Selecting this option opens the Field Settings dialog box. Here, you change the Subtotals option to None. After you click OK, your subtotals are removed.

Is there an easy way to fill the empty cells left by row fields?

When you turn a pivot table into hard data, you are left not only with the values created by the pivot table, but also the pivot table's data structure. For example, the data in Figure 12.4 came from a pivot table that had a tabular layout.

Figure 12.4

It would be impractical to use this data anywhere else without filling in the empty cells left by the row field.

	A	B	C	D
1		Market	Product_Description	Sum of Sales_Amount
2		BUFFALO	Cleaning & Housekeeping Services	66844.85
3			Facility Maintenance and Repair	69569.62
4			Fleet Maintenance	86460.11
5			Green Plants and Foliage Care	34831.13
6			Landscaping/Grounds Care	65465.46
7			Predictive Maintenance/Preventative Maintenance	127307.1
8		CALIFORNIA	Cleaning & Housekeeping Services	37401.34
9			Facility Maintenance and Repair	281198.37
10			Fleet Maintenance	337224.52
11			Green Plants and Foliage Care	830412.67
12			Landscaping/Grounds Care	248342.72
13			Predictive Maintenance/Preventative Maintenance	520155.76
14		CANADA	Facility Maintenance and Repair	294257.33
15			Fleet Maintenance	273174.68
16			Green Plants and Foliage Care	15965.5
17			Landscaping/Grounds Care	76751.08
18			Predictive Maintenance/Preventative Maintenance	116096.68

12

Notice that the Market field kept the same row structure it had when this data was in the row area of the pivot table. It would be unwise to use this table anywhere else without filling in the empty cells left by the row field, but how do you easily fill these empty cells?

Although your first thought might be to copy each market and paste it into the appropriate empty cells, keep in mind that there are 20 markets. You don't want to waste your time pasting market names into empty cells.

The best solution here is to use a simple formula. This formula, shown in Figure 12.5, is entered next to the first data item in the row field. The idea is to create a column next to the empty cells and fill it with a value. That value, in this case, is a market name.

Figure 12.5

The formula
=IF(B2="",A1,B2)
states that if the cell next to the formula is empty, use the cell above the formula. If not, use the cell next to the formula.

	A	B	C	D
1		Market	Product_Description	Sum of Sales_Amount
2	=IF(B2="",A1,B2)	BUFFALO	Cleaning & Housekeeping Services	66844.85
3			Facility Maintenance and Repair	69569.62
4			Fleet Maintenance	86460.11
5			Green Plants and Foliage Care	34831.13
6			Landscaping/Grounds Care	65465.46
7			Predictive Maintenance/Preventative Maintenance	127307.1
8		CALIFORNIA	Cleaning & Housekeeping Services	37401.34
9			Facility Maintenance and Repair	281198.37
10			Fleet Maintenance	337224.52
11			Green Plants and Foliage Care	830412.67
12			Landscaping/Grounds Care	248342.72
13			Predictive Maintenance/Preventative Maintenance	520155.76
14		CANADA	Facility Maintenance and Repair	294257.33
15			Fleet Maintenance	273174.68
16			Green Plants and Foliage Care	15965.5
17			Landscaping/Grounds Care	76751.08
18			Predictive Maintenance/Preventative Maintenance	116096.68

After you enter the correct formula, copy it down to the end of your dataset. As you can see in Figure 12.6, this method is a lot more efficient than copying and pasting market names for 20 markets.

You're not done yet. After you have filled in the gaps with your formula, highlight the entire column by clicking on the column letter, and then go up to the Ribbon and select Copy. Right-click on the column letter and select Paste Special, then Values, and then OK. This turns your formulas into hard data.

All you have to do at this point is delete the original column with the empty cells and add a header to the column you just created.

Is there an easy way to fill the empty cells left by row fields in many columns?

The method described for the preceding problem works fine for one column, but it could get tedious if you have to fill in several columns such as with the pivot table shown in Figure 12.7.

Figure 12.6
After your formula is entered, you can copy it all the way down to the end of your dataset to fill in the gaps.

	A	B	C	D
1		Market	Product_Description	Sum of Sales_Amount
2	BUFFALO	BUFFALO	Cleaning & Housekeeping Services	66844.85
3	BUFFALO		Facility Maintenance and Repair	69569.62
4	BUFFALO		Fleet Maintenance	86460.11
5	BUFFALO		Green Plants and Foliage Care	34831.13
6	BUFFALO		Landscaping/Grounds Care	65465.46
7	BUFFALO		Predictive Maintenance/Preventative Maintenance	127307.1
8	CALIFORNIA	CALIFORNIA	Cleaning & Housekeeping Services	37401.34
9	CALIFORNIA		Facility Maintenance and Repair	281198.37
10	CALIFORNIA		Fleet Maintenance	337224.52
11	CALIFORNIA		Green Plants and Foliage Care	830412.67
12	CALIFORNIA		Landscaping/Grounds Care	248342.72
13	CALIFORNIA		Predictive Maintenance/Preventative Maintenance	520155.76
14	CANADA	CANADA	Facility Maintenance and Repair	294257.33
15	CANADA		Fleet Maintenance	273174.68
16	CANADA		Green Plants and Foliage Care	15965.5
17	CANADA		Landscaping/Grounds Care	76751.08
18	CANADA		Predictive Maintenance/Preventative Maintenance	116096.68

Figure 12.7
You want to fill in all blanks in columns A through C.

	A	B	C	
1	Region	Market	Business_Segment	Product_D
2	WEST	CALIFORNIA	Housekeeping and Organization	Cleaning &
3			Landscaping and Area Beautification	Green Pla
4				Landscapi
5			Maintenance and Repair	Facility M
6				Fleet Mair
7				Predictive
8		PHOENIX	Housekeeping and Organization	Cleaning &
9			Landscaping and Area Beautification	Green Pla
10				Landscapi
11			Maintenance and Repair	Facility M
12				Fleet Mair
13				Predictive
14		SEATTLE	Housekeeping and Organization	Cleaning &
15			Landscaping and Area Beautification	Green Pla
16				Landscapi
17			Maintenance and Repair	Facility M
18				Fleet Mair
19				Predictive

12

This solution is not as intuitive as the preceding method, but it works nicely when you have several columns of blanks to fill.

You select a range in columns A, B, and C that extends from the first row with blanks to the row just above the grand total. In the present example, this is A3:C84.

Press the F5 key on your keyboard to activate the Go To dialog box. The Go To Special dialog box is a powerful feature that allows you to modify your selection based on various conditions. In the lower-left corner of the Go To dialog box, choose the Special button. This will activate the Go To Special dialog you see here in Figure 12.8. From here, you will you will choose the option for Blanks.

Figure 12.8
Using the Go To Special dialog box allows you to select all the blank cells to be filled.

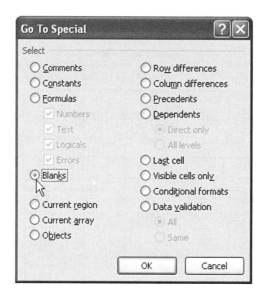

The result is that only the blank cells within your selection are selected.

Enter a formula to copy the pivot item values from the cell above to the blank cells. You can do this with four keystrokes, but it helps if you don't look at the screen while you perform them. Type an equal sign. Press the up-arrow key. Hold down the Ctrl key while pressing Enter.

The equal sign tells Excel that you are entering a formula in the active cell. Pressing the up-arrow key points to the cell above the active cell. Pressing Ctrl+Enter tells Excel to enter a similar formula in all the selected cells instead of just the active cell. As Figure 12.9 illustrates, with these few keystrokes, you enter a formula to fill in all the blank cells at once.

You still should convert those formulas to values. However, if you attempt to copy the current selection, Excel presents an error; you cannot copy a selection that contains multiple selections. By selecting Blanks from the Go To Special dialog box, you actually selected many areas of the spreadsheet.

You have to reselect the original range A3:C84. You can then press Ctrl+C to copy and choose Edit, Paste Special, Values to convert the formulas to values.

This method provides a quick way to easily fill in the outline view provided by the pivot table.

Figure 12.9
Pressing Ctrl+Enter enters the formula in all selected cells.

	A	B	C	
1	Region	Market	Business_Segment	Product_D
2	WEST	CALIFORNIA	Housekeeping and Organization	Cleaning &
3	WEST	CALIFORNIA	Landscaping and Area Beautification	Green Plar
4	WEST	CALIFORNIA	Landscaping and Area Beautification	Landscapi
5	WEST	CALIFORNIA	Maintenance and Repair	Facility M
6	WEST	CALIFORNIA	Maintenance and Repair	Fleet Mair
7	WEST	CALIFORNIA	Maintenance and Repair	Predictive
8	WEST	PHOENIX	Housekeeping and Organization	Cleaning &
9	WEST	PHOENIX	Landscaping and Area Beautification	Green Plar
10	WEST	PHOENIX	Landscaping and Area Beautification	Landscapi
11	WEST	PHOENIX	Maintenance and Repair	Facility M
12	WEST	PHOENIX	Maintenance and Repair	Fleet Mair
13	WEST	PHOENIX	Maintenance and Repair	Predictive
14	WEST	SEATTLE	Housekeeping and Organization	Cleaning &
15	WEST	SEATTLE	Landscaping and Area Beautification	Green Plar
16	WEST	SEATTLE	Landscaping and Area Beautification	Landscapi
17	WEST	SEATTLE	Maintenance and Repair	Facility M
18	WEST	SEATTLE	Maintenance and Repair	Fleet Mair
19	WEST	SEATTLE	Maintenance and Repair	Predictive

Why does my pivot chart exclude months for certain data items?

If you are plotting trends over time with a pivot chart, and there is no occurrence of a particular month, the pivot chart excludes that month entirely. However, in most cases, you want to show your audience a placeholder for that month, illustrating that no data is there.

For example, the chart in Figure 12.10 shows that in the Midwest, there is a trend from January through December. There is, however, no data for May and June. Therefore, the pivot chart excludes these months. It would be nice if this pivot chart would show all 12 months regardless.

12

Figure 12.10
May and June are not represented on the pivot chart.

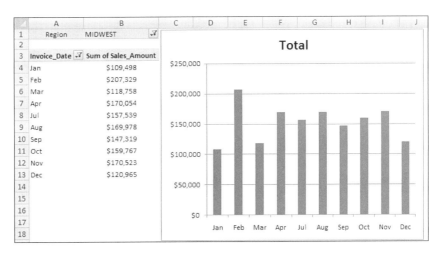

The solution to this problem is to set the pivot field to show all items with no data.

In this example, you right-click on Invoice Date. Then, in the activated dialog box, you place a check in the Show Items with No Data check box, as shown in Figure 12.11.

Figure 12.11
Right-click on Invoice Date and then, in the activated dialog box, place a check in the Show Items with No Data check box.

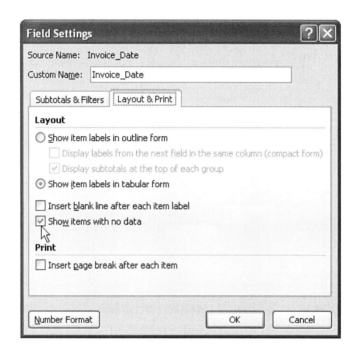

When your pivot field is set to show all items, your pivot table shows all 12 months, whether or not there is data in those months. The net effect is that you see May and June even though there is no data in those months, as shown in Figure 12.12.

Figure 12.12
When your pivot field is set to show all items, your pivot table shows all 12 months.

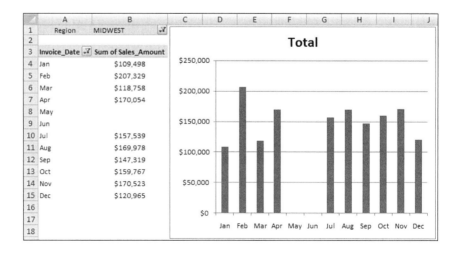

How do I add a rank number field to my pivot table?

When you are sorting and ranking a field with a large number of data items, it can be difficult to determine the number ranking of the current data item you are analyzing. Furthermore, you may want to turn your pivot table into hard values for further analysis. An integer field that contains the actual rank number of each data item could prove to be helpful in analysis outside the pivot table.

Click anywhere inside your pivot table; then go up to the Ribbon and select the Options tab. Here, you select Formulas and then Calculated Field.

In the Insert Calculated Field dialog box, give the field a name such as **MarketRank**. The formula should be =1. Choose the Add button to create the field, which is shown in Figure 12.13.

Figure 12.13
Adding a Rank field requires a simple calculated field that assigns the value of 1 to each market.

	A	B	C
1			
2			
3		Values	
4	Market ▾	Sum of Sales_Amount	Sum of MarketRank
5	CALIFORNIA	$2,254,735	1
6	FLORIDA	$1,450,392	1
7	CHARLOTTE	$890,522	1
8	NEWYORK	$873,581	1
9	CANADA	$776,245	1
10	MICHIGAN	$678,705	1
11	PHOENIX	$570,255	1
12	DENVER	$538,039	1
13	TULSA	$520,095	1
14	KANSASCITY	$473,597	1
15	DALLAS	$467,089	1
16	BUFFALO	$450,478	1
17	NEWORLEANS	$333,454	1
18	SEATTLE	$179,827	1

12

Initially, the MarketRank field looks fairly useless, reporting that all markets have a rank of 1. Right-click the Sum of MarketRank heading and choose Value Field Settings.

In the Value Field Settings dialog box, give the field a name such as **Rank**. Select the Show Values As tab. From here, change the setting for Show Data As to Running Total In. Because this field is used to rank the markets, change the Base Field to Market. Figure 12.14 shows the completed dialog box.

The result is a new data field that reports the relative rank of each market, as shown in Figure 12.15.

Figure 12.14
Change the Rank field to
be a running total within
market.

Figure 12.15
After the change to
Running Totals, the cal-
culated field properly
shows the rank of each
market.

Market	Sum of Sales_Amount	Rank
CALIFORNIA	$2,254,735	1
FLORIDA	$1,450,392	2
CHARLOTTE	$890,522	3
NEWYORK	$873,581	4
CANADA	$776,245	5
MICHIGAN	$678,705	6
PHOENIX	$570,255	7
DENVER	$538,039	8
TULSA	$520,095	9
KANSASCITY	$473,597	10
DALLAS	$467,089	11
BUFFALO	$450,478	12
NEWORLEANS	$333,454	13
SEATTLE	$179,827	14

CAUTION

The Rank field works only for the Market field. If you reshape the report to have Region replace
Market, you have to change the field options to change the base field to Region.

12

How do I hide calculation errors in my pivot table?

Often, when you employ a calculated field within a pivot table, you get calculation errors. These errors are typically caused by the values in the dataset. For example, in the pivot table shown in Figure 12.16, notice the division-by-zero errors.

Figure 12.16
This pivot table displays some unsightly division-by-zero errors.

	A	B	C	D
1		**Values**		
2	City	Service Hour per Dollar	Revenue	Contracted Hours
3	ABBEVILLE	0.05	$630	30
4	ABERDEEN	0.02	$2,258	49
5	ABILENE	0.03	$1,739	54
6	ACCORD	#DIV/0!	$0	10
7	ACKERMAN	0.03	$1,032	36
8	ACME	0.02	$490	12
9	ACTON VALE	#DIV/0!	$0	12
10	ACWORTH	0.06	$302	18
11	ADAIRSVILLE	0.03	$819	24
12	AMES	0.02	$2,090	45
13	AMHERST	#DIV/0!	$0	24
14	ANACORTES	0.05	$1,262	61
15	ANDREWS	0.03	$1,011	26
16	ANGELUS OAKS	#DIV/0!	$0	8
17	ANJOU	#DIV/0!	$0	42
18	ANKENY	0.04	$1,750	69
19	ANTHONY	0.04	$354	14
20	APACHE JUNCTION	0.04	$561	20
21	APOLLO	#DIV/0!	$0	2
22	APOPKA	0.06	$1,817	106

12

Although they are valid, these errors are unsightly and a bit distracting. You can easily hide calculation errors by tweaking the pivot table's configuration as follows:

1. Right-click on your pivot table and select PivotTable Options.
2. In the activated dialog box, select the Layout & Format tab.
3. Place a check next to For Error Values Show.
4. Enter a value you would like to see in place of the error values.

In the example illustrated in Figure 12.17, the error values will be replaced by the text NA.

After you make this change, your pivot table shows the universally understood not applicable value (NA) instead of ugly error values. You can see the difference in Figure 12.18.

Figure 12.17
You can set a value to show in place of error values.

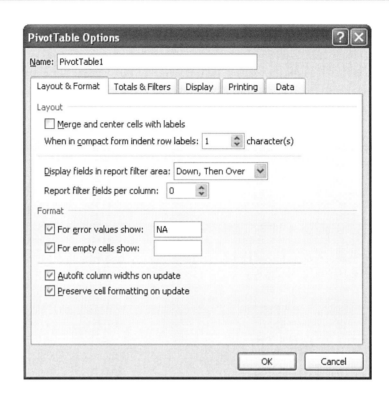

> **TIP**
> The PivotTable Options dialog box provides a similar option for empty cells. This option allows you to fill the empty values within your pivot table with a default value.

How can I reduce the size of my pivot table reports?

When you create a pivot table report, your workbook almost doubles in size. The reason is that Excel creates a cache or snapshot of your data and stores it with your workbook. This, in effect, creates a duplicate copy of your data specifically for your pivot table. In situations in which the datasets are large, all this duplication can lead to unwieldy workbooks that are difficult to distribute.

You can alleviate this problem by simply distributing the pivot table report without the source data that makes up its data source. To do this, you create your pivot table and then copy just the pivot table into a new workbook. Your clients can use the pivot table as normal, and your workbook is half as big.

So what happens if your clients need to see the source data? Well, they can simply double-click on the intersection of the row and column grand totals. This tells Excel to output the contents of the pivot table's cache into a new worksheet. So, with one double-click, your clients can re-create the source data that makes up the pivot table!

Figure 12.18
Your pivot table looks a
whole lot cleaner.

	A	B	C	D
1		Values		
2	City	Service Hour per Dollar	Revenue	Contracted Hours
3	ABBEVILLE	0.05	$630	30
4	ABERDEEN	0.02	$2,258	49
5	ABILENE	0.03	$1,739	54
6	ACCORD	NA	$0	10
7	ACKERMAN	0.03	$1,032	36
8	ACME	0.02	$490	12
9	ACTON VALE	NA	$0	12
10	ACWORTH	0.06	$302	18
11	ADAIRSVILLE	0.03	$819	24
12	AMES	0.02	$2,090	45
13	AMHERST	NA	$0	24
14	ANACORTES	0.05	$1,262	61
15	ANDREWS	0.03	$1,011	26
16	ANGELUS OAKS	NA	$0	8
17	ANJOU	NA	$0	42
18	ANKENY	0.04	$1,750	69
19	ANTHONY	0.04	$354	14
20	APACHE JUNCTION	0.04	$561	20
21	APOLLO	NA	$0	2
22	APOPKA	0.06	$1,817	106

How can I easily create a separate pivot table for each market?

One of the most common requests an analyst gets is to create a separate pivot table report for each region, market, manager, or whatever. These types of requests usually lead to a painful manual process in which you copy a pivot table onto a new worksheet and then change the filter field to the appropriate region or manager. You then repeat this process as many times as you need to get through each selection.

Creating separate pivot table reports is one area where Excel really comes to the rescue. Excel has a function called Show Report Filter Pages that automatically creates a separate pivot table for each item in your filter fields.

To use this function, simply create a pivot table with a filter field, as shown in Figure 12.19.

Place your cursor anywhere on the pivot table and then go up to the Ribbon to select the Options tab. On the Options tab, go to the PivotTable group and click the Options drop-down. Click the Show Report Filter Pages button, as demonstrated in Figure 12.20.

A dialog box opens, allowing you to choose the filter field for which you would like to create separate pivot tables. Select the appropriate filter field and click OK.

12

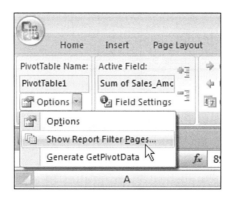

	A	B	C
1			
2	Market (All)		
3			
4	Sum of Sales_Amount	Sales_Period	
5	Product_Description	P01	P02	P0:
6	Cleaning & Housekeeping Services	80082.85	89750.17
7	Facility Maintenance and Repair	121303.92	305831.52
8	Fleet Maintenance	148565.44	297315.01
9	Green Plants and Foliage Care	75716.12	135529.12
10	Landscaping/Grounds Care	92352.89	99173.28
11	Predictive Maintenance/Preventative Maintenance	163843.66	189316.59
12	Grand Total	681864.88	1116915.69

Figure 12.20
Click the Show Report
Filter Pages button.

Your reward is a sheet for each item in your filter field containing its own pivot table. Figure 12.21 illustrates the result. Note the newly created tabs are named to correspond with the filter item shown in the pivot table.

> **NOTE**
> You can use Show Report Filter Pages on only one filter field at a time.

How do I avoid the need to constantly redefine my pivot table's data range?

You will undoubtedly encounter situations in which you have pivot table reports that are updated daily. That is, records are constantly added to the source data. When records are added to a pivot table's source dataset, you must redefine the range that is captured before the new records are brought into the pivot table. Redefining the source range for a pivot table once in a while is no sweat, but when the source data is changed on a daily or weekly basis, it can start to get bothersome. This is where a dynamic range can come in handy.

Figure 12.21

With just a few clicks, you can have a separate pivot table for each market!

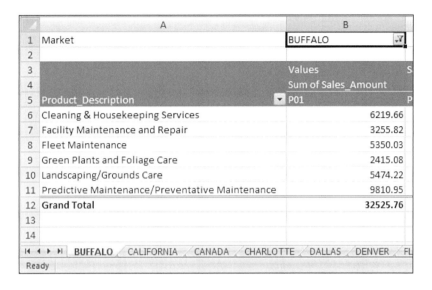

	A	B
1	Market	BUFFALO
2		
3		Values
4		Sum of Sales_Amount
5	Product_Description	P01
6	Cleaning & Housekeeping Services	6219.66
7	Facility Maintenance and Repair	3255.82
8	Fleet Maintenance	5350.03
9	Green Plants and Foliage Care	2415.08
10	Landscaping/Grounds Care	5474.22
11	Predictive Maintenance/Preventative Maintenance	9810.95
12	Grand Total	32525.76
13		
14		

BUFFALO / CALIFORNIA / CANADA / CHARLOTTE / DALLAS / DENVER / FL

Ready

A dynamic range is a named range that automatically shrinks or grows based on the number of rows and columns that exist in your dataset. The idea is that when you add rows or columns to your dataset, the dynamic range redefines itself so that the new rows are included.

Using a dynamic range with a pivot table enables you to add as many rows to your dataset as you need without the need to manually redefine the source range. The dynamic range does all the work for you.

To start building a dynamic range, you first need a range of data. In Figure 12.22, you see a data range that that will be added to each day. This data range is a perfect candidate for a dynamic range.

Figure 12.22

This dataset will grow daily.

	A	B	C	D	E	F
1	Region	Inovice #	Date	Sales Amount	State Tax	Total
2	West	11324	7/20/2007	$70	$6	$76
3	West	11325	7/21/2007	$343	$31	$373
4	North	11326	7/22/2007	$64	$6	$70
5	South	11327	7/23/2007	$169	$15	$184
6	North	11328	7/24/2007	$102	$9	$112
7	South	11328	7/24/2007	$102	$9	$112
8	South	11329	7/25/2007	$102	$9	$111
9	West	11329	7/25/2007	$102	$9	$111
10	West	11330	7/26/2007	$209	$19	$227
11	North	11331	7/27/2007	$162	$15	$176
12	South	11334	7/30/2007	$43	$4	$47
13	North	11335	7/31/2007	$191	$17	$208
14	West	11335	7/31/2007	$191	$17	$208
15						

12

Before building the pivot table, you need to create the dynamic named range. Select the Formulas tab on the application's Ribbon and then select the Define Name button. Selecting this button activates the New Name dialog box, shown in Figure 12.23.

Figure 12.23
Activate the New Name dialog box.

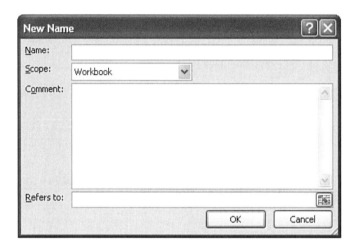

Then follow these steps:

1. In the Name box, enter a name for your named range. In this example, use the name **DynamicRange**.

2. In the Refers To box, enter the following Offset formula:
   =OFFSET(Sheet1!$A$1,0,0,COUNTA(Sheet1!$A:$A),COUNTA(Sheet1!$1:$1))

   This formula defines the range size based on the count of rows in column A and count of columns in row 1.

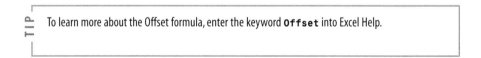

TIP
To learn more about the Offset formula, enter the keyword **Offset** into Excel Help.

When completed, your dialog box should look similar to the one shown in Figure 12.24.

3. Click OK to activate the named range.

4. Start a new pivot table, and in the Table/Range box, enter the name of your dynamic named range. In this case, you would enter **DynamicRange**, as demonstrated in Figure 12.25.

After creating your pivot table, you can add as many columns and rows as you want. All you have to do is refresh your pivot table, and the newly added rows and columns are picked up.

Figure 12.24
The completed dynamic
named range.

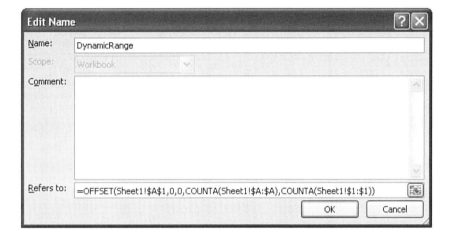

Figure 12.25
Use your newly created
dynamic named range as
your data source.

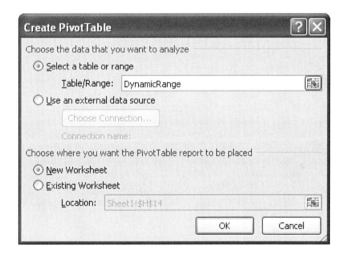

Finding Pivot Table Commands on the Ribbon

If you were accustomed to the PivotTable toolbar in Excel 97–Excel 2003, you might be initially frustrated by the new Ribbon interface.

This appendix provides a map. If you know where a command used to be in the legacy Excel interface, the tables in this chapter help you find the command in the new interface.

IN THIS CHAPTER

Inserting a Pivot Table 315

Finding Commands from the Legacy
PivotTable Toolbar 316

Inserting a Pivot Table

In previous versions of Excel, the entry point for creating a pivot table was always on the Data menu. After you selected PivotTable and PivotChart Report, you chose either a pivot table or pivot chart in the first step of the wizard.

In Excel 2007, there are two entry points for creating a pivot table:

- There is an icon and a drop-down at the start of the Insert ribbon. Click the top half of the icon to create a pivot table. Use the drop-down at the bottom of the icon to create either a pivot table or pivot chart (see Figure A.1).
- If you converted your dataset to a table using Ctrl+T, you can create a pivot table using the Table Tools Design ribbon. Choose Summarize with Pivot from the Tools group of this Ribbon.

Figure A.1
Use the Insert ribbon to create a pivot table or pivot chart.

Finding Commands from the Legacy PivotTable Toolbar

Previous versions of Excel offered a PivotTable toolbar, as shown in Figure A.2. Most of the commands were in the PivotTable drop-down on the left of the toolbar.

Figure A.2
The legacy PivotTable toolbar, showing the PivotTable drop-down.

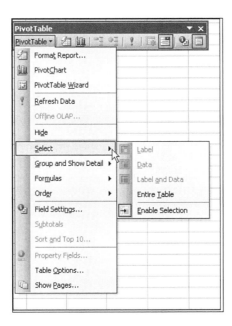

Table A.1 shows every command on the PivotTable toolbar and the location of the equivalent command in Excel 2007.

Table A.1 Commands on the PivotTable Toolbar	
Excel 2003 Command	**Excel 2007 Command**
PivotTable, Format Report	Pivot Table Tools Design, PivotTable Quick Styles

Excel 2003 Command	Excel 2007 Command
PivotTable, PivotChart	PivotTable Tools Options, Tools, PivotChart
PivotTable, PivotTable Wizard	Office icon, Excel Options, Customization, PivotTable
PivotTable, Refresh Data	PivotTable Tools Options, Data, Refresh, Refresh
PivotTable, Refresh Data	Table Tools Design, External Table Data, Refresh
PivotTable, Refresh Data	PivotChart Tools Analyze, Data, Refresh
PivotTable, Refresh Data	Data, Manage Connections, Refresh
PivotTable, Offline OLAP	PivotTable Tools Options, Tools, OLAP Tools, Offline OLAP
PivotTable, Delete	Row/Column shortcut menu, Delete
PivotTable, Select	PivotTable Tools Options, PivotTable Options, Table Options, Select
PivotTable, Select, Label	PivotTable Tools Options, PivotTable Options, Table Options, Select, Label
PivotTable, Select, Data	PivotTable Tools Options, PivotTable Options, Table Options, Select, Data
PivotTable, Select, Label and Data	PivotTable Tools Options, PivotTable Options, Table Options, Select, Label and Data
PivotTable, Select, Entire Table	PivotTable Tools Options, PivotTable Options, Table Options, Select, Entire Table
PivotTable, Select, Enable Selection	PivotTable Tools Options, PivotTable Options, Table Options, Select, Enable Selection
PivotTable, Group and Show Detail, Hide Detail	Data, Outline, Hide Detail
PivotTable, Group and Show Detail, Show Detail	Data, Outline, Show Detail
PivotTable, Group and Show Detail, Group	Data, Outline, Group, Group
PivotTable, Group and Show Detail, Group	Data, Outline, Group
PivotTable, Group and Show Detail, Ungroup	Data, Outline, Ungroup, Ungroup
PivotTable, Group and Show Detail, Ungroup	Data, Outline, Ungroup
PivotTable, Group and Show Detail, Ungroup	PivotTable Tools Options, Group, Ungroup
PivotTable, Formulas, Calculated Field	PivotTable Tools Options, Tools, Formulas, Calculated Field

A

continues

Table A.1 Continued

Excel 2003 Command	Excel 2007 Command
PivotTable, Formulas, Calculated Item	PivotTable Tools Options, Tools, Formulas, Calculated Item
PivotTable, Formulas, Solve Order	PivotTable Tools Options, Tools, Formulas, Solve Order
PivotTable, Formulas, List Formulas	PivotTable Tools Options, Tools, Formulas, List Formulas
PivotTable, Order, Move to Beginning	Cell shortcut menu, Move
PivotTable, Order, Move Up	Cell shortcut menu, Move
PivotTable, Order, Move Down	Cell shortcut menu, Move
PivotTable, Order, Move to End	Cell shortcut menu, Move
PivotTable, Order, Move to Column	Cell shortcut menu, Move
PivotTable, Field Settings	PivotTable Tools Options, Active Field, Field Settings
PivotTable, Subtotals	PivotTable Tools Styles, Layout, Subtotals
PivotTable, Sort and Top 10	Data, Sort & Filter
PivotTable, Property Fields	PivotTable Tools Options, Tools, OLAP Tools, Property Fields
PivotTable, Table Options	PivotTable Tools Options, PivotTable Options, Options
PivotTable, Table Options	PivotTable Tools Options, PivotTable Options, Table Options, Options
PivotTable, Show Pages	PivotTable Tools Options, PivotTable Options, Table Options, Show Pages
Format Report	PivotTable, Tools, Styles
Chart Wizard	Office Button, Excel Options, Customization, PivotTable
Hide Detail	Data, Outline, Hide Detail
Show Detail	Data, Outline, Show Detail
Refresh Data	Data, Manage Connections, Refresh
Refresh Data	PivotTable Tools Options, Data, Refresh
Refresh Data	Table Tools Design, External Table Data, Refresh
Refresh Data	PivotChart Tools Analyze, Data, Refresh

A

Excel 2003 Command	Excel 2007 Command
Hidden Items in Totals	*Removed from product.*
Always Display Items	*Removed from product.*
Field Settings	PivotTable Tools Options, Active Field, Field Settings
Show Field List	PivotTable Tools Options. Show/Hide. Field List

When a pivot chart was displayed in previous versions of Excel, a PivotChart drop-down replaced the PivotTable drop-down in the PivotTable toolbar, as shown in Figure A.3.

Figure A.3
The legacy PivotTable toolbar, showing the PivotChart drop-down.

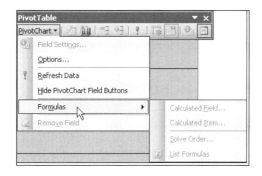

Table A.2 shows the commands on the PivotChart drop-down and their equivalent commands in Excel 2007.

Table A.2   Commands on the PivotChart Drop-Down

Excel 2003 Command	Excel 2007 Command
PivotChart, Field Settings	PivotTable Tools Options, Active Field, Field Settings
PivotChart, Options	PivotTable Tools Options, PivotTable Options, Options
PivotChart, Options	PivotTable Tools Options, PivotTable Options, Table Options, Options
PivotChart, Refresh Data	PivotTable Tools Options, Data, Refresh
PivotChart, Refresh Data	PivotTable Tools Options, Data, Refresh, Refresh
PivotChart, Refresh Data	Table Tools Design, External Table Data, Refresh

continues

Table A.2 Continued

Excel 2003 Command	Excel 2007 Command
PivotChart, Refresh Data	Table Tools Design, External Table Data, Refresh, Refresh
PivotChart, Refresh Data	PivotChart Tools Analyze, Data, Refresh
PivotChart, Refresh Data	PivotChart Tools Analyze, Data, Refresh, Refresh
PivotChart, Refresh Data	Data, Manage Connections, Refresh
PivotChart, Refresh Data	Data, Manage Connections, Refresh, Refresh
PivotChart, Hide PivotChart Field Buttons	*Removed from product.*
PivotChart, Formulas, Calculated Field	PivotTable Tools Options, Tools, Formulas, Calculated Field
PivotChart, Formulas, Calculated Item	PivotTable Tools Options, Tools, Formulas, Calculated Item
PivotChart, Formulas, Solve Order	PivotTable Tools Options, Tools, Formulas, Solve Order
PivotChart, Formulas, List Formulas	PivotTable Tools Options, Tools, Formulas, List Formulas
PivotChart, Remove Field	Field Menu, Remove, Remove Field

A

INDEX

Symbols

% of Column option (Sum of Revenue field), 73

% Of option (Sum of Revenue field), 75

% of Row option (Sum of Revenue field), 72

% of Total option (Sum of Revenue field), 73

A

Access data, building pivot tables from, 180-183

ActiveFilters property, 237

ActiveX controls, 218

activity by market, analyzing (case study), 35-38

Add Parameters dialog box, 196

AddFields method, 241

AllowMultipleFilters property, 238

Analysis Services Tutorial cube, 202

analyzing activity by market (case study), 35-38

Autofit Column Widths on Update option, suppressing, 229

automatic subtotals, 253-254

AutoShow option, 267-270

AutoSort, 100, 248

Average function, 66

averages, 276-277

axes (pivot charts), 146

B

blank cells
  replacing with zeros, 49-50
  summary calculations, 65-66

blank cells, eliminating, 248

browsers, viewing pivot tables in, 199

C

cache (pivot)
  pivot cache objects, building, 240
  refreshing, 17
  sharing
    overview, 41
    side effects of, 41-42

CalcItemsProblem macro, 261-262

calculated fields, 258-260
  case study: summarizing next year's forecast, 124-129
  creating with external formulas, 118-119
  definition, 117
  inserting directly into pivot tables, 119-124
  manually adding to data sources, 118
  rules for use, 135-136
  troubleshooting, 296

calculated items, 260-263
  creating, 129-133
  definition, 117
  rules for use, 136-137

calculation options
  percentage growth from previous month, 278
  percentage of specific items, 278
  percentage of total, 277
  running totals, 278-279

calculations. *See also* functions; macros
  calculated fields
    case study: summarizing next year's forecast, 124-129
    creating with external formulas, 118-119

definition, 117
inserting directly into
pivot tables, 119-124
manually adding to
data sources, 118
rules for use, 135-136
calculated items
creating, 129-133
definition, 117
rules for use, 136-137
cell references, 135
constants, 135
cube formulas, 211-213
deleting, 137
documenting, 139
editing, 137
errors, hiding in pivot
tables, 307
named ranges, 135
operator precedence,
134-135
percentages
percentage growth
from previous
month, 278
percentage of specific
items, 278
percentage of
total, 277
running totals,
278-279
referencing totals, 135
running totals
% Difference From
option, 72
% of Column
option, 73
% Of option, 75
% of Row option, 72
% of Total option, 73

Difference From
option, 71
Index option, 75-77
overview, 70-71
Running Total In
option, 72
solve order, changing,
138-139
subtotals
adding multiple,
69-70
suppressing, 68
summary calculations
blank cells, 65-66
functions, 66-67
worksheet functions, 135

**Cannot group that
selection (error
message), 294**

case studies
analyzing activity by
market, 35-38
consolidating and
analyzing datasets,
176-179
converting pivot tables to
values, 56-60
creating order lead-time
report, 88-89
creating top 10 report,
113-114
grouping text fields,
90-92
preparing data for pivot
table analysis, 25-26
report showing invoice
frequency and revenue
distribution by product,
148-152
revenue by line of
business reports, 77-80

summarizing next year's
forecast, 124-129
synchronizing two pivot
tables with one combo
box, 225-229

cells
blank cells
eliminating, 248
replacing with zeros,
49-50
summary calculations,
65-66
data ranges, handling
with VBA, 235-236
empty cells, filling,
299-302
named ranges, 135
references, 135

**Change PivotTable Data
Source dialog box, 40-41**

charts. *See* **pivot charts**

**classic PivotTable,
activating, 169**

Clear command, 42-43

Clear method, 244

**ClearAllFilters
method, 237**

clearing
filters, 106
pivot tables, 42-43

ClearTable method, 237

Code window (VBA), 233

color gradients, 286-287

Column field, 174-175

**Column Labels drop
zone, 29**

columns
Autofit Column Widths on Update option, suppressing, 229
column area, 15
Column field, 174-175
Column Labels drop zone, 29
headings, 292

commands
finding, 316-320
quick reference table, 316-320
Ribbon commands, 9

compact layout, 52-53

CompactLayoutColumn Header property, 238

CompactLayoutRow-Header property, 238

CompactRowIndent property, 238

compatibility issues, 293
Compatibility Checker, 18-19
Compatibility mode, 18, 190

conditional formatting, 157-166

connecting to OLAP cubes, 202-205

consolidating and analyzing datasets (case study), 176-179

consolidation ranges, multiple
case study: consolidating and analyzing datasets, 176-179
Column field, 174-175
Page fields, 175

Row field, 174
selecting, 168-174
Value field, 175

constants in calculations, 135

controls
ActiveX controls, 218
form controls, 218-220

Convert to Formulas tool, 211-213

converting
pivot tables to cube formulas, 211-213
pivot tables to values, 56-60

ConvertToFormulas method, 237

copying pivot tables, 298-299

Count function, 66, 292

Count Nums function, 67

Create Cube File Wizard, 208-210

Create PivotTable dialog box, 27-28

CreatePivot macro, 242-243

CreatePivotDataBar macro, 286-287

CreatePivotTable method, 240-241

CreateSummaryReport-UsingPivot macro, 244-246

.cub file extension, 209

cube formulas, 211-213

cubes (OLAP)
connecting to, 202-205
cube formulas, 211-213

definition, 201-202
dimensions, 205
hierarchies, 205
levels, 205
limitations of OLAP pivot tables, 207
measures, 206
members, 206
offline cubes, creating, 207-210
structure, 205-206

Custom Lists dialog box, 101-102

custom sorts, 101-102

customizing pivot tables
blank cells, replacing with zeros, 49-50
compact layout, 52-53
default pivot table features, 46
field names, 51
number format, 47-48
outline layout, 54
overview, 45
running totals, 70-71
% Difference From option, 72
% of Column option, 73
% Of option, 75
% of Row option, 72
% of Total option, 73
Difference From option, 71
Index option, 75-77
Running Total In option, 72
styles
choosing default styles, 64
creating, 62-63

modifying, 64
overview, 61
subtotals
adding multiple,
69-70
supressing, 68
summary calculations,
65-67
table styles, 47
tabular layout, 54-55

D

data bars, 286-287

Data Field Settings dialog box, 48

data ranges
dynamic ranges, 310-312
handling with VBA,
235-236

data sources
calculated fields
adding manually, 118
case study:
summarizing next
year's forecast,
124-129
creating with external
formulas, 118-119
inserting directly into
pivot tables, 119-124
disparate data sources,
analyzing, 167
case study: consolidat-
ing and analyzing
datasets, 176-179
multiple consolidation
ranges, 168-175
external data sources,
179-180
Microsoft Access,
180-183
SQL Server, 183-187

preparing for pivot table
reporting
case study, 25-26
data spread across
columns, 23
effective data source
design, 24
field formatting, 24
gaps and blank cells,
23-24
overview, 21
section headings,
22-23
tabular layouts, 22

**data visualizations,
286-287**

databases
database-centric
layouts, 22
OLAP (Online
Analytical Processing)
cubes
connecting to,
202-205
cube formulas,
211-213
definition, 201-202
dimensions, 205
hierarchies, 205
levels, 205
limitations of OLAP
pivot tables, 207
measures, 206
members, 206
offline cubes, creating,
207-210
structure, 205-206

date fields
grouping, 84-85
by month and year, 86
by week, 86-88

case study: creating
order lead-time
report, 88-89
two date fields in one
report, 88
grouping by month,
263-265
grouping by week,
265-267

Date Filters, 109-111

**default pivot table
features, 46**

default styles, 64

**Defer Layout Update
tool, 42, 293**

**deferring layout
updates, 42**

deleting
calculations, 137
pivot tables, 154

Developer ribbon, 232

dialog boxes. *See* **specific
dialog boxes**

**% Difference From
option (Sum of Revenue
field, 72**

**Difference From
option (Sum of Revenue
field), 71**

**dimensions of OLAP
cubes, 205**

**disparate data sources,
analyzing, 167**
case study: consolidating
and analyzing datasets,
176-179
external data sources,
179-180
Microsoft Access,
180-183
SQL Server, 183-187

multiple consolidation ranges
Column field, 174-175
Page fields, 175
Row field, 174
selecting, 168-174
Value field, 175

DisplayAllMember PropertiesInTooltip method, 237

DisplayContextTooltips property, 238

DisplayFieldCaptions property, 238

DisplayMemberProperty Tooltips property, 238

distributing pictures of pivot charts, 154

docking PivotTable Field List, 93

documenting formulas, 139

drag-and-drop functionality, 34-35

drop zones
Column Labels, 29
Report Filter, 29
Row Labels, 29
Values, 30

dynamic ranges, 310-312

E

editing
calculations, 137
macros, 220-225
styles, 64

empty cells, filling, 299-300, 302

enabling
Developer ribbon, 232
VBA, 231-232

error messages
Cannot group that selection, 294
The PivotTable field name is not valid, 291

Excel 4 summary reports, 2-4

Excel 97 compatibility issues, 288

Excel 2003 pivot tables, 190

Excel 2007
Compatibility Checker, 18-19
Compatibility mode, 18, 190

Excel Services, publishing pivot tables to, 193-199
Excel Services features, 196-197
features disallowed in Excel Services, 198
preparation, 194
requirements, 194
step-by-step process, 194-196
viewing pivot tables, 199

Excel Services Options dialog box, 195-196

executive overviews, creating with AutoShow option, 267-270

external data sources, 179-180
Microsoft Access, 180-183
SQL Server, 183-187

external formulas, creating calculated fields with, 118-119

F

Field Settings dialog box, 70, 94

FieldListSortAscending property, 238

fields
adding to Report Filter area, 103
adding to reports, 29-32
addressing issues, 257
calculated fields, 258-260
case study: summarizing next year's forecast, 124-129
creating with external formulas, 118-119
definition, 117
inserting directly into pivot tables, 119-124
manually adding to data sources, 118
rules for use, 135-136
troubleshooting, 296
calculated items, 260-263
Column, 174-175
date fields, grouping, 84-85
by month, 263-265
by month and year, 86
by week, 86-88, 265-267
case study: creating order lead-time report, 88-89
two date fields in one report, 88

formatting, 24
grouping, 83, 294
numeric fields, grouping,
89-90
Page fields, 175, 272
PivotFields, filtering
manually, 275-276
PivotTable Field List
docking/
undocking, 93
drop zone
drop-downs, 94
Fields drop-down, 94
filtering pivot tables
with, 106-108
rearranging, 93
sorting pivot tables
with, 98
rank number fields,
305-307
renaming, 51
Row, 174
Sum of Revenue: Show
Values As options,
70-77
text fields, grouping,
90-92
ungrouping, 92
Value, 175
files
.cub file extension, 209
.xls format, 18
.xlsm extension, 232
filling empty cells,
299-302
Filter (Customer) dialog
box, 114
filtering, 279-284
creating filters, 33-34
pivot tables, 102
case study: creating
top 10 report,
113-114
Date Filters, 109-111

Field List filters,
106-108
Label Filters, 108-109
Report Filter area,
adding fields to, 103
selecting/clearing
filter items, 106
Value Filters, 111-112
with multiple
items, 104
with single item,
104-105
PivotChart Filter
Pane, 144
PivotFields, 275-276
recordsets with
ShowDetail option,
270-272
reports, 279-284
finding commands,
316-320
For Error Values Show
option, 307
form controls, 218-220
Format Data Series dialog
box, 149
formatting
fields, 24
numbers, 47-48
pivot charts, 146-148
pivot table reports,
252-253
formatting pivot tables,
157-166
formulas. *See* **calculations**
functions. *See also*
calculations; macros
AddFields, 241
Average, 66
in calculations, 135
Clear, 244
ClearAllFilters, 237

ClearTable, 237
ConvertToFormulas, 237
CreatePivotTable,
240-241
Count, 66, 292
Count Nums, 67
DisplayAllMemberProp-
ertiesInTooltip, 237
INDEX, 227
Max, 67
Min, 67
Product, 67
RowAxisLayout, 237
StdDev, 67
SubtotalLocation, 237
Sum, 66, 241-243
Var, 67
VarP, 67

G

Go To Special dialog box,
57-58
grand totals,
suppressing, 250
grouping
date fields, 84-85
case study: creating
order lead-time
report, 88-89
by month, 263-265
by month and year, 86
by week, 86-88,
265-267
two date fields in one
report, 88
fields, 83, 294
numeric fields, 89-90
text fields, 90-92
Grouping dialog box,
85-87, 90

H

headings
  column headings, 292
  section headings, 22-23
hiding calculation
  errors, 307
hierarchies of OLAP
  cubes, 205

I

icon sets, 286-287
Import Data dialog box,
  182, 187
INDEX function, 227
Index option (Sum of
  Revenue field), 75-77
InGridDropZones
  property, 238
Insert Calculated Field
  dialog box, 121-122,
  125-128, 305
Insert Calculated Item
  dialog box, 129-131
inserting pivot tables, 315
invention of pivot
  tables, 5-6
invoice frequency,
  showing by product,
  148-152
items, calculated
  creating, 129-133
  definition, 117
  rules for use, 136-137

J-K-L

Jobs, Steve, 6

keywords, Set, 236

Label Filter dialog box,
  108-110

Label Filters, 108-109

layers, adding to
  reports, 32

LayoutRowDefault
  property, 238

layouts
  changing, 285-286
  compact layout, 52-53
  database-centric
    layouts, 22
  deferring layout
    updates, 42
  outline layout, 54
  overview, 52
  tabular layouts, 22, 54-55

levels of OLAP
  cubes, 205

limitations of pivot table
  reports, 17-18

lines, comparing, 75

linked datasets, 154-156

List Formulas command,
  139-140

lists, PivotTable Field
  List
  docking/undocking, 93
  drop zone drop-
    downs, 94
  Fields drop-down, 94
  filtering pivot tables
    with, 106-108

rearranging, 93
  sorting pivot tables
    with, 98
Live Preview feature, 48
Lotus 1-2-3 summary
  reports, 2-4
Lotus Improv, 5

M

macro recorder
  (VBA), 234

macros. *See also*
  calculations; functions
  benefits of, 215
  CalcItemsProblem,
    261-262
  CreatePivot, 242-243
  CreatePivotDataBar,
    286-287
  CreateSummaryReport
    UsingPivot, 244-246
  definition, 215
  form controls, 218-220
  modifying, 220-225
  PivotExcel97
    Compatible,
    272-275, 288
  ProductLineReport,
    254-256
  recording, 216-217
  RefreshData example,
    217
  ReportByMonth,
    264-265
  ReportByWeek, 266-267
  RetrieveTop3Customer
    Detail, 270-272
  security, 217-218
  SynchMarkets example,
    225-229

Top5ByRegionReport, 273-275

Top5Markets, 268-270

TopNthCusts example, 221-225

TwoDataFields, 259-260

Macros dialog box, 232

manual sort order, 276

manual sorts, 100-101

ManualUpdate property, 240

market activity, analyzing (case study), 35-38

markets, creating separate tables for each market, 309-310

Max function, 67

maximums, 276-277

measures of OLAP cubes, 206

members of OLAP cubes, 206

memory, pivot cache, 17

methods. *See* **functions; macros**

Microsoft Access data, building pivot tables from, 180-183

Min function, 67

minimums, 276-277

Modify Table Quick Style dialog box, 63

modifying. *See* **editing**

months
displaying all, 303-304
grouping fields by, 86, 263-265

Move Chart dialog box, 143

Move PivotTable dialog box, 43-44

moving pivot charts, 143

multiple consolidation ranges
case study: consolidating and analyzing datasets, 176-179
Column field, 174-175
Page fields, 175
Row field, 174
selecting, 168-174
Value field, 175

N

named ranges, 135

names of fields, changing, 51

New Formatting Rule dialog box, 161-163

New Name dialog box, 312

number formats, 47-48, 248-249

numeric fields, grouping, 89-90

O

object variables, 236

object-oriented syntax (VBA), 234

objects
object variables, 236
object-oriented syntax (VBA), 234
pivot cache objects, building, 240

Office Services. *See* **Excel Services**

offline OLAP cubes, creating, 207-210

OLAP (Online Analytical Processing) cubes
connecting to, 202-205
cube formulas, 211-213
definition, 201-202
dimensions, 205
hierarchies, 205
levels, 205
limitations of OLAP pivot tables, 207
measures, 206
members, 206
offline cubes, creating, 207-210
structure, 205-206

opening pivot tables in older versions of Excel, 293

operator precedence, 134-135

Options ribbon, 96-98

order lead-time reports, creating, 88-89

outline layout, 54

Outline view, 252

P

Page fields, 175, 272

Paste Values feature, 153

percentages
percentage growth from previous month, 278
percentage of specific items, 278
percentage of total, 277
running totals, 278-279

pivot cache
pivot cache objects,
  building, 240
refreshing, 17
sharing
    overview, 41
    side effects of, 41-42

pivot charts
alternatives to
    deleting underlying
      pivot table, 154
    distributing picture of
      pivot chart, 154
    linked datasets,
      154-156
    turning pivot table
      into hard values, 153
capabilities, 141-142
case study: report
  showing invoice
  frequency and revenue
  distribution by product,
  148-152
changing location of, 143
creating, 142-145
data field placement,
  145-146
definition, 141
effect of changes to
  underlying pivot
  table, 145
formatting limitations,
  146-148
PivotChart Filter
  Pane, 144

pivot table reports
AutoShow option,
  267-270
averages, minimums, and
  maximums, 276-277
calculation errors,
  hiding, 307

case study: report
  showing invoice
  frequency and revenue
  distribution by product,
  148-152
creating for each region
  or model, 272-275
data fields
    adding, 29-32
    addressing issues, 257
    calculated data fields,
      258-260
    calculated items,
      260-263
    date fields, grouping
      by month, 263-265
    date fields, grouping
      by week, 265-267
data visualizations,
  286-287
defined, 11
filtering, 33-34, 279-284
layers, 32
layout, 285-286
limitations, 17-18
macros
    benefits of, 215
    definition, 215
    form controls,
      218-220
    modifying, 220-225
    recording, 216-217
    RefreshData
      example, 217
    security, 217-218
    SynchMarkets
      example, 225-229
    TopNthCusts
      example, 221-225
order lead-time reports,
  creating, 88-89
page fields, 272

percentages
    percentage growth
      from previous
      month, 278
    percentage of specific
      items, 278
    percentage of
      total, 277
    running totals,
      278-279
PivotFields, filtering
  manually, 275-276
rearranging, 32-33
refreshing, 40
resizing, 308
revenue by line of
  business reports, 77-80
revenue by product
  reports, 246-248
    automatic subtotals,
      253-254
    blank cells,
      eliminating, 248
    final formatting,
      252-253
    grand totals,
      suppressing, 250
    number format,
      248-249
    Outline view, 252
    ProductLineReport
      macro, 254-256
    sort order, 248
    subtotals, suppressing,
      249-250
    summaries, 251-252
    table layout, 248
seasonality reports, 73
ShowDetail option,
  270-272
sorting, 276

summaries, 251-252

top 10 reports, creating, 113-114

pivot tables

advantages, 12-13

building in VBA, 239

AddFields method, 241

CreatePivot macro, 242-243

CreatePivotTable method, 240-241

CreateSummary-ReportUsingPivot macro, 244-246

ManualUpdate property, 240

pivot cache objects, 240

pivot table size, 244-246

Sum function, 241-243

calculations. *See* calculations

changing, 243

clearing, 42-43

columns

column area, 15

headings, 292

compared to Lotus 1-2-3 or Excel 4 summary reports, 2-4, 7-8

compatibility, 18-19

conditional formatting, 157-166

converting to values, 56-60

copying, 298-299

creating, 26-28, 309-310

customizing

blank cells, replacing with zeros, 49-50

compact layout, 52-53

default pivot table features, 46

field names, 51

number format, 47-48

outline layout, 54

overview, 45

running totals, 70-77

styles, 61-64

subtotals, 68-70

summary calculations, 65-67

table styles, 47

tabular layout, 54-55

data ranges

dynamic ranges, 310-312

handling with VBA, 235-236

deferring layout updates, 42

defined, 11

deleting, 154

empty cells, filling, 299-302

Excel 97 compatibility issues, 288

Excel 2003 pivot tables, 190

excluded months, displaying, 303-304

external data sources, 179-180

Microsoft Access, 180-183

SQL Server, 183-187

fields

adding, 29-32

addressing issues, 257

calculated data fields, 258-260

calculated items, 260-263

Column, 174-175

grouping, 83-92, 263-267, 294

Page fields, 175, 272

rank number fields, 305-307

renaming, 51

Row, 174

ungrouping, 92

Value, 175

filtering, 102

case study: creating top 10 report, 113-114

Date Filters, 109-111

Field List filters, 106-108

Label Filters, 108-109

with multiple items, 104

Report Filter area, adding fields to, 103

selecting/clearing filter items, 106

with single item, 104-105

Value Filters, 111-112

inserting, 315

invention of, 5-6

layers, 32

layouts

compact layout, 52-53

outline layout, 54

overview, 52

tabular layout, 54-55

limitations, 17-18

multiple consolidation ranges

case study: consolidating and analyzing datasets, 176-179

Column field, 174-175

Page fields, 175
Row field, 174
selecting, 168-174
Value field, 175
new features, 2
OLAP (Online
Analytical Processing)
cubes
connecting to,
202-205
cube formulas,
211-213
definition, 201-202
dimensions, 205
hierarchies, 205
levels, 205
limitations of OLAP
pivot tables, 207
measures, 206
members, 206
offline cubes, creating,
207-210
structure, 205-206
opening in older versions
of Excel, 293
pivot cache, sharing,
41-42
PivotTable Field List
docking/
undocking, 93
drop zone
drop-downs, 94
Fields drop-down, 94
filtering pivot tables
with, 106-108
rearranging, 93
sorting pivot tables
with, 98
preparing data for
case study, 25-26
data spread across
columns, 23

effective data source
design, 24
field formatting, 24
gaps and blank cells,
23-24
overview, 21
section headings,
22-23
tabular layouts, 22
publishing to Excel
Services, 193-199
Excel Services fea-
tures, 196-197
features disallowed in
Excel Services, 198
preparation, 194
requirements, 194
step-by-step process,
194-196
viewing pivot
tables, 199
publishing to web,
191-192
rearranging, 32-33
redefining, 176
refreshing, 216, 291-292
refreshing all pivot
tables simultane-
ously, 297-298
refreshing automati-
cally, 297
relocating, 43-44
report filters
creating, 33-34
report filter area, 16
reports. *See* pivot table
reports
row area, 15
running totals
% Difference From
option, 72
% of Column
option, 73

% Of option, 75
% of Row option, 72
% of Total option, 73
Difference From
option, 71
Index option, 75-77
overview, 70-71
Running Total In
option, 72
sharing
with Excel Services,
193-199
with other Office
versions, 189-191
as web pages, 191-192
sorting
AutoSort, 100
custom sorts,
101-102, 298
with Field List hidden
drop-down, 98
manual sorts, 100-101
with Options ribbon,
96-98
subtotals
adding multiple,
69-70
suppressing, 68
synchronizing two pivot
tables with one combo
box, 225-229
table styles, 284-285
troubleshooting
calculated fields, 296
Cannot group that
selection (error
message), 294
column headings, 292
Count function, 292
data displayed twice,
294-295
Defer Layout Update
option, 293

deleted data items in filter area, 295-296

disappearing data, 291-292

The PivotTable field name is not valid (error message), 291

version compatibility, 293

turning into hard data, 298-299

turning into hard values, 153

values area, 14-15

version 10 pivot tables, 191

version 12 pivot tables, 190

viewing in browsers, 199

when to use, 13-14

PivotChart drop-down, equivalent Ribbon commands, 319-320

PivotChart Filter Pane, 144

PivotChart Wizard, 169

PivotColumnAxis property, 238

PivotExcel97Compatible macro, 272-275, 288

PivotFields, filtering manually, 275-276

PivotRowAxis property, 238

PivotTable and PivotChart Wizard command, adding to Quick Access toolbar, 169

PivotTable Field List

docking/undocking, 93

drop zone drop-downs, 94

Fields drop-down, 94

filtering pivot tables with, 106-108

rearranging, 93

sorting pivot tables with, 98

PivotTable Field List dialog box, 28, 42

PivotTable Options dialog box, 49

PivotTable toolbar, equivalent Ribbon commands, 316-319

precedence of operators, 134-135

preparing data for pivot table reporting

case study, 25-26

data spread across columns, 23

effective data source design, 24

field formatting, 24

gaps and blank cells, 23-24

overview, 21

section headings, 22-23

tabular layouts, 22

PrintDrillIndicators property, 238

Product function, 67

ProductLineReport macro, 254-256

Project Explorer, 232

properties. *See* specific properties

Properties window (VBA), 233

Publish as Web Page dialog box, 192-193

Q-R

Quick Access toolbar, 169

ranges

dynamic ranges, 310-312

handling with VBA, 235-236

named ranges, 135

rank number fields, 305-307

rearranging

pivot tables, 32-33

PivotTable Field List, 93

Record Macro dialog box, 216-217

recording macros, 216-217

recordsets, filtering with ShowDetail option, 270-272

redefining pivot tables, 176

references (cell), 135

RefreshData macro, 217

refreshing

pivot cache, 17

pivot table reports, 40

pivot tables, 216, 291-292

refreshing all pivot tables simultaneously, 297-298

refreshing automatically, 297

region reports, creating, 272-275

relative importance, tracking, 75-77

relocating pivot tables, 43-44

renaming fields, 51

replacing blank cells with zeros, 49-50

Report Filter area, 16, 29, 103

ReportByMonth macro, 264-265

ReportByWeek macro, 266-267

reports
  AutoShow option, 267-270
  averages, minimums, and maximums, 276-277
  calculation errors, hiding, 307
  case study: report showing invoice frequency and revenue distribution by product, 148-152
  creating for each region or model, 272-275
  data fields
    adding, 29-32
    addressing issues, 257
    calculated data fields, 258-260
    calculated items, 260-263
    date fields, grouping by month, 263-265
    date fields, grouping by week, 265-267

  data visualizations, 286-287
  defined, 11
  filtering, 33-34, 279-284
  layers, 32
  layout, 285-286
  limitations, 17-18
  macros
    benefits of, 215
    definition, 215
    form controls, 218-220
    modifying, 220-225
    recording, 216-217
    RefreshData example, 217
    security, 217-218
    SynchMarkets example, 225-229
    TopNthCusts example, 221-225
  order lead-time reports, creating, 88-89
  page fields, 272
  percentages
    percentage growth from previous month, 278
    percentage of specific items, 278
    percentage of total, 277
    running totals, 278-279
  PivotFields, filtering manually, 275-276
  rearranging, 32-33
  refreshing, 40
  resizing, 308
  revenue by line of business reports, 77-80

  revenue by product reports, 246-248
    automatic subtotals, 253-254
    blank cells, eliminating, 248
    final formatting, 252-253
    grand totals, suppressing, 250
    number format, 248-249
    Outline view, 252
    ProductLineReport macro, 254-256
    sort order, 248
    subtotals, suppressing, 249-250
    summaries, 251-252
    table layout, 248
  seasonality reports, 73
  ShowDetail option, 270-272
  sorting, 276
  summaries, 251-252
  top 10 reports, creating, 113-114

resizing pivot table reports, 308

RetrieveTop3Customer-Detail macro, 270-272

revenue by line of business reports, 77-80

revenue by product reports, creating, 246-248
  automatic subtotals, 253-254
  blank cells, eliminating, 248
  final formatting, 252-253

grand totals,
suppressing, 250
number format, 248-249
Outline view, 252
ProductLineReport
macro, 254-256
sort order, 248
subtotals, suppressing,
249-250
summaries, 251-252
table layout, 248

revenue distribution,
showing by product,
148-152

ribbons, 9
Developer, 232
Options, 96-98

row area, 15

Row field, 174

Row Labels drop zone, 29

RowAxisLayout
method, 237

Running Total In
option (Sum of Revenue
field), 72

running totals, 278-279
% Difference From
option, 72
% of Column option, 73
% Of option, 75
% of Row option, 72
% of Total option, 73
Difference From
option, 71
Index option, 75, 77
overview, 70-71
Running Total In
option, 72

S

Salas, Pito, 5-6

seasonality reports, 73

section headings, avoiding
data in, 22-23

security, 217-218

Select Table dialog
box, 181

Set keyword, 236

sharing
pivot cache
overview, 41
side effects of, 41-42
pivot tables
with Excel Services,
193-199
with other Office
versions, 189-191
as web pages, 191-192

ShowDetail option,
270-272

ShowDrillIndicators
property, 239

ShowTableStyleColumn-
Headers property, 239

ShowTableStyleColumn-
Stripes property, 239

ShowTableStyleLast-
Column property, 239

ShowTableStyleRow-
Headers property, 239

ShowTableStyleRow-
Stripes property, 239

size of pivot tables,
determining, 244-246

slicing the measures
(OLAP), 206

Solve Order dialog box,
138-139

solve order of
calculations, changing,
138-139

Sort dialog box, 98-100

sorting pivot tables, 96,
248, 298
AutoSort, 100
custom sorts, 101-102
with Field List hidden
drop-down, 98
manual sorts, 100-101,
276
with Options ribbon,
96-98

SortUsingCustomLists
property, 239

*Special Edition Using Excel
2007*, 218

*Special Edition Using
Microsoft Excel
2007*, 19

SQL Server data, building
pivot tables from,
183-187

StdDev function, 67

StdDevP function, 67

styles
choosing default
styles, 64
creating, 62-63
modifying, 64
overview, 61
table styles, 47, 284-285

SubtotalLocation
method, 237

subtotals
adding, 69-70, 253-254
suppressing, 68, 249-250

Sum function, 66, 241-243

Sum of Revenue field, Show Values As options, 70-71
% Difference From, 72
% Of, 75
% of Column, 73
% of Row, 72
% of Total, 73
Difference From, 71
Index, 75, 77
Running Total In, 72

summaries, creating, 251-252

summarizing next year's forecast (case study), 124-129

summary calculations
blank cells, 65-66
functions, 66-67

suppressing
grand totals, 250
subtotals, 68, 249-250

SynchMarkets macro, 225-229

synchronizing two pivot tables with one combo box (case study), 225-229

T

table layout, 248

table styles, 47, 284-285

TableStyle2 property, 239

tables. *See* pivot tables

tabular layouts, 22, 54-55

text fields, grouping, 90-92

The PivotTable field name is not valid (error message), 291

toolbars
PivotTable toolbar, 316-319
Quick Access toolbar, 169

tools, VBA tools, 233-234

top 10 reports, creating, 113-114

Top5ByRegionReport macro, 273-275

Top5Markets macro, 268-270

TopNthCusts macro, 221-225

totals
grand totals, suppressing, 250
percentage of total, 277
referencing, 135
running totals, 278-279
% Difference From option, 72
% of Column option, 73
% Of option, 75
% of Row option, 72
% of Total option, 73
Difference From option, 71
Index option, 75-77
overview, 70-71
Running Total In option, 72

subtotals
adding, 69-70, 253-254
suppressing, 68, 249-250

troubleshooting
calculation errors, 307
pivot tables
calculated fields, 296
Cannot group that selection (error message), 294
column headings, 292
Count function, 292
data displayed twice, 294-295
Defer Layout Update option, 293
deleted data items in filter area, 295-296
disappearing data, 291-292
The PivotTable field name is not valid. (error message), 291
version compatibility, 293

trusted locations, 217-218

TwoDataFields macro, 259-260

U

undocking PivotTable Field List, 93

ungrouping fields, 92

updates, deferring, 42

user interfaces, 218-220

V

Value field, 175

Value Field Settings dialog box, 305

Value Filter dialog box, 112

Value Filters, 111-112

values
  converting pivot tables to, 56-60
  values area, 14-15
  Values drop zone, 30

Var function, 67

variables, 236

VarP function, 67

VBA (Visual Basic for Applications), 231
  AutoShow option, 267-270
  averages, minimums, and maximums, 276-277
  building pivot tables in, 239
    AddFields method, 241
    CreatePivot macro, 242-243
    CreatePivotTable method, 240-241
    CreateSummary-ReportUsingPivot macro, 244-246
    ManualUpdate property, 240
    pivot cache objects, 240
    pivot table size, 244-246
    Sum function, 241-243

data fields
  addressing issues, 257
  calculated data fields, 258-260
  calculated items, 260-263
  date fields, grouping by month, 263-265
  date fields, grouping by week, 265-267
data ranges, handling, 235-236
Developer ribbon, 232
  enabling, 231-232
Excel 2007 new features, 237-239
filters, 279-284
macro recorder, 234
macros. *See* macros
manual sort order, 276
object-oriented syntax, 234
object variables, 236
Outline view, 252
overview, 231
page fields, 272
percentages
  percentage growth from previous month, 278
  percentage of specific items, 278
  percentage of total, 277
  running totals, 278-279
pivot table formatting, 252-253
PivotFields, filtering manually, 275-276

revenue by product reports, creating, 246-248
  automatic subtotals, 253-254
  blank cells, eliminating, 248
  final formatting, 252-253
  grand totals, suppressing, 250
  number format, 248-249
  Outline view, 252
  ProductLineReport macro, 254-256
  sort order, 248
  subtotals, suppressing, 249-250
  summaries, 251-252
  table layout, 248
ShowDetail option, 270-272
summaries, creating, 251-252
table styles, 284-285
tools, 233-234
Visual Basic Editor
  Code window, 233
  Project Explorer, 232
  Properties window, 233
workbooks, creating, 250-251

version 10 pivot tables, 191

version 12 pivot tables, 190

viewing pivot tables in browsers, 199

views, Outline, 252

Visual Basic Editor
Code window, 233
Project Explorer, 232
Properties window, 233

Visual Basic for
Applications. *See* VBA

W

web pages, publishing
pivot tables as, 191-192

week, grouping fields by,
86-88, 265-267

wizards, 27
Create Cube File
Wizard, 208-210
PivotChart Wizard,
activating, 169

workbooks, creating,
250-251

X

x-axis (pivot charts), 146

xlAfter filter, 281

xlAfterOrEqualTo filter,
281

xlAllDatesInPeriodApril
filter, 281

xlAllDatesInPeriodAugust
filter, 281

xlAllDatesInPeriod-
December filter, 281

xlAllDatesInPeriod-
February filter, 281

xlAllDatesInPeriod-
January filter, 281

xlAllDatesInPeriod-
July filter, 281

xlAllDatesInPeriod-
June filter, 281

xlAllDatesInPeriod-
March filter, 281

xlAllDatesInPeriodMay
filter, 281

xlAllDatesInPeriod-
November filter, 281

xlAllDatesInPeriod-
October filter, 281

xlAllDatesInPeriod-
Quarter1 filter, 281

xlAllDatesInPeriod-
Quarter2 filter, 281

xlAllDatesInPeriod-
Quarter3 filter, 281

xlAllDatesInPeriod-
Quarter4 filter, 281

xlAllDatesInPeriod-
September filter, 281

xlBefore filter, 281

xlBeforeOrEqualTo filter,
281

xlBottomCount filter, 281

xlBottomPercent filter,
281

xlBottomSum filter, 281

xlCaptionBeginsWith
filter, 281

xlCaptionContains filter,
282

xlCaptionDoesNotBegin-
With filter, 282

xlCaptionDoesNot-
Contain filter, 282

xlCaptionDoesNotEnd-
With filter, 282

xlCaptionDoesNotEqual
filter, 282

xlCaptionEndsWith
filter, 282

xlCaptionEquals
filter, 282

xlCaptionIsBetween
filter, 282

xlCaptionIsGreaterThan
filter, 282

xlCaptionIsGreaterThan-
OrEqualTo filter, 282

xlCaptionIsLessThan
filter, 282

xlCaptionIsLessThanOr-
EqualTo filter, 282

xlCaptionIsNotBetween
filter, 282

xlDateBetween filter, 282

xlDateLastMonth
filter, 282

xlDateLastQuarter
filter, 282

xlDateLastWeek
filter, 282

xlDateLastYear filter, 282

xlDateNextMonth
filter, 283

xlDateNextQuarter
filter, 283

xlDateNextWeek
filter, 283

xlDateNextYear filter, 283

xlDateThisMonth
filter, 283

xlDateThisQuarter
filter, 283

xlDateThisWeek filter, 283

xlDateThisYear filter, 283

xlDateToday filter, 283

xlDateTomorrow filter, 283

xlDateYesterday filter, 283

xlNotSpecificDate filter, 283

.xls files, 18

.xlsm file extension, 232

xlSpecificDate filter, 283

xlTopCount filter, 283

xlTopPercent filter, 283

xlTopSum filter, 283

xlValueDoesNotEqual filter, 283

xlValueEquals filter, 283

xlValueIsBetween filter, 283

xlValueIsGreaterThan filter, 283

xlValueIsGreaterThanOr-EqualTo filter, 283

xlValueIsLessThan filter, 283

xlValueIsLessThanOr-EqualTo filter, 283

xlValueIsNotBetween filter, 284

xlYearToDate filter, 284

Y-Z

y-axis (pivot charts), 146

zeros, replacing blank cells with, 49-50

THIS BOOK IS SAFARI ENABLED

INCLUDES FREE 45-DAY ACCESS TO THE ONLINE EDITION

The Safari® Enabled icon on the cover of your favorite technology book means the book is available through Safari Bookshelf. When you buy this book, you get free access to the online edition for 45 days.

Safari Bookshelf is an electronic reference library that lets you easily search thousands of technical books, find code samples, download chapters, and access technical information whenever and wherever you need it.

TO GAIN 45-DAY SAFARI ENABLED ACCESS TO THIS BOOK:

- Go to **http://www.quepublishing.com/safarienabled**
- Complete the brief registration form
- Enter the coupon code found in the front of this book on the "Copyright" page

If you have difficulty registering on Safari Bookshelf or accessing the online edition, please e-mail customer-service@safaribooksonline.com.